Natural
Remedies
Dogs and
Cats
Wish You
Knew

Natural Remedies Dogs and Cats Wish You Knew

A Holistic Care Guide

DR. VIV HARRIS

Ulysses Press

Published in the United States by
ULYSSES PRESS
P.O. Box 3440
Berkeley, CA 94703
www.ulyssespress.com

First published as *The Healthy Animal Handbook: Holistic Health for Cats and Dogs* in 2006 in New Zealand by Random House New Zealand.

ISBN10: 1-56975-637-6 3679 6711 2/08
ISBN13: 978-1-56975-637-9
Library of Congress Control Number: 2007905469

Acquisitions Editor: Nick Denton-Brown
Managing Editor: Claire Chun
Editor: Amy Hough
Editorial Associates: Lauren Harrison, Elyce Petker
Production: Steven Zah Schwartz, Judith Metzener, Tamara Kowalski
Index: Sayre Van Young
Text design: Sarah Elworthy
Illustrations: Deborah Hinde
Cover design: Double R Design
Cover photography: © Michael Pettigrew/iStockphoto

Printed in the United States by Bang Printing

10 9 8 7 6 5 4 3 2 1

Distributed by Publishers Group West

Disclaimer: The information in this book is not intended to replace the advice of your veterinarian. The author or publisher cannot be responsible for unsupervised treatments administered at home. If in any doubt, seek a professional opinion.

Contents

Acknowledgments

My career as a holistic veterinarian has been an exhilarating and exciting pioneering journey. I spent the first few years of practice just trying to survive and learn the basic veterinary principles, the grassroots knowledge and the platform experience from which to branch out into other parts of the profession. Much of this vital knowledge came from the patient and supportive teachings of my bosses at my first veterinary job—thanks Andy and Alex!

Once I had experience in the basics, I grew interested in other ways of treating the problems we encountered, especially using traditional complementary therapies such as herbal medicine and homeopathy. There were very few well-known holistic veterinarians when I began the quest for this knowledge more than fifteen years ago, and many accolades need to go to the great holistic vets I met along the way. These people inspired me with their humble yet loving and devoted approach to finding ways to treat those difficult veterinary problems that conventional medicine could not adequately address.

The members of the Australian Association of Holistic Veterinarians included some amazingly talented, progressive and inspiring holistic vets. Meeting them and attending their excellent conferences each year provided a time for learning and for a meeting of minds, enabling my own knowledge and expertise to grow. Having the freedom to take these pearls of wisdom back to my own practice and start using them right away cemented the knowledge, and I feel really privileged to have had the opportunity to develop and grow from this experience. A special thanks to the staff at my veterinary clinic, who put up with me coming back from each workshop or conference armed and dangerous with a new modality to put into practice. They not only put up with me as I did this, but they also supported their use and enthusiastically shared them with clients. We got very used to sad animals and owners coming to the clinic in a last-minute effort to find relief for a seemingly untreatable condition, and leaving with hope and a whole bunch of things to try, often regaining a reasonable quality of life for the animals, allowing them to carry on until their natural time was up.

And many thanks to my wonderful clients who would listen intently to all my ramblings, and (usually!) do what I suggested. It was not unusual for them to find in their animals' improved health the inspiration to go on and try these holistic suggestions on themselves. It always gave me huge satisfaction to explain these health principles to owners in the context of their animals then find they would go out and seek the very same help for themselves from practitioners who treated humans. Thanks also to my family and friends, who have tirelessly supported me in my business and in my search for knowledge. Running a veterinary clinic and breaking away from the traditional way of doing things is never easy, and they were always there to support me, especially Mom, Dad, Chris, Warren and Peter.

Finally, the biggest thanks of all go to my very special animal friends, who have helped, guided and saved my life many times over, teaching me simple and profound lessons that books and advice could never match. Their experiences and examples have given me the answers to many life questions that I have been able to share with clients and family in their moments of need. Thank you Holly, Rua, Ebony, Mitzi, Dink, Sam, Tarquin, Trillo, Bru Bru, Oscar, Blackie and most of all Jackson, my one very, very special dog for this lifetime. Jackson was a dog that touched everybody's lives—everyone who met him recognized his specialness, and even now, years later, people still talk about him with awe. He came into my life when he was really needed, taught me so much, and gracefully left when he felt I was in good hands. A fine and noble dog.

Preface

When I set out to write a book, I wanted to write about the way I worked as a veterinarian, how I saw veterinary medical problems, how I looked at cases and the way I chose to treat them. Instead the book has become bigger than this, a consolidation of a way of thinking, of approaching medicine from an entirely different angle from the way I was taught at veterinary school all those years ago. The basics are still the same, those crucial first principles that our excellent veterinary education taught us, but the approach is different.

Rather than focusing on just the physical presentation of symptoms and the suppression or removal of these symptoms, this way of looking at problems also embraces the emotional, mental and spiritual parts of each individual. To me it seems a far more commonsense approach, one that is much more closely aligned with the laws of nature. By embracing all parts of the whole, and combining our conventional approach to medicine (involving surgery, lifesaving drugs and diagnostics) with complementary medical models such as acupuncture, homeopathy, flower essences and nutrition, our toolboxes as veterinarians and as animal owners are far more comprehensive and effective than if we were relying on just one type of medical system.

A holistic approach brings together the very best of both these worlds—conventional and complementary—allowing us to take each animal as an individual, assess its particular needs and produce a treatment or preventive program for each individual situation. Lumping all symptoms, age ranges or breeds into one collective body, with rigid treatment options, does away with this individuality, and may be the reason many chronic disease processes often do not respond adequately to a purely conventional approach.

The holistic approach delivers sensible, thorough and individualized advice for preventing disease (or "dis-ease") via high quality nutrition, excellent lifestyle practices and correcting body imbalances. It uses treatment options that support the body, rather than simply hiding symptoms, which often drives the imbalance deeper into the system, resulting in far more serious health consequences. The theory is simple: create *balance* (or optimal health) in the body, which results in a healthy immune system. When the immune system is in balance (optimally healthy), the whole body tends to be in balance, and disease (or rather "dis-ease") cannot be present.

This book is about creating balance on all levels—physical, emotional, mental and spiritual—and about what to do if there is imbalance, with the aim of regaining the balance and therefore good health. In the first part of the book, the concepts of holistic medicine are introduced and preventive health measures outlined. The second part of the book is devoted to treatments and how to regain this balance.

As domestic animals, our pets are heavily reliant on our abilities to provide them with the care they need to live happy and healthy lives; they often can't resolve health issues on their own. So it's up to us to inform ourselves about the remedies they wish we knew—natural and holistic ones, administered with love.

Key

🐾 **tip**

🐶 **recipe**

! warning

? question

✴ **important note**

Chapter 1
What is holistic health?

The need for balance

Most of us have heard the word "holistic," but how many of us really know what it means? Essentially it means just what it says—holistic (or wholistic) simply means "the whole" rather than the parts. When we relate this to our bodies or our pets' bodies, it means we look at the whole of the being, and how it integrates and relates to every part of itself, not just the parts that may be showing a symptom, such as the sore foot, upset stomach or dry coat. All parts are interrelated and nothing happens in isolation—we are a product of the whole, of all that has happened to our beings in the past and all that will happen to us in the future.

Taking a holistic approach also means we don't just focus on the physical aspects of our bodies—we also consider the emotional, mental and spiritual parts of ourselves and of our pets. Health is not just in the physical body, but in the emotions, the thoughts and the spiritual body. Good health means we are in *balance*, that all our parts are healthy, balanced and functioning to their full potential. An imbalance of any of these parts will often result in illness, leading to various symptoms. Physical signs of "dis-ease" or illness may often be the last to appear. Illness often begins in the mental, emotional or spiritual parts and, if left unchecked, moves inwards to our physical body where it settles as some form of physical illness, such as a cold, pain, stiffness or worse.

In the United States, our conventional medical system is classified as "Western" medicine as opposed to "Eastern" medicine, that is, the ancient Chinese, Indian and old Asian philosophies. In

Western human medicine, we tend to focus mainly on the physical aspects of our being, and this is also the case in Western veterinary medicine. We tend to look at most physical ailments in isolation, rather than looking at all the other parts of our makeup. For example, we wonder why our livers have stopped working when we've eaten a very poor diet for most of our lives, have been extremely angry at the world, have had a hard-driving personality and have never really stopped to smell the flowers along life's pathway.

The body is an amazing work of art. It constantly tries to heal itself, to regain equilibrium (or homeostasis) and continue its daily functioning. It often gives us clues of increasing frequency and intensity that we need to change what we are doing if we are not creating a nurturing environment for all parts of ourselves—physical, mental, emotional and spiritual. These clues may range from recurring colds to frequent headaches or skin allergies. To ignore these mild clues and cover up the warning signs with paracetamol, steroids and nasal decongestants, without addressing *why* they are happening and rectifying them, can drive the imbalance of health deeper into the inner parts of the body, possibly leading over time to far more serious body malfunctions.

Our Western medical thinking has many merits and I don't mean to sound "anti-Western," but it is possible to look at medicine in a far more integrative and bigger way by taking the best of Western and other forms of medicine and combining them to produce a holistic approach.

Western medical history

Over the last 150 years or so the Western style of medicine has conditioned us to fix our health only when the physical part is broken, ignoring the fact that the root of the problem may be in our mental, emotional and spiritual parts. We take out what we see as the bad part, put in a new part and carry on as before, without considering why it "broke" in the first place.

This is due largely to the thinking that developed around the industrial revolution, from the late seventeenth to the nineteenth century. Bodies were viewed in a similar way to the machines that were revolutionizing the industrial world. Medical thinking accepted this analogy, and although there were many wonderful discoveries in the field of medicine, there was an evolving model of our bodies as machines, without assets such as emotions, mental thought or a spiritual life. A lack of recovery meant that an appropriate surgical technique had not been developed, a drug had not been found that made the symptoms go away, or the engine had just stopped working. Very little regard was given to vital holistic principles such as nutrition appropriate for the condition, or addressing the possible underlying reasons why the body was sick, such as stress, mental anguish or spiritual starvation.

When I talk about the spiritual I don't mean "religious," but a connection with the universal energy of life, being a part of the world energy rather than just a part of one's own life. When the Western medical model is used we are each seen as a totally separate being rather than being intricately connected to the web of all lives. We view ourselves in isolation, and don't recognize that all our thoughts and actions will have an impact on everyone else. By recognizing our connection to the universal energy we become aware that doing things just for ourselves and acting cruelly or without regard for others will eventually have an impact back on us, because we are all connected in some way.

So how does this relate to animals? Well, it is accepted that most of the more advanced mammals (if not all animals) have emotions, varying degrees of mental thought and a spiritual part. Debate about whether animals have a soul or feelings has raged for hundreds of years as humans have tried to disconnect themselves from the way they treat animals—especially farm animals, which are often treated as machines to produce an end product for consumption. Cruel practices such as tail docking and overcrowding were all excused by the explanation that they are "just animals," devoid of feelings or senses. These practices were carried out to improve farm systems rather than the quality of life of the individual animal. Animals have been the losers since farming became an intensive business, with the "bottom line" being more important than their physical, mental or emotional health.

Fortunately, there is now a growing awareness of animal welfare in both the farming and the companion animal worlds. The American Veterinary Medical Association has become increasingly active in animal welfare issues on the farm, and more legislation is now available to prosecute people who do not provide the necessities of life for their animals. All this points to a growing awareness that our animal friends are not just machines to produce a product, whether it be milk, meat or friendship. As with our own bodies, we are realizing that there is a better way to view animal health. Like us, animals are integrated, whole beings with not just a physical body but with mental, emotional and spiritual bodies. We are starting to think in a holistic way.

A "whole" approach

Holistic health considers all the things that go into the environment and have a direct or indirect impact on the body. In the case of animals this includes where they live, what sort of shelter or accommodation they have, whether they are confined for much of the day or allowed to run free, how much company they have, human or otherwise, and how much "entertainment" they have. The mental and emotional health of an animal cannot flourish if it is tied to a kennel for most of the day and rarely gets out to run and play; such a situation often results in behavioral problems, which can lead to physical problems. An example of this is when a dog develops lick granulomas on its front legs. Because it is bored, the animal continuously licks at one patch, usually on the front paw, which results in thickening of the skin in that area and often infection.

Puppies that are confined to dog runs in the crucial early weeks and months of life, when mental and emotional health is hugely affected, may be timid and fearful all their lives, resulting in behavioral and personality disorders. Exercise that is appropriate for age and body type not only improves physical health, it also has an effect on mental and emotional health, providing not just entertainment but also stimulation of the body's hormones and a sense of well-being.

A holistic approach always includes nutrition, because the foods that are eaten, the quality of the food and the nutrients going into the body will determine the overall health of that body on all levels. Emotional and mental health, for example, are closely linked to a good quality diet, especially an adequate intake of B complex vitamins, magnesium and many of the essential fatty acids that are often found in foods such as flaxseed and fish oils. Nutritional research has blossomed in the last few decades, and the medical profession (including the veterinary profession) now recognizes the critical role played by the foods we eat and the nutrient balance in our bodies.

A preventive approach

Holistic health also involves taking a preventive approach—maintaining an excellent diet, doing exercise that is appropriate to age and body type and stimulating the mind for emotional and mental well-being—to keep us in balance. If our bodies are in balance we are in good health, and there is no need for remedies and drugs to reestablish this balance. I often call this the "precarious point of balance," because it becomes more and more difficult to achieve as we get older, requiring more effort as the point of balance changes according to the day, the seasons and what is happening in our lives.

Practitioners of traditional Chinese medicine recommend a "tune up" at the beginning of each season. They will analyze the pulse to determine which body system may be slightly out of balance, and use herbs, acupuncture, massage and exercises to rebalance the body so that it can cope in the best way for that season. This is a truly holistic approach, integrating all parts of the being—physical, mental, emotional and spiritual—and keeping the body well so it is less likely to break down.

Unfortunately, in general Western medicine the focus is on treating things once they have gone out of balance, i.e., the "ambulance at the bottom of the cliff" approach. This is changing, however, in both veterinary science and in human medicine. Wellness programs providing education and health advice are being developed, although they are not as specific and as individually effective as the traditional Chinese approach, which is tailored for each individual depending on their pulse diagnosis. The Western approach still tends to address the needs of the general population rather than the specific needs of a particular body. All beings are very different in their needs, which are dynamic and changeable, so it is difficult to produce a commercial diet or specific treatment that will cater for all body types in an age range.

Where did the complementary therapies come from?

In contrast to generally recognized Western medicine, which is only a few hundred years old, the roots of most complementary medicine or health philosophies go back many centuries. These ancient forms of medicine were based on many years of observation, as well as experimentation with foods, herbs and lifestyle. They are truly holistic in their nature, addressing not only the physical state but the emotional, mental and spiritual states. They have traditionally used things that were available in their environment and appropriate for their climate and country, and their medical systems were closely integrated into their everyday lives. This reinforces the idea of a preventive approach—staying healthy through an appropriate diet, exercises, meditation, etc.—rather than fixing a health problem once it has happened.

Ayurvedic medicine

Some of the earliest medical philosophies originated in India, where a deeply philosophical medical system evolved that included iridology (making diagnoses by examining changes in the iris of the eye), a form of acupuncture, diet, herbs and exercises such as yoga. The traditional Indian health system, known as Ayurveda, recognizes various body types and mixes, each with its individual characteristics, needs and recommendations for creating balance. Like other holistic systems of health, the Ayurvedic system caters to the individual, and it looks at all levels of the being—physical, emotional, mental and spiritual.

Traditional Chinese Medicine

Traditional Chinese medicine (sometimes referred to as TCM) is another very ancient medical system, based on 5,000 years of observation and use. TCM uses acupuncture, diet (where food is used as medicine for rebalancing the body), herbs and exercises (such as tai chi and qi gong), involving all body systems and again looking at all aspects of the being. It also totally integrates its medical system and philosophies into everyday life, from morning exercises to balance and raise energies to how foods are prepared and what is eaten, depending on the individual or the season.

A basic concept in TCM is the energy flow around the body (known as qi or chi, both pronounced "chee") and the need to maintain the balance of this qi energy in all areas of your life. How you relate to the surrounding world is also integrated—the body is not viewed as a separate being, unrelated to all that is around it, but is intrinsically part of all life systems. Thus, all actions have corresponding reactions, which always have an impact on the individual to some degree. Even the flow of energy through one's home is recognized in the system known as feng shui, which is also based on the underlying concepts of qi energy flow. The well-known yin-yang symbol represents the balance needed in all systems, the dynamically changing nature of this balance and how everything has components of its opposite within the system.

The yin-yang symbol depicts the nature of opposites, the light (yang) and dark (yin), how within the light there is dark, and within the dark there is light, as well as the dynamic nature of things as they move from one state to another. It shows the interdependence of one state on the other, for without light there is no dark, and without dark there is no light. This concept comes from observing the sun's movement through the sky over the course of a year, the top being the summer solstice, with the maximum light levels, and the beginning of the decline of light to the winter solstice at the bottom, the time of maximum darkness.

Herbalism and homeopathy

European herbalism and North American Indian medical systems have also been around for many centuries. These systems have tended to rely mostly on plants and herbs as treatment options and dietary recommendations. Herbalism, or the use of plants as medicine, was used not only to treat health problems but to keep a person well by cleansing the system or supporting it during times of stress such as pregnancy or recovery from illness or wounds. Another system, homeopathy, started to evolve in the sixteenth century, and later developed largely through the influence of a German physician, Samuel Hahnemann. It became a part of European medical culture, later spreading to North America with European migrants.

Combining the different systems

By integrating these complementary modalities into the Western medical system we give ourselves a far greater range of tools with which to treat all types of problems. We can borrow this ancient knowledge for treatments, and we can use the philosophies and systems for preventing health problems, combining them with Western medical philosophies to create a wonderful treasure trove of preventive and treatment options. By taking the best of many centuries of medical knowledge and combining it with modern Western medicine, we can create a new system of health care that looks at all parts of our lifestyle—one that focuses not just on our physical bodies but addresses our mental, emotional and spiritual needs, providing a truly holistic way to live.

Current Western medical knowledge and the huge advances of the last two to three hundred years in sanitation, anatomy, anesthesia, drug development and genetics, are highly valuable resources. Because we live in the "modern" world, these advances in medicine suit our current "modern" lives. Many of the ancient medical theories and approaches are simply not appropriate for the way we live in the twenty-first century, but at the same time there are some very useful treatments and philosophies that we can adapt and use to complement the modern Western system. In this way we can provide a more complete and "whole" approach to staying well and treating any problems that arise.

Summary

Holistic health:

- Relates to the WHOLE of the individual, not just parts.
- Looks at the physical, emotional, mental and spiritual aspects of the individual.
- Focuses on creating BALANCE (homeostasis) in the body.
- Addresses the important basics of health such as nutrition, exercise, grooming and a healthy emotional and mental environment.
- Acts in a preventive way, aiming to keep the individual optimally healthy so the body does not need to produce symptoms to warn of an imbalance.
- INTEGRATES the best of Western medicine with the best of the traditional medical systems (such as traditional Chinese medicine, Ayurveda, herbalism and homeopathy) to provide a much more comprehensive understanding of health as well as giving us many, many more treatment options which work with the body rather than against it.
- Is often also known as "complementary" or "integrative" medicine.

Western medical thinking tends to focus on the suppression of symptoms and the treatment of problems once they have happened rather than focusing on prevention and creating balance on all levels. While Western medicine has an enormously valuable role to play, it is definitely not the whole story.

Chapter 2
The holistic approach to basic pet care

Keeping your pets well

By combining both ancient and modern health care knowledge, it is possible to come up with a simple and effective plan that involves both preventive care and treatment options for our animal friends. Our first aim is to keep our four-legged friends well, and in the unlikely event that they become unwell we can then choose a treatment option that works deeply and effectively without creating side effects, and focuses on regaining the balance in the body that was lost temporarily. It is not necessary to have an in-depth knowledge of systems such as traditional Chinese medical philosophy in order to keep your pet well, but it is a fascinating way to view life, our bodies and the environment, and has much to teach those of us who live in a climate of excess and imbalance.

The importance of the immune system

The immune system is a crucial "part" of the body. It is an integrated system involving many of the internal organs, such as the spleen, liver and thymus gland, as well as blood cells, lymphatics and the bone marrow. The immune system protects the body from invading pathogens (such as bacteria and viruses) by creating an immune response, fighting infection and removing foreign invaders from the body. Any weakness in the immune system can result in significant health issues: if it is underactive, the body can succumb to infections and serious chronic diseases; if it is overactive, the body can be destroyed by its own defenses, resulting in autoimmune diseases causing blood cell, joint and organ destruction that, if not reversed, can lead to death.

A holistic approach recognizes the huge impact the immune system has on the health of the body, and focuses on keeping it as healthy as possible. The immune system is very sensitive to toxins, poor diet and stress, and prolonged exposure to these things can seriously weaken it, leaving the body susceptible to recurrent infections and degenerative diseases. You can't dissect an immune system from a body, because as mentioned, it is the integration of many areas in the body. This is why a disease that directly attacks the immune system, like AIDS (Acquired Immune Deficiency Syndrome), is so devastating—without an optimally functioning immune system the body cannot be in healthy balance.

Keeping well

Keeping our animal friends well is all about keeping their bodies and minds in balance. There are four main ways of doing this:

- Diet
- Exercise
- Grooming and cleaning
- Mental and emotional stimulation (i.e., entertainment and love)

Diet

There is no truer adage than "you are what you eat." What we put into our bodies and those of our animal friends is the crucial link between good health and bad health. There are other factors, of course, but there is no doubt that the long-term use of a poor or unbalanced diet can accelerate aging, degenerative diseases and susceptibility to infections by affecting all the body systems, especially the immune system. Diet can keep the body serviced and energized, and more importantly, in balance. Using food as a form of treatment or "medicine" is very much part of both traditional Chinese medicine and Indian Ayurvedic philosophy. Food can be used to warm up or cool down the body, and the foods that are eaten need to change with the seasons and the environment. It is far more than eating breakfast, lunch and dinner—we can adapt particular foods to prevent and even treat certain disease states. In traditional Chinese medicine, diet is a core focus in rehabilitation and prevention of disease, and as one might expect in a system that has been around for 5,000 years, the concept has been developed to a very sophisticated level.

The types of food appropriate when under stress or during pregnancy, birth, lactation, growth and old age vary enormously, and they can make a huge difference on the body's ability to function efficiently.

In Western medicine, there is increasing use of particular foods or nutrients (functional foods and "nutraceuticals") for the treatment of certain conditions. An example of this is the use of glucosamine, found in animal cartilage, which can help relieve the symptoms of arthritis.

The subject of diet is thus a very important one, and it is covered in detail in Chapter 3.

Exercise

"Use it or lose it" is another very true adage when it comes to our bodies. Exercise is not only essential for keeping the muscles and circulation in balance, but also important for our animal friends' mental and emotional health. In Western medicine, exercise is regarded as necessary to build muscle strength, keep the heart healthy, stimulate internal organ functioning and oxygenate the body. In traditional Chinese medicine, exercise stimulates the flow of qi energy, which is the central concept in TCM. When the qi energy is flowing at the correct rate and in the correct direction along the correct pathways, balance is achieved, and therefore, good health.

Appropriate exercise for each stage in life

Exercise needs to be appropriate for age and body condition, or damage to the body may occur. One example of this is over-exercise in fast-growing, large breed dogs, especially at the age of five to ten months when maximum growth is occurring. Over-exercise at this time, combined with "overnutrition" (too much food energy, or an imbalance of important minerals) and susceptible genetics can lead to severe and often permanent damage of the cartilage lining in joints. I usually recommend no more than a 20-minute (not too strenuous) walk a day until the dog is a year old, in addition to letting it run around at home as it likes.

Regular routines

Most animals respond well to a regular routine of daily walks at a similar time, over familiar areas, mimicking wild territorial roaming to guard their territory. Even cats that are confined to the indoors, as in apartment living, can be taken for walks in a safe area, and can even be trained to wear a walking harness so they can be controlled in traffic or unfamiliar areas. Sticking to a similar time each day allows the animal's body to adjust to the routine, and means their bowels and bladder will be used to being emptied on a regular basis.

It is important to engage in a form of exercise that is enjoyable for both owner and pet, safe and appropriate for the animal's breed and stage in life and active enough to get the heart rate up, the circulation going and the bowels moving. Exercise should also provide a chance to play, smell the roses (or other animals!) and realize there is a wonderful world to enjoy and be part of. In other words, the aim is to make sure not only the physical body, but also the animal's mental, emotional and spiritual state is being cared for. A truly holistic experience!

Grooming and cleaning

Just as exercise helps get the qi energy moving around the body and stimulates circulation and blood flow, so does grooming. Just under the skin and in the muscles are thin-walled vessels that carry the lymph around the body. Lymph plays a big part in immunity, and the lymph vessels drain the surrounding areas, removing waste and toxins and taking them to the liver, where if all systems are functioning well, they are processed and removed from the body. Appropriate massage by brushing the coat, as well as direct massage to the muscles, can stimulate the flow of the lymph, improving drainage and helping the body remove toxins.

Grooming cleans the skin

Grooming is also vital for the health of skin and hair. It removes the surface build-up of dead skin cells and dead hair and stimulates the tiny blood vessels below the skin's surface, bringing nutritive materials to repair and grow the hair and skin. Regular brushing helps keep the hair and fur untangled and smooth by distributing the hair oils along the shaft—this is very important in long-haired animals because a simple, small knot can lead to more extensive matting and knotting. This can become very uncomfortable, and it is often necessary to shave the mats of hair and fur right down to the skin surface. This may need to be done under sedation or even anesthetic because many cats (and dogs!) vigorously resent this procedure and bite and scratch.

If you have a long-haired pet, or even one with a medium-length fluffy coat, get them used to being groomed daily right from birth. This will not only prevent knots forming but will help keep the skin, the hair and indeed the whole body healthy. Animals with short coats also benefit from regular grooming, which removes shed hair and provides general skin, blood vessel and lymphatic stimulation. The coat will feel softer and look shinier, because the spreading of the skin oils along the hair shaft smooths the small scales on the hair shaft and encourages the hair to lie flat and reflect the light, which is what makes the coat look shiny. Grooming also provides important bonding time.

Molting and shedding

Most animals have an outer coat comprised of strong, coarse guard hairs, which helps protect the coat and skin from the elements, and a softer, fluffier undercoat that helps to insulate the skin and keep the animal warm. The ratios of the two differ markedly from breed to breed and also depend on the climate, how much the animal lives outdoors and its state of health.

Every hair has a life cycle which also varies in length depending on breed, age, season and state of health. Once its growth is finished, it will die and fall out of the hair follicle. If the surrounding hairs are all dying at the same time and falling off the body, which often happens with seasonal changes such as the arrival of spring, the shedding is obvious and the loss of dead hair far more recognizable than at other times. As long as there are no bald areas and the skin is looking healthy, there is nothing to worry about, and brushing with an appropriate brush or comb should still be done on a daily basis. The shedding will eventually slow as the new hair cycles begin.

Shedding is a premium time for matting and knots to occur, so be very diligent with your brushing, ensuring the shed undercoat is removed each day. Don't just brush over the top of the coat, because it's often the fluffy undercoat hair that mats most easily. A good comb is often the best way to remove this undercoat, because brushes tend to skim over the top of it. You need to get right down to the skin surface under the shed hair and gently remove the hair and any dead skin cells.

The surface skin cells also have a life cycle, and more cells are often shed during the molt. Grooming helps to remove these sloughed, dead skin cells as well as the shed hair, thus cleaning the coat and reducing scaly build-up. Regular removal of shed hairs also decreases the likelihood of fur being ingested and causing digestive upsets (furballs).

Sebaceous glands—producing the skin's oil

The sebaceous glands in the skin are very important because they produce the oils that keep the skin surface and the hairs healthy and smooth and prevent them from drying out. Underproduction of these oils can result in cracking of the skin and lack of shine on the hair. Regular grooming stimulates this oil production and spreads the oil evenly over the coat and along the hair shafts.

When the skin is aggravated by scratching and excessive licking, the sebaceous glands tend to become overactive and produce too much oil, resulting in a greasy coat. The normal skin bacteria tend to multiply as well and react with the oils, which results in the oils becoming rancid and producing a smell resembling dirty socks or rancid butter. This smell is associated with a lot of skin problems. It is known as secondary seborrhea, because it is secondary to the biting and scratching of the skin, which often starts because of a primary allergy. When the skin is irritated and out of balance, vigorous grooming is not recommended because it will irritate the skin even more. In fact, the skin needs to be allowed to heal and recover, so be very careful when brushing—use a soft brush to remove excess scurf and debris, and avoid raw areas.

Washing and shampooing

If your animal friend has a normal coat and you live in a clean environment, regular weekly shampooing is generally not recommended because it will strip the coat of essential oils and can create skin problems such as dryness or even an allergic reaction.

Washing and shampooing is generally only necessary if your pet has rolled in something revolting, if you live in a highly polluted environment such as near a main road, if you have cigarette smokers in the household or if you use a lot of toxic household cleaners. In these situations your animal's coat will accumulate these toxins and they need to be washed off regularly to reduce absorption into the body.

The other reason to shampoo your pet is if there is some form of allergy such as secondary seborrhea, which requires regular treatments with a special shampoo to calm the oil glands, reduce the bacterial load on the skin surface and settle the excess shedding of superficial skin cells. The use of these shampoos is regarded as a type of treatment course, and it is done every five to seven days. The shampoo is lathered up well and left on for 15 to 20 minutes to process, then rinsed off.

Because the secondary seborrhea can be very itchy in its own right, as well as the primary allergy that started it all off in the first place, it is really important to treat both the secondary symptoms and the primary allergy. There is more on this in the section on skin problems in Chapter 5.

If your pet has a normal coat without any itching or dryness, you probably only need to wash it once every one to two months. Use a gentle, neutral pH shampoo, and make sure it is rinsed off well afterward. This frequency of shampooing will remove oil build-up, debris and any particles of dust that may contain toxins from the environment. You can towel-dry your pet afterward or just take your dog for a walk; they are usually dry when they return home.

The use of hairsprays and other human-based shampoos and hair products is not recommended. I advise using only shampoos and conditioners that are recommended for animals and available from your veterinarian, since they have been specially formulated for animal skin and hair. The exception would possibly be a very mild baby shampoo, and only if the skin and coat are normal.

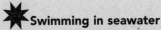

Swimming in seawater
It is important to rinse the salty water off the coat after swimming if at all possible, since it can sometimes cause itchiness as the coat dries and the salt may be left on the skin in high concentrations.

Ask your veterinarian or nursing staff to recommend a suitable shampoo for your pet; there are a dazzling array of shampoos and coat conditioners available, and they have the training and product knowledge to recommend the right one for your pet.

Clipping and trimming

Clipping or trimming animals' coats can be a controversial topic. Animals that are bred for very cold climates have a correspondingly thick insulating undercoat, and long, thick guard hairs. If they are brought to live in a warm or hot climate, this coat is not necessary, and it can even be dangerous because the animal can overheat. Shaving the coat right back to the skin level is one possibility, while stripping the insulative undercoat is another, less drastic-looking option. There are professional dog groomers who will do this, or if you have the time and inclination, it can be done at home with a special stripping knife or comb. Clipping is best done at the very beginning of summer to allow the coat to grow back before the next winter or cooler season. If there is a cold spell before this, you may need to get a dog coat for your pet, since its system will not be used to the lack of insulation.

Always try to remove excess hair down inside the ear canals by pulling or plucking—too much hair in the canals can prevent drainage of the outer ear and may lead to ear infections.

Unlike humans, dogs and cats don't have sweat glands in the skin, and cooling is achieved by panting, and to a degree by dilation of the blood vessels near the skin surface, especially on the ears. The pads of the feet sweat a little, but overheating or hyperthermia can happen very quickly—especially in a confined space like a closed car on a hot day—and it is often fatal. A thick coat will definitely contribute to this overheating, so clipping or thinning is highly recommended in the warmer months or areas. A shorter coat also makes washing and treating for fleas much easier, and there is less to clean up around the house when the animal sheds its hair!

Mental and emotional stimulation through attention and entertainment

As part of the holistic approach, we need to address our four-legged friends' emotional and mental health. All the things discussed so far help these in an indirect way. For example, nutrition will affect the emotions and mental capacity if certain minerals and vitamins are lacking or if the blood sugar is too low. A lack of exercise can lead to boredom and obsessive behaviors, while grooming not only improves the health of the skin and coat, but the attention the animal gets while you are brushing or washing it can have an important positive effect on its emotional health.

We all need attention and love from those around us, and animals are no different—they require both mental and emotional feeding to be balanced and healthy. Many animal behavioral problems arise from either a lack of or too much attention and entertainment; again, it is important to get the mix right.

Dogs tend to be reliant on their owners for their emotional and mental stimulation. They will often attach themselves to one person and become his or her shadow, so to speak, following him or her everywhere and becoming distressed if parted. Separation anxiety is a very real issue for many dog owners, and to a lesser extent cat owners, since cats seem to be more self-reliant. The flower essences (described in detail in Chapter 4) can be effective in normalizing this anxiety and achieving balance in the emotional response. I have often used these in my veterinary practice to treat cases of separation anxiety resulting in destruction in the house, or barking and obsessive behavior.

Where do these behaviors come from, and how do I treat them?

Each animal has its own personality, which is a product of its genetics or breeding as well as its surroundings and upbringing. For example, certain breeds of dog tend to be more nervous and suspicious than others. If a dog of this type did not have enough positive learning experiences as it was developing from puppyhood into adulthood, or if it has experienced negative effects such as abuse and cruelty, it may become a fear-biter or possibly aggressive. (Note, however, that some dogs can become aggressive even with an ideal upbringing.) Most behavioral problems have complex histories and trying to normalize these behaviors can be very difficult. Treatment often involves management and retraining, and sometimes the use of a flower essence mixture to help correct the underlying emotional imbalances. Behavioral problems and solutions are discussed in more detail in Chapter 5.

Your pet's emotional and mental health develops from a young age (see Chapter 7 for more on raising puppies and kittens holistically). As an adult, ongoing love and attention is crucial. Every day your pet needs to recognize that it is wanted and where it stands as a part of your family (or "pack"); as owners, you become the other members of its pack. This is how dogs tend to structure their social groups, and many behavioral problems in dogs are related to confusion about where they stand in the social hierarchy, or "pecking order." Some aggression problems relate to the dog's desire to be more dominant over particular family members, resulting in biting and growling, and often directed at the smaller or more timid members of the family. This highly undesirable behavior must be rectified as soon as it surfaces—the longer it goes on, the harder it is to change. It is difficult to give specific advice, since most aggressive dogs require professional help from a behavioralist or trainer.

Early on, in very, very mild cases, rectifying this behavior may be possible with a few firm words or simple dominance techniques such as getting the person who is being targeted to feed the dog, making it sit or submit before it receives the reward of food, or making it sit before a door is opened, with the reward of being able to go out the door. Making the positive outcomes reward-based is generally a win-win situation because it is clear when the dog has done what you want it to do and when it hasn't. Again, it is difficult to give specific advice, because each case of aggression is very different. Professional behavioralists or trainers are the best people to deal with these problems, especially if the dog is dangerous.

Training dogs is as much about the owner as it is about the dog. When professional dog trainers or behavioralists go into a home, they see situations as they arise and advise the owners to respond in a particular way—this is just as important as training the animals. Dogs need clear, firm, consistent training techniques that cannot be confused, and they need to know they can expect a reward at the end.

A lack of love and attention can lead to obsessive-compulsive disorders in dogs, as it can in humans. Dogs that are insecure in their environment may bark or pace fence lines obsessively; in their minds they are often just doing their job of protecting the family (or "pack"), but have taken this far past the "normal" stage. Other things like overgrooming and compulsive licking that leads to the creation of sore and raw patches are often due to anxiety or boredom. A sense of security and routine in the home goes a long way toward preventing these.

In cats, stress in the home may lead to behavioral problems, especially overgrooming, which can result in baldness down the hind legs and back. Some years ago I had a client with a cat that had licked and pulled all the hair out from down its back, under its stomach and down the hind legs. The cat was anxious and generally unrelaxed, but questioning the owners revealed none of the common sources of stress in cats, such as neighboring cats giving it a hard time, or renovations being done in the home. With further questioning, however, it turned out that one of the partners in the relationship had lost their job and there was a lot of stress in the household. The cat was picking up on this and taking it out on itself, literally "pulling its hair out." I prescribed a Bach flower essence to help calm the cat, and once the owners were aware of the effect their problems were having, they managed to reduce the stress in the home. The cat gradually settled and became far more relaxed; it stopped overgrooming, and all its hair grew back.

In summary, appropriate levels of attention are a very important part of a holistic approach to pet care. The animal should not have too much attention, to the extent that it becomes insecure about doing things on its own, or too little, which can result in anxiety and possibly aggression. Nobody wants a difficult family member, especially if it's a 150-pound Rottweiler, so attend to any behavioral problems early on, and give your pet the love and affection it deserves.

Summary

Diet
- "You are what you eat."
- Diet is a vital part of a holistic approach to health.
- A poor diet can accelerate aging and degenerative diseases and increase the chances of immune system imbalances.
- Food can be used to rebalance the body and treat certain conditions.

Exercise
- "Use it or lose it."
- Exercise is important for health on all levels—physical, emotional, mental and spiritual.
- Exercise needs to be appropriate for age and body condition.
- Routine exercise encourages normal body functioning.

Grooming and cleaning
- Grooming stimulates the oil glands in the skin and the lymphatics while removing old hair and dead skin cells.
- It massages the skin and muscles.
- Time spent grooming your animal friend is important for its emotional health.
- Brushing evenly distributes the skin oil over the hairs, protecting them and creating a shiny coat.
- Washing with a medicated shampoo is an important part of treating some skin conditions.
- Normal skin only needs washing every one to two months with a normal shampoo.
- Only use shampoos that are designed for animal skin; do not use human shampoos.

Mental and emotional stimulation through attention and entertainment
- Attention and entertainment are important for the emotional and mental health of your pet.
- Give appropriate levels of attention; too much can be as bad as too little.

Chapter 3
Nutrition and diet—the cornerstones of health

Preventing illness or "dis-ease" in your pet is reliant on several things, including exercise, grooming, attention and entertainment, but by far the most important is what it is fed. An appropriate diet for your animal friend is the foundation and real basis of life, because without the correct nourishment, the body cannot function at its best.

How do you know what to feed your pet? Animal foods are a multimillion-dollar industry, and there are new foods being developed all the time in an effort to grab a slice of this lucrative business. There are numerous choices—canned foods, dry foods, semi-frozen foods, homemade diets—so what do you choose to provide the optimum health for your four-legged friend? Let's start with some background information.

Dietary requirements are based on the individual animal—its body type, age, level of exercise, preferences, state of health, and whether it's pregnant, lactating (making milk), growing or recovering from an illness. These requirements can change from day to day and season to season, and it is important to supply the dietary variations necessary to address these changes. In the wild, cats and dogs (especially) are able to eat prey, as well as herbs, berries and various plants that help meet their changing requirements. Domestic cats and dogs, especially those that live in apartments or homes with small backyards, are unable to do this, so their owner needs to provide all the necessary nutritional components of their diets. It is also important to remember that domestic cats and dogs are quite removed from their wild forebears, having adapted to a totally different environment, and it is necessary to adapt their diets accordingly. Bearing this in mind, we need to take account of their changing needs and watch for any changes in health that may indicate a need to alter their diet.

What they are supposed to eat

Dogs are generally considered to be omnivorous (eating both meat and plant material), while cats are considered to be mainly carnivorous (mainly eating meat). Dogs in the wild will forage for eggs, plant material, fruit and even herbivore feces, as well as eating mammals, birds and possibly some insects. Cats are very much designed to be carnivores, with their retractable claws designed to secure prey; the particular configuration of their teeth (long, deeply rooted canine teeth for grabbing and holding prey, teeth for cutting and shearing, and a few teeth for grinding); short digestive tract; and very acidic stomach juices for digesting meat. If plants are eaten in the raw state, they mostly pass through the digestive system as roughage or "fiber," which has its uses in providing material for the animal's own beneficial intestinal bacteria to grow on, reducing intestinal pH and discouraging "bad" intestinal bacteria from growing. In domesticated pets promoting healthy intestinal bacteria can be achieved by providing fiber in the diet (such as oat bran), rather than something like yogurt. Most of the beneficial yogurt bacteria are destroyed in the highly acidic stomach, whereas the fiber passes through relatively unchanged into the large intestine.

In the wild, when a dog kills a small mammal it will generally eat the contents of the gut, which include semi-digested plant material and grains; then the internal organs, which provide concentrated levels of nutrients (especially the liver, kidneys and brain); then they chew on the muscle meat, bones and skin. Chewing not only helps digestion by mixing in the enzyme-rich saliva and breaking the pieces of food into manageable sizes, it cleans the teeth as well.

When deciding on a suitable diet for your pet, you need to consider what its body is designed to eat and try to provide a diet that is as close to this as possible. Of course, when you live in the center of a city, it can be difficult to find a freshly killed rabbit or mouse every day. However, you can mimic the animal's natural diet to a certain extent by giving it a well-balanced diet and fresh, unprocessed foods with supplements derived from complex natural food sources.

Each species has specific nutritional requirements that must be accounted for. For example, cats need approximately twice as much protein in their diet as dogs; they have a special daily dietary need for the amino acids (protein building blocks) taurine and arginine, and they cannot make vitamin A in their bodies. Dogs are far more adaptable to changes in protein and levels of carbohydrate in their diet.

Homemade vs. commercial diets

Providing a balanced and sensible view on what to feed your cat or dog is not easy when you have one foot in the world of conventional veterinary medicine and one foot in the world of complementary medicine. The two sides often have very different views on whether "commercial" or "homemade" diets are best, both with strong arguments for and against. My aim is to bring the best of both sides together and apply some simple and practical guidelines to a very complex topic.

Exactly what food is fed to an animal is entirely dependent on that particular animal, and proof of whether or not a diet suits an animal can be found in how healthy it is in the long term, on all levels—physical, mental and emotional. Indicators of this are weight levels; body condition; the results of blood tests and physical examination; condition of the skin, eyes and teeth; as well as energy and activity levels.

Commercial diets

Commercial diets are foods that are prepared and packaged for sale, usually in supermarkets, pet stores and veterinary clinics. They are processed in various ways to allow for shelf life and storage, and vary in quality. Some locally produced generic brands use whatever ingredients are available at the time, while the "super premium" foods follow strict formulas, using the same ingredients in each batch of a particular food product. The latter are generally more expensive since the ingredients may have to be sourced from different locations and the price also covers the cost of the research and testing that is undertaken to ensure quality control and palatability.

The Association of American Feed Control Officials (AAFCO) has developed official pet food regulations and testing guidelines for the United States. These provide protocols to ensure foods are formulated so that essential nutrients meet recommended levels, and include guidelines for feeding trials. Labeling, ingredient lists and health claims for pet foods are regulated through AAFCO and the Food and Drug Administration (FDA). When buying commercial food, at the very least make sure it is AAFCO tested, and preferably one of the "super premium" brands usually found in veterinary clinics, which often tend to be of a higher and more consistent quality than some supermarket brands.

The pros

The positive aspect of using good quality, appropriate commercial food is that due to stringent production rules and quality control, these foods usually provide consistent levels of all the necessary nutrients appropriate to the animal's needs. During important stages in your pet's life, such as growth, pregnancy and lactation, and in diet-critical conditions such as kidney failure, urinary tract problems and diabetic control, you can be assured that the animal's specific dietary needs are being met. In addition, many animal owners barely have time to prepare food for themselves, let alone their animal friends, so the prepared commercial foods are also very convenient. It is far better to use a high quality commercial food than a poorly balanced homemade diet where the ingredients are not of good quality and appropriate supplements are not included.

The cons

However, the negative aspects of many commercial diets also need to be considered. There is a huge range of ingredient quality in pet foods, which can result in a drop in nutritional quality. Commercial foods may be highly processed, and many contain dyes, flavorings, colorings and preservatives to enable the product to be stored for longer, increase its visual appeal (mostly to owners) and increase its palatability. Obviously the more an animal likes to eat a food, the more likely the owners are to buy it.

Most commercial foods are cooked or dried, which changes the structure of most of the ingredients and sometimes leads to compounds forming that can have a negative effect on the immune system and the body as a whole. Essential fatty acids especially are very sensitive to heat damage, and can go from a very important dietary component to a heat-denatured oil that has the potential to cause serious health problems in the long term. Excessive cooking of proteins and starches together can also lead to potentially health-damaging compounds. Cooking and processing can improve the digestibility of some foods, especially grains, but the high levels of extended heating required to produce many commercial foods change them dramatically, often for the worse.

Animals can react as humans do to some colorings and preservatives in food, resulting in behavioral and physical problems such as hyperactivity, altered immune function and allergies. So the more food is cooked, dried and processed, the more the ingredients are changed, and the more the "natural vitality" (biological vitality) of the food is lost as it goes from one state to another. This is why many people prefer to create their own homemade diets.

Homemade diets

Creating a well-balanced, nutritionally appropriate homemade diet is a viable alternative to commercial pet foods. Done correctly, it can be a very powerful component in the holistic approach to health. It is something I recommend when I am sure the owner will follow the recipes closely and be diligent in using the supplements correctly.

The pros

The positive aspects of creating a well-balanced and appropriate homemade diet are many. Owners can play an active part in creating food for their animal friends, and can learn about various important foods and supplements that may also benefit their own health. Natural diets can be made from fresh, organic ingredients (which are often nutritionally superior to non-organic produce), and micronutrients can be added from complex sources such as seaweeds, yeasts and plant oils, rather than refined chemical additives.

Meats can be fed raw or lightly cooked so that the proteins are not denatured excessively; the grains and carbohydrate sources can be cooked or ground to enhance digestibility, but prepared separately from the meat and combined just before serving, or fed separately at a different mealtime. Supplements are also added just before serving to avoid damage to the heat-sensitive oils and reduce interactions between ingredients. Raw vegetables can be put into a blender or juicer and pulverized to help break down the plant structure, making them easier to digest without destroying too many vitamins through cooking. Raw, meaty bones provide dental exercise and help keep teeth and gums healthy, as well as some calcium if the bones are crunched up and eaten. It is *really* important *not* to cook bones since they tend to splinter and can be very dangerous internally, sometimes perforating the gut. (Raw bones can potentially do this but it is less likely.)

The conventional academic approach to feeding recommends a "complete and balanced" mix of foods at every meal, which is what the commercial foods try to provide. This means the recommended amounts of proteins, fats, carbohydrates, minerals and vitamins, etc. are supplied in every meal, every day.

In his book *Give Your Dog a Bone*, Ian Billinghurst takes a different approach. He recommends providing all the necessary nutrients over several meals. This tends to mimic the situation in the wild, where a high-protein (meat) meal may be ingested one day, and there may be just eggs, plant material and other foraged nutrients over the following day or so until the next meat meal becomes available. This system allows the various internal organs to rest between concentrated meaty meals, thus reducing overwork in the long term.

At the end of the day, it is the overall long-term health of the animal that determines whether or not a diet is suitable, which means regular veterinary checks to pinpoint any problems so they can be rectified before any permanent damage is done.

There is a lot to be said for the "energetic (or biological) vitality" of food. This energy is taken into the body and transferred via the digestive processes into vitality of the body. You won't find anything about this aspect of nutrition in the text books, since it is not something that is easily tested in a laboratory, but it has been a feature of many ancient health systems for centuries, and something I have noted for many years. All foods have an energetic quality or vitality, but things like excessive cooking, processing and the addition of substances like artificial colorings, preservatives and flavorings seriously deplete this vitality. "Living" foods, such as fresh sprouted grains and seeds, are high in vitality. They contain increased levels of enzymes and vitamins, as well as starches that have been converted to simple sugars, proteins that have been converted into free amino acids, and free fatty acids that have been created from fats, making these foods more digestible and energetically more useful.

The cons

However, the negative aspects of a homemade diet also need to be addressed. Overcooking, poor ingredient quality and choices, omitting the supplements and not varying the ingredients can all be potential problems and reduce the quality of the nutrition received. Even small deviations in the type and quality of ingredients can affect the completeness and balance of the diet, even if a variety of foods are used over a period of time. Catering to changes in metabolic rates, weight fluctuations and different nutritional needs can be difficult unless these things are all understood. This is why I recommend having homemade diets checked for suitability by an animal nutritionist or veterinarian if they are to be used exclusively. These professionals can produce a diet specifically for your pet's needs.

In special situations like rapidly growing large breed dogs, it is important not to "overdo" the nutrition, which can lead to accelerated growth rates and result in serious bone and joint problems. It is also essential to supply the correct ratios of calcium to phosphorus at the correct times, and unless you follow recipes or procedures closely this may be compromised. In these situations, using appropriate large breed growth formulas of the super premium foods or well-balanced puppy diets is the most reliable way to go. Pet owners are often very enthusiastic to begin with when making natural diets, following the recipes closely and providing all ingredients diligently, but with time some parts of the recipe may be omitted or changed, and this is when deficiencies can arise.

Using food as medicine

In traditional Chinese medicine, foods are used as "medicines" to help heal different problems and support the body as it heals itself. All foods have a thermal nature, in that they can be warming foods, cooling foods or neutral foods. This means you can choose cooling foods to feed your pet if it has a "hot" condition such as inflammation, infection or fever, and warming foods for "cold" conditions, such as those that occur in many old animals during recovery from illness or surgery, or when the weather is cold. The aim as always is to bring the body back into balance.

It is interesting to reflect on the way people choose to eat certain kinds of foods at different times of the year. For example, we tend to eat a lot of salads and raw foods (cooling foods) in hot weather, and more casseroles and cooked foods (warming foods) in colder weather. Cooking puts heat into the food, and when you eat it this heat goes into the body, so if you have a "hot" condition like inflamed, itchy skin, eating dried or well-cooked food will add more heat to an already hot body, thus worsening the problem. The best foods for these conditions are raw, uncooked foods with a cooling thermal nature. The table below shows a few of the more common foods and their thermal nature. When you are preparing a home-made diet and your pet has a particular problem, choose foods that will help bring balance to the system.

The thermal nature of certain foods (adapted from information in Healing with Whole Foods, by Paul Pitchford[5])

Type of food	Thermal nature	Use
Meats Chicken	Warming	In elderly animals, during lactation and recovery from giving birth; also to treat poor appetites
Lamb	Warming	To increase energy and internal warmth, during lactation, for anemia and low body weight
Beef	Neutral	For general weakness, wasting (as with diabetes), and for thin animals. Generally not so good for kidney or liver disorders
Pork	Cooling	In thin, nervous, weak animals; for constipation, dry coughs, wasting stages of diabetes, inflammatory bowel problems

Type of food	Thermal nature	Use
White fish	Neutral	Improves appetite; for indigestion
Sardines	Neutral	For blood circulation, and as a mild diuretic. An excess can cause heat conditions
Grains Barley	Cooling	Benefits digestion
Corn	Neutral	Improves appetite, regulates digestion, promotes healthy teeth and gums, nourishes and supports the kidneys
Millet	Cooling	Strengthens the kidneys, aids digestion, balances over-acid conditions; antifungal, useful for *Candida albicans* overgrowth
Oats	Warming	For diarrhea, hepatitis, indigestion, abdominal bloating, general weakness
Rice	Neutral	Increases energy; good for depression, diarrhea, nausea, diabetes
Wheat	Cooling	For insomnia, irritability, emotional instability; encourages growth, weight gain and fat formation; good for frail, elderly or growing young animals. Can provoke allergic reactions, especially if rancid or refined
Vegetables Carrot	Neutral/warming	Good for lungs, digestion, liver, diarrhea; stimulates the removal of wastes, acts as a mild diuretic; contains an oil that destroys roundworms; carrot juice heals burns; also used for treating cancer and acts as an anti-inflammatory
Celery	Cooling	For inflammation of the liver, eye, bladder (cystitis), skin; helps reduce fevers; also good for arthritis and nerve inflammation

Type of food	Thermal nature	Use
Onion	Neutral/warming	Lowers blood pressure, inhibits allergic reaction, reduces phlegm in nose and throat
Parsley	Slightly warming	For kidney and urinary problems (but not severe kidney inflammation); strengthens adrenal glands, optic nerves; good for early ear infections
Pumpkin	Warming	For diarrhea, eczema, edema; regulates blood sugar levels so is useful for diabetes and hypoglycemia; promotes discharge of mucous from lungs, bronchi and throat; regular use can benefit bronchial asthma
Garlic	Warming	Aids circulation; inhibits viruses and amoebae; eliminates worms, unfavorable bacteria and yeasts including *Candida albicans*; promotes growth of healthy intestinal flora
Potato	Neutral	Reduces inflammations, helps relieve arthritis, helps improve general energy levels
Lettuce	Cooling	Good for digestion and lactation; mildly diuretic; relaxes the nerves without affecting the digestion; a mild sedative
Cucumber	Cooling	Diuretic, counteracts toxins, lifts depression, cleanses the blood, purifies the skin and acts as a digestive aid
Legumes Soybean	Cooling	Improves kidney function, circulation, pancreatic function (helps with diabetes), skin eruptions; lowers fever, acts as a diuretic
Lentil	Neutral	Diuretic, beneficial to the heart and circulation

Type of food	Thermal nature	Use
Mung beans	Cooling	Detoxifies the body; good for the liver and gallbladder; helps treat diarrhea, conjunctivitis, painful urination, heatstroke and inflamed skin conditions
Sprouted mung, alfalfa	Extremely cooling	Useful for inflammation, especially of the skin, also excessive personality (i.e., overactive, loud, robust); helps detoxify the body

If you had a young, very active, noisy dog with a red, smelly, inflamed skin, you could choose foods that would help treat these problems and rebalance the body by cooling it down from the inside. These would include raw vegetables such as celery, raw greens, sprouts, cucumber and carrots; grains such as millet; legumes such as soybeans; and meats such as white fish, beef (a neutral to warming meat, less so if fed raw) or pork (a cooling meat but expensive and needs to be cooked because of parasites, which adds heat).

Dogs find it difficult to digest raw grains and vegetable matter, but cooking helps soften the walls of the plant cells and aids digestion. Remember, though, that cooking adds heat to the food and then to the body, so in "heat" conditions (hot, smelly, exudative conditions) it is necessary to balance digestibility with reduced levels of cooking.

Older animals tend to have "cold" body conditions—they tend to be thinner, searching out the heater or that patch of sunshine, move more slowly and have dry skin. These "cold" conditions require warming foods to balance the system and add warmth to the body internally. Foods such as cooked chicken or lamb, cooked grains such as oats or rice and warming vegetables such as pumpkin, carrots and garlic are helpful.

The seasons also affect what foods are recommended. In the warmer weather, feeding your animals more cooling and raw foods will balance the summer heat, especially if they have "heat" tendencies such as seeking cool floors and shade all the time, inflammatory conditions and excess smell about their bodies. In winter, feed more cooked, warming foods, especially to animals that hug the heater or are generally thin and weak.

Meeting the needs of the individual

As we have seen, every animal has differing requirements that change with the seasons and with their state of health. Food companies are now beginning to recognize this, producing an ever-increasing range of prescription diets—diets for kidney problems, skin problems and so on. These are, however, predominantly made up of dried foods, or canned foods that have been cooked and processed so they can be stored. Consequently, they tend to have lost a lot of the initial food vitality.

An advantage of these super premium foods is that they are taste tested and animals will actually eat them. Cats in particular can be very fussy, especially when they are unwell, and at this time it is even more important that they eat something. I stress to animal owners that while fresh food diets are preferable, if your pet simply will not eat them, and they cannot afford not to eat (i.e., if they are older, or very thin animals) then you may need to try the good-quality commercial foods just to keep them going.

If an old animal stops eating a downward spiral begins, and if they go two or three days without food it is often very difficult to get them eating again. When cats go for more than 36–48 hours without eating (especially if they are very fat or very thin) the body starts to go into starvation mode and the metabolic changes that begin can make the animal's condition a lot worse.

If your cat is unwell and has stopped eating, it is very important to get it to a veterinarian sooner rather than later, especially if it is old and frail, so that the vet can start syringe- or tube-feeding it. Dogs seem to cope better with periods of anorexia (reduced appetite), but again, if they are not eating, see your veterinarian to find out why and get some dietary suggestions to aid recovery.

Formulating a homemade diet

There are a number of very important points to remember if you are using a homemade diet recipe. These recipes are in effect basic guidelines, and they may not take into account an animal's individual needs, which can be highly changeable. At the same time, they are designed to provide the correct proportions of each food group, and substituting different ingredients may change the overall nutritional analysis, possibly for the worse.

Not all owners have the knowledge or ability to adjust recipes to suit their individual pet's energy requirements while maintaining the correct ratios and balance in the diet. Computer formulation of diets is recommended, as this can indicate if the diet is complete and balanced for a general group of animals (see "References and further reading," page 274, for useful websites). However, this also has its limitations as computer formulations rely on standard values that may differ from the actual food used (for example, food quality can vary even between the same cuts of meat). They also do not include food trials, which reveal how an animal reacts to a particular diet when fed it exclusively over a period of time.

Homemade diets can also be more expensive, depending on where you source the ingredients, although buying dry ingredients in bulk without compromising on freshness can reduce the cost. There are also definite "fashions" in nutrition, with information changing all the time, and what may be acceptable today may be out of favor tomorrow!

Having said all this, you may be tempted not to bother with homemade foods, but it is definitely worthwhile if you have the motivation and knowledge, and are prepared to pay careful and consistent attention to recipe detail. A fresh, organic, biologically appropriate diet (i.e., one that suits your particular animal) will play a huge part in your pet's overall health.

The most common dietary situation is where you need to sustain an adult pet in a comfortable environment, with moderate levels of activity, and this is not very demanding in terms of nutrition and diet formulation. During growth, the last trimester of pregnancy, the first half of lactation (making milk), and for hard physical work or during certain illnesses, the diet needs to be far more precise with regard to food energy and optimal ranges of essential nutrients.[1]

The terminology of nutrition

Some background on nutrition terminology will be useful[2]:

- **A complete diet** is one in which each nutrient essential for health is present.

- **A balanced diet** is one in which each nutrient is present in the correct amount and proportion. High-quality commercial foods achieve this balance and completeness at every meal. Many good homemade diets are complete, but unless they are analyzed in a laboratory or via a computer they may not be properly balanced. But does every meal need to be complete and balanced? Or is it enough to achieve this completeness and balance over several days or several meals as many wild animals appear to do? There are differing views on this point, but personally I believe the ideal diet has a variety of foods which overall provide completeness and balance. Because of this I suggest a variety of similar ingredients and the use of different recipes and mixes. It is important to have regular health checks to ensure appropriate performance of the diet.

- **Digestibility** measures how "available" a food is to the animal and how much it is absorbed. Cooking generally improves the digestibility of plant materials and grains by splitting the cell walls and making the cell contents more available to digestive enzymes in the digestive system. Cooking also generally improves the digestibility of proteins to a point, but overcooking can have the reverse effect. Overcooking (as in the drying of commercial foods) can greatly affect digestibility and amino acid content, and may contribute to the graying of patches or lines in the coat. Overcooking of eggs also damages their proteins and lowers their digestibility. Sprouting seeds and grains increases their digestibility, as does grinding and soaking. Some indigestible contents may be needed to provide fiber and bulk to the bowel, as described earlier. Combinations of different proteins will increase the overall quality of the food and its digestibility. A basic guide to the digestibility of food is what comes out the other end of the animal; if the feces are large and bulky and the animal is always hungry and is losing weight, the food can be assumed to have low digestibility and is therefore not as "available" to the animal.

- **Palatability** is how tasty a food is to the animal. Adding oils and fats often increases the palatability of the food.

- **Antioxidants** help prevent spoilage and degeneration of food. Preservatives in commercial food can vary in toxicity, but the more commonly used preservatives today are vitamin E, vitamin C and rosemary oil. The use of vitamin E in natural diets will help preserve the oil additives, but they also need to be kept in the dark and ideally in the fridge. If raw food is used, it MUST be fresh and kept refrigerated for short periods only. Raw meat can potentially carry bacteria that is harmful to humans and animals, as well as several different types of parasite. Light cooking will destroy most of these nasties, but refrigeration of the cooked product afterward is also necessary. Burning fat can result in cancer-forming products called benzopyrenes, and cooking may destroy many of the vitamins found in vegetables.

- **Component interactions**—varying the level of one of the main food groups (i.e., proteins, carbohydrates or fats)—will affect the levels of the other components. There can also be interactions between certain plant components and minerals which can make the minerals unavailable to the animal.

Basic food groups

When making a homemade diet, for completeness, one should include items from each of the five food groups[3]:
1. A protein source, preferably an animal source.

2. A carbohydrate source from cooked cereal grain (also contains fiber).
3. A fat source, either animal fat or vegetable oils.
4. A mineral source, especially calcium.
5. A multi-vitamin source.

1. Proteins

Use high-quality proteins such as eggs, lean meat, cottage cheese, torula yeast, organ meats (such as liver, heart, kidney, tripe or gizzard), beef, lamb, chicken and fish. Secondary protein sources that can be used for dogs are beans (or legumes) such as soybeans, kidney beans, chickpeas and adzuki beans. The final food should contain 25 to 30% cooked meat for dogs and 35 to 50% cooked meat for cats. Liver can be used once or twice a week (as no more than half the meat portion) as it provides many useful nutrients[3].

2. Carbohydrates

These are mainly used to provide energy but some sources can contribute significant amounts of protein, fiber and fat. The usual sources are cooked cereals such as rice, corn, wheat, potato, barley and millet. Excellent cereals with reasonable protein levels are quinoa, amaranth and soybeans (a legume). The carbohydrate to protein ratio should be at least 1:1 to 2:1 for cat foods, and 2:1 to 3:1 for dog foods. If extra fiber is needed, peas or bran (rice, oat or wheat) can be used[3].

3. Fats

Fats provide essential fatty acids as well as a dense energy source. When extra calories are needed but the volume of food cannot be increased, adding an extra fat source will allow this. Too much fat will result in a very energy-dense diet, which can lead to obesity. Changing the various cuts of meat can markedly increase the fat content of food, hence the primary protein source (usually meat) will affect the amount of fat in the diet. When the meat used is "lean" then an additional fat source such as vegetable fat can be used for at least 2% of the formula weight for dogs and 5% of the formula for cats[3]. Soybean or safflower oil is often used since these oils are high in linoleic acid (an omega-6 fatty acid), and I also like to add some flaxseed oil for extra omega-3 fatty acids. Cats need more dietary fats than dogs because they need a more energy-dense diet, as well as arachidonic acid, an essential fatty acid that is mostly found in animal fats.

4. Minerals

These are an essential additive to most homemade diets because the foods alone cannot be eaten in large enough volumes to provide a balanced ratio of minerals, especially calcium and phosphorus. A meaty diet (where the protein levels are equal to or greater than the carbohydrate levels) usually contains sufficient phosphorus, so you only need to add a calcium supplement such as calcium carbonate (lime flour) (0.5 g/day for a 10-pound cat and at least 2.0 g/day for a 35-pound dog)[3]. Where the protein levels (usually meat) are lower than the carbohydrate levels you usually need to add a calcium and a phosphorus supplement such as dicalcium phosphate (at a ratio of about 2 parts calcium to 1 part phosphorus), using the same dose rate as you would for calcium carbonate[3].

Nutritional yeast contains relatively high levels of phosphorus compared to calcium, so if you are using the dog and cat powder mixes described later in this Chapter, I suggest using a calcium-only product such as calcium carbonate as the main calcium source to balance this[4]. The many other microminerals that are needed can be found in a kelp supplement as well as in nutritional yeast, or to be reliable, a human or specialized animal mineral/vitamin supplement. These supplements can be expensive but they are non-negotiable as additives to a homemade diet. Imbalances in these micronutrients (too much or too little) can be dangerous and can seriously affect the health of your animal friend, especially during crucial times such as late pregnancy, growth and lactation.

5. Vitamins

Like minerals, vitamins are non-negotiable additives to the homemade diet as the foods alone rarely provide the required balance. Use either human multivitamin tablets (an adult over-the-counter vitamin and mineral tablet that contains no more than 200% of the daily recommended allowances for people is all right for both cats and dogs at $^1/_2$ to 1 tablet per day[3]) or a supplement mix from sources such as yeast, kelp and lecithin. I prefer these minerals and vitamins from a complex natural source such as kelp, alfalfa powder, blue-green algae (spirulina) or barley grass powder, but they may be cumbersome to use and unpalatable to some animals, and may also have variable levels of the important minerals and vitamins, depending on the source.

So, bringing all this together, we can devise a recipe containing the following:

1. A source of protein, with the final food containing not less than 25–30% meat for dogs and 35–50% meat for cats. Liver can be used two to three times a week, but not as more than half the meat. If the meat is cooked or if you feed a homemade diet exclusively, then a taurine supplement (200–500 mg per day) is necessary for cats (cooking can damage this amino acid[3]). Muscle meats seem to be deficient in taurine, which is most abundant in brain and organ meats. Including mackerel and heart in the diet will help supplement this necessary protein component in cats[4].

2. A source of carbohydrate that provides sufficient energy (along with the other ingredients) and fiber for the needs of the animal, at one to two times the amount of protein source for cats and two to three times the amount of protein source for dogs.

3. A source of animal fat for cats (supplying arachidonic acid) as well as a vegetable fat source to supplement linoleic acid and the omega-3 fatty acids (alpha-linolenic acid).

4. A source of obvious calcium and possibly phosphorus (if the meat level is less than the carbohydrate level). Also a source of the microminerals and vitamins (a human multivitamin mix or a mix of complexes such as kelp, primary yeast and lecithin granules).

5. A source of choline, which may be added.

6. Sufficient energy to maintain body weight at the correct level (you should not be able to see the ribs, but you should be able to *just* feel them). This energy requirement will vary with exercise levels, metabolic rate, state of health and stage of life. This is why it can be tricky making your own diets—estimating the amount of energy required can be difficult without calorie counting. The basic guideline is that if the animal is getting too

fat, reduce the energy density of the food by lowering the fat levels or reducing the volume of food (although this may also reduce the critical levels of essential proteins, minerals and vitamins).

Supplements

If you are preparing a homemade diet using the appropriate meats, vegetables and grains for your pet's age and state of health, you also need to include special supplements to add essential minerals and vitamins to the diet. These can come from a multi-vitamin-mineral tablet or from the more complex foods that are rich in minerals and vitamins. However, one problem is that the levels of these important minerals and vitamins vary between sources, so it can be difficult to be sure of the exact amount they provide. In higher-demand situations such as lactation, late pregnancy and growth, a continued imbalance of these critical nutrients may cause significant health problems.

The following are some of the possible complex food sources for these nutrients.

Sea vegetables

Sea vegetables, or seaweeds, are a very rich form of many of these essential minerals and vitamins. They are spectacularly useful as food additives, supplying all the hundred or so minerals and trace elements that our blood contains, in a form that is easily used by the body. It is also interesting to note that even if seaweeds grow in polluted seawater, they don't absorb the pollutants as many land vegetables do. In fact, they detoxify and transform a certain number of toxic metals, enabling the body to excrete them harmlessly via the intestines.

Seaweeds are especially high in calcium, iodine and iron. Kelp has four times the iron of beef and between 100 and 500 times more iodine than shellfish; the seaweeds wakame, arame and hijiki have ten times the calcium of milk, while sea lettuce has 25 times the iron of beef[5]. Kelp can be bought in a powdered form, and although it has quite a strong taste, this is dissipated when it is added to other foods.

Essential fatty acids

The body also needs essential fatty acids, which are used to produce healthy skin and hair, support thyroid and adrenal activity, and bolster immunity. They also promote healthy blood, nerves and arteries, and are critical in the transport and breakdown of cholesterol. Essential fatty acids can also be used as natural anti-inflammatory agents and are useful in the treatment of skin and joint inflammation.

Deficiencies in essential fatty acids can lead to skin problems (such as dry, flaky skin), dry hair, hair loss, liver problems, irritability, increased susceptibility to infections, infertility and retarded growth. The three main essential fatty acids that are required in the diet are:

- Linoleic acid (an omega-6 fatty acid);
- Arachidonic acid (omega-6), and
- Alpha-linolenic acid (omega-3 fatty acid).

The essential fatty acids are also important in blood clotting; the omega-6 fatty acids encourage clotting, while the omega-3 fatty acids reduce clotting, therefore it is very important to have a balance between the two. Omega-3 fatty acids are especially important for the health of the circulatory system, blood and blood vessels, for regulating cholesterol and other fats, and they can encourage blood flow to tissues damaged by lack of circulation.

Two primary examples of omega-3 fatty acids are EPA (eicosapentaenoic acid) and DHA (docosahexaenoic acid), which are found in high levels in oily fish. These fatty acids are important in blood vessel renewal, brain development, growth and learning ability. Human studies have shown that feeding mothers fish oils during pregnancy and lactation aids fetal and infant brain development markedly, as 50% of the brain's DHA is formed before birth and 50% accumulates during the first year of life[5]. Other sources of omega-3 fatty acids are plant sources such as flaxseed, pumpkin seed, soy products and dark-green vegetables such as parsley, kale and Swiss chard.

Omega-6 fatty acids are found in nuts, grains, seeds, most vegetables, fruit and animal products. Along with the other fatty acids, they are important in the synthesis of hormone-like substances known as prostaglandins, which affect every cell and organ in the body. There are different types of prostaglandins. Gamma-linolenic acid (GLA), an omega-6 fatty acid that produces a type of prostaglandin called PG1, is effective against inflammatory conditions such as eczema, arthritis and autoimmune disease, can alleviate "dry eye," helps the immune system function properly, activates T-cells (which destroy cancer and other unwanted substances in the cells of the body) and helps regulate the action of insulin, so is useful for diabetics.

The highest sources of GLA are spirulina and the seeds of borage, black currant and evening primrose, which are ingested as oils. It is very important that these oils are taken in a non-rancid form, as rancidity or oxidation will create free radicals in the body, which contribute to aging and weaken immunity. They should be stored in an airtight container in a cool, dark place such as a refrigerator, or even in capsule form, which helps reduce rancidity. It is also very important not to heat the oils or cook with them as the heat destroys their structure and therefore their function.

Arachidonic acid, another type of omega-6 fatty acid, is obtained from direct sources such as meat, eggs and peanuts. Arachidonic acid produces a type of prostaglandin called PG2, as well as releasing leukotrienes into the blood. Too much PG2 can lead to pain and inflammation and encourage the blood to clot, and while normal levels of leukotrienes help heal wounds, an excess can contribute to asthma, dermatitis, rhinitis and lupus (systemic lupus erythematosus, or SLE). At normal levels, arachidonic acid and PG2 help cell proliferation, but taken to extremes they can be directly linked to cancer and tumors.

Anti-inflammatory drugs such as aspirin block the production of PG2, thus reducing pain, inflammation and fever, but they also block the production of PG1, which is itself anti-inflammatory. It is more useful in the long term to increase the production of PG1 and PG3, which effectively reduces PG2 production, as well as providing their own anti-inflammatory action and other valuable properties. Dietary supplements of foods with PG1 and PG3 precursors (such as flaxseed, borage and evening primrose oils, fish oils, seeds and nuts) will ensure the balance is favorable.

Dogs and cats cannot synthesize linoleic acid or alpha-linolenic acid, so the diet needs to supply these important nutrients. In addition, cats cannot make arachidonic acid, so they need to obtain it from animal fats. It is, however, important not to overdo dietary oils, as this can lead to obesity and sometimes blood and body fat disorders.

Summary

The important omega-6 fatty acids are:
- Linoleic acid, which is sourced from nuts, seeds, vegetables, fruit and animal products, and can convert into gamma-linolenic acid (GLA).
  - Direct sources of GLA are spirulina, evening primrose oil, borage oil and black currant oil;
  - GLA converts to PG1, which acts as an anti-inflammatory and as pain relief.
- Arachidonic acid, which is sourced from meat, dairy products and eggs.
  - Arachidonic acid converts to PG2, which at normal levels helps cell proliferation, but an excess can result in inflammation and pain.

Important omega-3 fatty acids are:
- Alpha-linolenic acid, which is sourced from flaxseeds, pumpkin seeds, soy products, dark-green vegetables and some marine plants.
- Eicosapentaenoic acid (EPA) and docosahexaenoic acid (DHA), which are both found in certain marine fish oils; direct sources are fish such as salmon, sardines and tuna. Alpha-linolenic acid can also convert into EPA and DHA.
  - EPA and DLA convert to PG3, which relieves pain and inflammation.

Paul Pitchford's *Healing with Whole Foods*[5] is a very useful book for anyone who wants to learn more about this subject. Much of the information in this and the following section is taken with permission from Chapters 9 and 10 of his book.

Nutritional (or brewer's) yeast

Nutritional yeast, or brewer's yeast, is another supplement in the natural diet that is full of important nutrients. It is very high in many of the B vitamins and in protein. In the higher-quality nutritional yeast that is grown on a B12-enriched medium, the vitamins are incorporated into the living food rather than added at the end. This makes it easier for the body to assimilate them, as they are already partially "digested."

Although nutritional yeast is high in many nutrients it can be deficient in others that are needed for balance. For example, yeast has a high phosphorus level, which can upset the phosphorus/calcium balance, so added calcium is needed to correct this imbalance. The best kinds of nutritional yeast to buy are the high-grade ones known as "primary" yeasts (for example, torula yeast) that are produced specifically as nutritional supplements, not just as a byproduct of beer brewing. These yeasts are less processed and not as bitter as brewer's yeast, thus making them more palatable and higher in nutrients, with more protein and fat than brewer's yeast.

Nutritional yeast is not recommended as food if an animal has an existing condition in which there are high levels of Candida-like yeasts on the body, since it can worsen these. This applies, for example, to yeasty skin and ear conditions, or where the animal is retaining fluid or has edematous swellings. Nutritional yeast has also had bad press as a food that causes allergies. Although it is possible to be allergic to nutritional yeast, I have found this to be uncommon; there are other foods that are far more allergenic, and more likely to cause problems. In animals that are generally healthy, nutritional yeast can be an extremely useful food supplement, and it often forms the basis of the food supplements recommended in homemade natural diets.

Calcium

It is important to ensure the appropriate balance of phosphorus and calcium, because too much or too little of one or the other can create problems in the bones and many other tissues. There is a greater demand for these minerals in growing, pregnant and lactating animals, and if these needs are not met in quality and quantity, deficiencies can arise. The result can be problems with bone and joint formation and strength, muscle contraction and a range of other body functions.

Sources of calcium for natural diet recipes:

- **Bone meal**—buy the powdered version that is for human use, rather than the garden variety, which may be contaminated. Concern has been raised in recent times that bone meal may be contaminated with organisms associated with BSE or "mad cow disease." It also varies in quality, and can be difficult to find.
- **Dicalcium phosphate**—this is a non-animal-derived alternative to bone meal. Use about two-thirds the amount stated for bone meal. Use when the protein fraction is less than the carbohydrate fraction of the diet.
- **Eggshell powder**—wash and dry empty eggshells, bake them at around 300°F for about 10 minutes to make them dry and brittle, then grind them to a fine powder. One eggshell dries to about 1 tsp powder. Use 5 tsp eggshell powder in place of each $1/4$ cup bone meal[4].
- **Calcium carbonate**. This only contains calcium and no phosphorus, and it may be unpalatable to some animals. Use it when the protein fraction of the diet is equal to or greater than the carbohydrate fraction.

If large breed, rapidly growing dogs do not receive an optimal balance of calcium and phosphorus (and a controlled level of food energy intake) in the first 12 to 15 months of life in particular, there is a very real risk of permanent joint and bone deformities. These can lead to degenerative joint disease, pain and lameness later in life, or acute lameness as they grow. Too much calcium can be as damaging as too little. When it is combined with "overnutrition" (where an energy-dense diet is fed, i.e., too many calories, causing rapid growth) and susceptible genetics, serious bone and joint deformities can occur. In the wild, dogs and growing puppies have to hunt and do not tend to eat protein- and calcium-rich prey every day, so their growth is controlled as the dietary levels of many nutrients fluctuate. So getting the balance right is crucial, especially in these fast-growing, large breeds of dog.

Companies that produce high-quality animal foods do huge amounts of research and have formulated diets specifically for this rapid growth phase, providing the correct amounts of both calcium and phosphorus, and other levels of nutrition to regulate growth and keep it within the normal range. If a homemade diet is used, the recipes need to be followed closely, without changing quantities and ingredients, to ensure the ratios remain in balance. One solution is to stick to a top quality large breed food for that crucial first 12 months. When requirements are not as critical, one can switch to a good homemade diet, making sure the recipes and guidelines are adhered to strictly.

Vitamin E

Vitamin E is added to the diet to act as a natural preservative to the oil mixes, as well as for its important healing properties. It acts as an antioxidant, protecting the vitamin A and essential fatty acids in the diet so that they retain their health-supporting properties. Rancid or oxidized oils taste bitter and smell "off"; they are very unhealthy and should be avoided.

Lecithin

Lecithin plays an especially important part in the maintenance of healthy brain, nervous system, liver, heart and kidney tissues.

Lecithin supplementation has been found to help nervous system dysfunction, poor memory, brain or nervous system tissue damage, poor motor function, poor fat-soluble vitamin assimilation, and skin problems such as eczema, allergies and skin infections[5].

Research and clinical trials have shown lecithin supplementation to be helpful for improving immunity, sexual function and male fertility, weight distribution and nerve problems, and lowering the requirements of insulin in diabetics[5].

Alternative supplement suggestions

If your animal does not accept dog or cat powders, or you have to omit the yeast, use a multivitamin supplement designed for humans, or the very high quality animal vitamins. It is difficult to find comprehensive mixes of the latter, and they can be expensive, but they are well worth it. If kelp is unpalatable to your animal you can substitute alfalfa powder and powdered liver in equal proportions in the dog powder ($^1/_4$ cup of each); see below for recipes for dog and cat powders.

Encouraging cats to eat the new diet

- Introduce the new food gradually, mixing it with the usual food over a period of a week or two, gradually increasing the proportions of the newer tastes.
- The powder and oil supplements are often the most difficult to introduce, so again, start by mixing small amounts into the usual food and slowly increase them until you reach the required daily amounts.
- Try fasting your pet for a day or so—an empty stomach helps to change old habits. However, do not do this with elderly or unwell animals unless you have checked with your veterinarian.
- Try warming the food so it is slightly steaming, but not so hot as to burn the tongue; the smell in the rising steam will encourage your pet to eat. Note: Cats will not eat if they can't smell the food, so a blocked nose can make a cat stop eating for quite some time—get it seen!
- Try adding very smelly foods like sardines or tuna; the novel smell often appeals, and many cats love fishy smells.
- Try some of the commercially available food tempters that have meaty smells. These can be sprinkled on top of the food, and they often get the cat eating.

Homemade diets

Here are a couple of very basic homemade diet recipes, with the supplements based on the powders and oils suggested in *Dr. Pitcairn's Complete Guide to Natural Health for Dogs and Cats*[4], by Richard Pitcairn and Susan Hubble Pitcairn. For more recipes and greater detail I suggest you refer to his or similar books that provide ideas for recipe variety, as well as puppy and kitten recipes.

The problem with printing recipes as a general guideline is that they are not specific for the individual. As said before, each individual has a specific requirement depending on their age, metabolic rate and state of health. If possible, get a nutritionist to create a recipe for your animal's requirements. They can provide correct levels of energy and nutrients. There are also computer programs available for this and the one I have used here is courtesy of Dr. Sean Delaney, who created a program called Balance IT© (see *www.balanceit.com*). You can enter your animal's details and create a homemade diet specific for its needs, knowing it provides all the essential components for good health.

It is important to follow the recipes closely and not to substitute too many ingredients, as this will throw the ratios of protein and other nutrients out of kilter. The supplements are also very important. The main part of the diet will provide the gross protein, carbohydrate and fat components but the supplements provide a lot of the micronutrients, minerals and vitamins that are crucial to make the body function normally.

Some animals love these diets and thrive magnificently on them, while others have definite tastes and getting them to eat different food can be a little difficult. I always suggest persevering, perhaps mixing the natural diet with a commercial food for a while, and reducing the stronger-tasting parts of the diet, such as the powder mix, for a few days in the introductory stage. Most dogs really love this food and do extremely well on it, but cats, many of which are fussy eaters, may take a little longer to adapt to the new tastes. Our feline friends have trained us very well to feed them what they want, and owners often go to extremes to get them food they will eat. Changing their diet can be difficult as cats are enormously routine-based animals, and even a small change in their diet can make them refuse food.

 Basic dog natural diet

This is designed for a healthy three-year-old neutered male dog weighing 40 pounds, with moderate exercise levels and a normal metabolic rate. The amount below is enough to feed the dog over one day. The recipe can be doubled or tripled to make several days' worth of food, which should be stored in the refrigerator. Add the daily amount of supplements just before serving, not into the bulk version.

approx. 1 cup ground beef (95% lean, 5% fat)
1/4 cup beef liver
approx. 1 1/2 cups brown rice, cooked
approx. 1 cup carrots or other vegetables

Supplements

1 tbsp dog oil (see page 60)
2 tbsp dog powder (see page 60)
100 IU vitamin E capsule
1½ multivitamin tablets
Cook the rice and the meat separately. Cool them, then combine. Add the vegetables and the supplements and serve. Makes about 3½ cups of food (daily amount).

This diet provides:
- 28% protein calories (typical commercial pet food range is 20–30%);
- 30% fat calories (typical commercial pet food range is 20–30%);
- 41% carbohydrate calories (typical commercial pet food range is 40–60%);
- 989 kcal (the estimated calorie requirement is approximately 979 kcal/day, but this is a guideline only. There can be a variation of plus or minus 50% in the actual amount the dog needs to maintain its weight. Consult your veterinarian to see if this diet is suitable for your dog).

If you used ground beef with 25% fat (instead of 5%) the diet would become very incomplete, with 13% protein, 46% fat and 41% carbohydrate, and a total energy level of 1259 kcal. Feeding these proportions over a period of time would cause serious health issues.

 ## A lower-calorie diet for the same-sized dog

3½ cups cooked rolled oats
approx. ⅓ cup skinless chicken, boiled lightly (or 95% lean ground beef)
approx. ⅛ cup vegetables such as carrots, broccoli, sprouts (raw)

Supplements

1 tbsp dog oil (see page 60)
2 tbsp dog powder (see page 60) or a multivitamin tablet
100 IU vitamin E capsule

Cook the oats and meat separately, cool, then combine. Add the vegetables and the daily supplements.

This diet contains:

- 24% protein;
- 29% fat;
- 47% carbohydrate;
- 704 kcal (estimated daily need is 979 kcal/day—again, highly variable).

 Essential supplements

Dog powder mix[4]

2 cups nutritional yeast

1 cup calcium carbonate powder (or $1\frac{1}{2}$ cups steamed bone meal)

$\frac{1}{2}$ cup kelp powder

$\frac{1}{2}$ cup lecithin

1000 mg vitamin C (or $\frac{1}{4}$ tsp sodium ascorbate)

Mix all the ingredients together. Place in an airtight jar and store in cool, dark place. Note: the kelp can be replaced with alfalfa and liver powder in equal proportions.

Dog oil mix[4]

$1\frac{3}{4}$ cups cold pressed safflower, canola or sunflower oil (ideally organic)

$\frac{1}{4}$ cup cod liver oil

100 IU vitamin E capsule (to preserve the oil)

Mix the first three ingredients together, then puncture the vitamin E capsule and squeeze the oil from the capsule into the mixture. Store in the refrigerator.

 Basic cat natural diet

This diet is designed for a three-year-old 10-pound neutered cat of normal weight and normal metabolic rate. The following is sufficient for one day's food.

approx. $\frac{1}{2}$ cup lean ground beef (95% lean, 5% fat)

approx. $\frac{1}{2}$–$\frac{3}{4}$ cup brown rice, cooked

approx. $\frac{1}{3}$ cup skinless chicken, lightly cooked

2 tbsp carrots

Supplements

1 tsp cat powder (see below)
1 tsp cat oil (see below)
500 mg taurine supplement
50 IU vitamin E (pierce a 100 IU capsule and squeeze half the oil over the food)
1 multivitamin tablet
Cook the rice and meat separately, and cool. Pulverize the rice in a blender, then blend in the vegetables so the cat can't pick them out of the meat. Mix with the meat, then add the supplements.

This diet provides:

- 32% protein calories (typical commercial pet food range is 25–35%);
- 28% fat calories (typical commercial pet food range is 25–35%);
- 46% carbohydrates (typical commercial pet food range is 30–50%);
- Total calories per day is 250 kcal (calculated requirement is 260 kcal/day, which can vary considerably depending on the individual).

 ## Essential supplements

Cat powder mix[4]

$^1/_2$ cup nutritional (primary) yeast
$^1/_4$ cup calcium carbonate (or $^3/_4$ cup steamed bone meal)
$^1/_4$ cup kelp powder
$^1/_4$ cup lecithin
1000 mg vitamin C powder
Mix together and place in an airtight jar. Store in a cool, dark place. Note: if kelp is unpalatable to the cat it can be replaced with alfalfa and liver powder in equal proportions.

Cat oil mix[4]

$^3/_4$ cup cold pressed olive oil
$^1/_4$ cup cod liver oil
2 tbsp flaxseed oil

50 IU vitamin E capsule (to preserve the oil)

Mix the first three ingredients together, then pierce the vitamin E capsule and squeeze the contents into the mixture. The vitamin E acts as a natural preservative for the oil. Store in the refrigerator.

Amounts to feed

The amount to feed your cat depends on:

- The energy levels of the food
- The metabolic rate of your pet
- Your pet's exercise levels

Generally:

- If the cat is getting too fat, reduce the volume of food
- If it is getting too thin, increase the volume of food
- You should not see the cat's ribs but should just be able to feel them

General notes

- It is very important to use the supplements with the basic meat/grains/vegetable mix.
- Feed the meat raw, or lightly cooked (but not overcooked) if you are worried about bacteria or parasites.
- Cook the grains well to assist with digestion.
- Vegetables are best grated or finely chopped, and can be either raw or very lightly steamed. Remember, the more you cook or process foods the more damage you do to the quality of the food.
- Avoid heating the oil mixes in any way, especially if you are using flaxseed oil, as this can damage the essential fatty acids and negate the benefits of the oil.
- Organic vegetables, grains and meats are best, and you can also try growing your own without pesticides or insecticides.
- Store the powders and oils in a cool, dark, dry place and use them within six months.

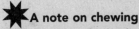**A note on chewing**

It is important for both dogs and cats to have lumps of meat or bones to chew daily to keep their teeth healthy. Raw, meaty bones form an important part of your animal friend's diet. The action of gnawing on meat or bones not only massages the gums but the friction of chewing removes the early stages of tartar and stimulates saliva flow. Get your pet used to chewing for at least five to ten minutes daily to keep its teeth and gums healthy, starting from a very young age. Introducing large lumps of meat or bones at an older age can be difficult, as often the animal does not know what to do with them, and it may bury or just leave them.

! A word of caution: *Never* feed your pet cooked bones, and if your dog or cat has a problem with eating bones (such as diarrhea or constipation) it may be safer to stick to cleaning their teeth with a toothbrush or giving them rubber chew bones. Occasionally bone fragments can damage teeth, cause perforations or obstructions in the stomach, or scratch the inner lining of the intestines.

Specific needs of cats

- Cats require certain protein-building blocks (amino acids) every day, and if these are not received daily, serious health issues will arise. Taurine, for example, is an amino acid that cats can only obtain through their diet; it is crucial for heart and eye health, and insufficient amounts can result in heart failure and blindness. Taurine is easily destroyed by heat and cooking and may be bound up and made unavailable in high-fiber diets. Therefore if food is processed in any way this vital amino acid will need to be added to the diet.
- Cats require higher levels of protein than dogs.
- Cats cannot make arachidonic acid; it all needs to come from the food they eat.

- Cats require several B vitamins and preformed vitamin A, which is mostly found in high levels in animal tissue (meats).

Do not feed dog food to cats because it generally does not contain the necessary levels of these nutrients. If you feed your cat a good-quality commercial food that has all the required nutrients, do not add supplements as this will alter the balance of the entire diet, usually for the worse.

Can I feed a vegetarian diet to my cat?

Feeding a cat a vegetarian diet can be very complicated, and finding alternative protein sources can be difficult and expensive. Cats are obligate carnivores and in the wild live almost exclusively on animal-derived foodstuffs. If you insist on your cat being vegetarian, it is essential to provide supplements to ensure all its crucial dietary needs are met. Many of the essential amino acids, such as taurine, for example, are not easily available in non-animal protein sources, and must be added.

Basically, it really isn't the best to feed a cat a diet that excludes meat and animal products. However, there are some nearly or completely vegetarian commercial foods on the market, which are formulated to include all the required nutrients.

Palatability

Taste is another very important point with cats—they can be really fussy! Failing to feed a variety of tastes to your cat up to the age of about six months may result in a fussy adult cat, as most taste preferences are set by six months of age. Most of the commercial foods have been taste-tested and are acceptable to the majority of cats—obviously there is no point in producing a food that is not palatable and therefore won't sell.

Cats initially use their sense of smell to explore food so any form of snuffle or nasal congestion, such as occurs with a viral infection, can be a problem. Often, a cat simply will not eat if it can't smell its food. This is where it can be useful to use tricks such as heating the food so the rising steam amplifies the smell, including strong-smelling foods such as sardines or other fish, or adding some of the food-flavoring tempters that are designed for this very situation.

When cats stop eating their food

It is very important that cats do not go without food for more than 24 to 36 hours because their systems will start going into starvation mode. This can be very damaging to the liver, especially with overweight cats, as the body fat is mobilized all at once and ends up clogging the liver. If the cat is thin and old it can be equally damaging, as it simply does not have the reserves to cope. Cats also tend to take in a lot of their daily water with their food, so if they are not eating they can become dehydrated quickly, which is serious if the kidneys are not working very well in the first place.

The main message here is that if your cat stops eating always check with your veterinarian to try and determine why. As noted above, smell is very important to cats, and if it has an infection or any other problem that interferes with its sense of smell you might be able to tempt it to eat with warmed or smelly food, or taste enhancers. If the problem is more serious or long term the cat may need to be hospitalized and syringe-fed special concentrated food to help it recover. Syringe feeding simply means using a large syringe and dripping liquid food into the cat's mouth; this can be the difference between recovery and degeneration of the cat's condition.

There are special convalescence foods available, which are designed to provide a concentrated liquid food source. These can be squeezed through the end of a syringe and into the side of the cat's mouth, and they are very useful in helping to rehabilitate the animal. Often, once syringe feeding begins it gets the ball rolling, and the cat will start eating again on its own.

There are a dazzling array of prescription foods available for almost all health problems, from kidney disease to being overweight, and they are often a viable nutritional solution to help support the animal's system while it is unwell. At the end of the day, however, the most important thing is that the cat eats something. If it won't eat the prescription foods then give it what it will eat, even if it isn't ideal for their condition. Many cats can be very staunch about their eating habits, especially old cats—they are incredibly fussy, and trying to persuade them to eat a different type of food can be very challenging.

Specific needs of dogs

Dogs' systems are a lot more forgiving than cats' when it comes to types of food and the frequency with which they are received. As dogs are historically scavengers and omnivores, their systems have obviously adapted to cope with a wide range of foods at irregular times. Often in the wild a dog would only be able to kill another animal every few days, and between kills would survive on foraged eggs, animal feces, insects and small animals.

A dog's body can adapt to the various types of protein it receives, and the overall amount it needs is less than in a cat's diet. Dogs will adapt to a vegetarian diet much more easily than a cat, as long as the essential dietary elements are present. They don't digest whole grain well, which is why most grains fed to dogs need to be well cooked or ground, to mimic the partial digestion that occurs in the gut of herbivorous prey.

Age-related nutrition

1. Young animals

As noted earlier, growing puppies and kittens require very specific dietary ingredients to grow in an optimal way. They require increased levels of protein for growth, as well as the correct balance of calcium and phosphorus for bone and joint development.

Large breed puppies, which have the potential to grow very fast, require a carefully balanced diet that is not so energy-dense that it accelerates growth and has the potential to create joint damage. To achieve this moderation in growth rate it is best to use either a properly formulated homemade diet—one that contains the appropriate supplements and is not too high in energy—or one of the super premium commercial foods that are designed for large breed dogs.

As a veterinarian I have seen the effects of an improper diet in the first 12 months of life, which can lead to a lifetime of joint and bone problems. For this reason I am a little nervous about recommending a homemade puppy diet for large breeds of dog. It is essential that the diet is prepared correctly, with all the supplements and proportions configured accurately. If there is any doubt about whether the correct natural diet can be achieved, my usual recommendation is to use a well-researched, well-balanced, large breed growth food until the dog is at least a year old.

Smaller breed dogs have different needs. Accelerated growth is not generally a problem since there is much less bone elongation and it occurs more slowly because the leg bones are shorter. Small breed dogs may need more concentrated foods because their stomach capacity is smaller, meaning they fill up quickly but also empty quickly. These dogs need to eat relatively often to provide the required nutrition. It is advisable to stick to growth formulas in the first year of life, after which the puppy can go onto adult maintenance foods, which have normal protein levels, normal calcium and phosphorus levels, and an average calorific level. This advice also applies to kittens.

It is useful to get cats used to eating a variety of foods, including cereals and vegetables, from an early age, which usually means they do not become fussy as adults. Getting kittens used to chewing raw meaty bones also increases the chance that they will continue chewing bones as adults. This helps to keep the teeth clean and gums healthy, as well as stimulating the flow of digestive enzymes and saliva.

> A simple way of determining if an otherwise healthy animal is getting too much or too little food is to monitor its weight. This is most easily done by checking the covering of fat over the rib area. The ideal covering is when you cannot see the ribs but can just feel them. Get used to running your hands over this area and getting a feel for your pet's normal rib covering. If it is getting hard to find the ribs, you need to consider a lower-calorie diet; if they are too prominent, you need to increase the calorie input.

2. Adults

Adult maintenance foods are designed for animals of average weight, average levels of exercise and average metabolic rates, from the age of approximately 12 months to around nine or ten years. The average family pet does very well on adult maintenance foods, with weight and energy levels maintained in the normal range. Animals with high exercise levels, such as working dogs or very active family dogs, may require a higher-calorie food to meet their higher energy expenditure.

Maintaining the correct weight

Some animals have a very efficient metabolism and burn up food more quickly than others, so they may also require higher-calorie food to keep their weight within the normal range. The premium or active commercial diets will provide this extra level of nutrition. If your pet is being fed a homemade diet you can either feed it more of the usual foods or add a little more fat by using extra vegetable oils or leaving fat on the meat. Make sure the overall proportions are checked by your vet or nutritionist, however, because adding extra fat can also change the protein and carbohydrate levels.

Weight loss can also be due to a health problem, so always check with your veterinarian if the loss is sudden or there are other clinical signs such as vomiting, diarrhea or appetite loss. Your vet can rule out any health problems and recommend a suitable diet to help the animal regain weight. If your pet has suddenly gotten fat, also check with your vet as the weight gain may be due to retained fluid or a mass (i.e., cancer) or even pregnancy! Again, the vet will determine the cause and recommend a suitable weight loss diet if it is just the result of too many calories for their output. There are special weight loss prescription diets that are low in calories but help make the animal feel full. A low-calorie homemade diet can be achieved by halving the oil content, removing all visible fat from meat, reducing the volume of food by about a third, and most important, *no snacks*—just a high-nutritional quality, low-fat, high-bulk diet. Often effective weight loss can occur when the animal is fed normal amounts of food but has all snacks and treats removed from its diet.

In cats, sudden weight loss accompanied by an increase in appetite may be due to *hyper*thyroidism, which requires veterinary attention. In dogs, weight gain combined with skin problems and lethargy can indicate *hypo*thyroidism, which again requires veterinary attention.

It is important not to put your pet on a crash diet. This is especially important for fat cats as it can cause serious health problems, including liver failure. The best way to reduce your pet's weight is slowly, over a medium to long length of time. Keeping your dog within the correct weight range is very important for the health of joints and for the circulatory system. Arthritic problems are amplified enormously if the animal is carrying more weight than it should, and there is often a marked reduction in pain and stiffness when excess weight is shed. It has also been shown that keeping your dog lean right from the start can help reduce or slow the onset of joint disease.

3. Geriatric animals

Cats over ten years old and dogs over eight or nine are considered "geriatric" or "senior," although this is very much a generalization. Some animals are old before this, and some are very healthy and fit well into their later years. From a dietary perspective, the generally accepted trend is to reduce protein levels in older animals, because the kidney function tends to reduce with time; reduce fat levels, because animals tend to be less active with age (or feed them the amount necessary to maintain optimal body weight), and feed lower amounts of sodium, because too much can affect the heart and kidneys.

As your pet ages it is important to have regular veterinary checkups so your vet can pinpoint any health problems and make recommendations early on, which will lead to a much more effective outcome than late intervention.

Kidney problems

The kidneys filter the waste products from protein metabolism, so as the function of the kidney units reduces so does the kidneys' filtering ability. The toxic byproducts of digestion thus remain in the bloodstream rather than being voided via the urine. This means the toxins circulate all around the body, causing damage wherever they go. Reducing the dietary intake of protein reduces the load on the kidneys, and helps to reduce the toxic load on the body. It also helps to preserve kidney function, since the kidneys do not have to work so hard. There is a balance required here—the body requires a certain amount of protein each day to function, so reducing the intake too much can also have health consequences.

One of the problems with kidney disease is that in its early stages there may be no obvious clinical signs. It is not until the disease is quite advanced that symptoms such as increased water intake, reduced appetite, loss of weight or mild dehydration become obvious. A rule of thumb is that if your pet is in the senior age range, but its kidney function seems good, feed it the "senior" foods that are slightly reduced in protein, or reduce the meat proportion in the homemade diets and increase the fat and carbohydrates by using fatty meat and extra grains (well cooked). Ensure any dietary changes are checked by your veterinarian. As the kidneys degenerate your vet can advise on the most appropriate diet. (See "Kidney problems," page 203).

Joint disease and arthritis

Older animals are often less active due to joint pain, lower energy levels or sheer laziness, so weight gain can be a problem. If your pet has joint disease it is crucial to reduce weight, as well as looking at nutritional and pharmaceutical treatments for the problem. Nutritional supplementation in arthritis can be very useful.

The commonly used supplements are glucosamine and chondroitin (important components in the cartilaginous linings of the joint), antioxidants such as vitamin E and vitamin C, selenium (to reduce free radical damage in joints), various minerals, and herbs such as devil's claw, to help with inflammation (for more on this see the section on arthritis in Chapter 5). Supplements like green mussel extract and bovine cartilage can also be useful. There are commercial supplement mixes available that supply these helpful products, and they are a critical component in treating joint disease. Ask your vet about these.

As discussed above, supplementation of omega-3 and omega-6 essential fatty acids can also help reduce inflammation. In addition, the omega-3 fatty acid EPA (found in fish oils) interrupts the production of certain enzymes that cause damage to the cartilage lining of the joints. I often recommend a fish oil mixed with evening primrose oil as part of a whole approach to helping relieve inflammation in joint problems. Once this cartilage is damaged its cushioning effect on the joint surfaces lessens and the bony ends of the joints grind on one another, resulting in severe inflammation, bony spur formation and a reduced range of movement. Nutritional therapy in arthritic disease focuses on improving cartilage health and reducing the inflammation that occurs in damaged joints.

Other problems

Other aging problems can be related to heart disease or degeneration, and a low-salt diet can be useful in controlling symptoms in the early stages of disease. Again, there are prescription diets for this which provide the optimum proportions of sodium and other minerals for stabilization of the condition. Many older animals have multiple conditions at the same time, and often the veterinarian needs to focus on the most problematic one, using the appropriate diet to help the body.

Many older animals feel the cold and have reduced body weight, and feeding warming foods and more cooked foods can help this. It is important to avoid things like sprouts and spirulina in these older animals, as they can be very cooling, and in an already "cold" animal they can stress the body further. Always make sure there is plenty of water available for these older animals, especially if they have problems with their kidneys; if water is restricted for any reason it can push them over the edge into kidney failure.

4. Pregnancy and lactation

Pregnancy puts great demands on the mother's body, so increasing many of the important nutritional elements is essential to maintaining optimum health during pregnancy, for the birth and for a healthy supply of milk to feed the offspring. Huge changes occur in the body during pregnancy, to meet the demands of the growing fetuses. The mother's body produces more blood to circulate through the placenta, and more pressure is put on her organs to feed the fetuses and remove wastes, so if there are existing health problems these may be amplified in pregnancy.

Nutritionally, it is important to consider a more energy-dense diet, increased levels of calcium and phosphorus (in appropriate ratios) for developing bones, as well as increased levels of fatty acids (especially fish oils), which have been shown in human studies to aid fetal nervous system development.

The normal recommendation is to feed the animal adult maintenance foods for the first two-thirds of the pregnancy, then growth formula during the last third, or a growth formula all the way through the pregnancy and during lactation[3]. These recommendations are very general; always be guided by your veterinarian's advice. Growth foods tend to be higher in calories as well as minerals such as calcium and phosphorus. Lactation requires increased dietary levels of most minerals and vitamins, as well as an increase in energy, so it is important that the animal remains on a growth diet at this time to provide all these extra nutritional requirements. If you are using a good-quality commercial diet, do not add extra nutrients because this will upset the proportions and can cause problems.

The growing puppies or kittens will receive all the nutrition first and the mother next, so if the continuing diet is inferior it will eventually weaken the mother, thus increasing the possibility of future pregnancy and birth problems.

There is also much to be said for maximizing both the mother's and the father's health for six to 12 months before conception, as they will pass on their inherent vitality to the offspring. A high-quality, well-balanced diet in this pre-conception phase will hugely increase the mother's chances of conception and a trouble-free pregnancy, as well as the father's ability to produce good-quality sperm. (For more on this see Chapter 7, "Raising puppies and kittens holistically.")

Summary

- Sound and appropriate nutrition is the foundation of good health.
- The "best" diet for your animal friend is one that keeps it in optimal health over a long period of time. This means adapting the diet to the changing needs of the animal.
- Indicators of appropriate diet are weight levels, body condition, blood tests, skin, eye and tooth condition, and energy levels.
- Good-quality commercial diets are regulated to provide appropriate balanced nutrition at every meal. But:
  - ❖ They are highly processed by cooking or drying, which alters the structure of the nutrients, sometimes negatively;
  - ❖ The quality of the ingredients varies;
  - ❖ They may contain colorings, preservatives and flavorings that may be harmful to the health of the animal;
  - ❖ They are often low in "biological vitality" as a result of processing.
- Homemade diets made with high biological value ingredients, appropriate for the animal they are intended for, and well-balanced using supplements from natural sources, with minimal processing, are highly recommended in the holistic approach to health. Poorly assembled homemade "natural" diets made with inferior ingredients and not containing correct levels of supplements are not!
- Meat-only diets are not suitable for pets.
- Raw (not cooked!) meaty bones are a very useful part of a natural diet.
- All foods have a thermal nature (warming, neutral or cooling) and can be chosen to help rebalance the body in disease states.
- Each species and each life stage requires a different type of diet.
- Make sure your pet has regular vet checkups to ensure its diet is suitable for its age, lifestyle and condition.

Chapter 4

Holistic therapies

Preventive medicine is all about keeping your pet's system in balance so it does not become sick. There are times, however, when things don't go according to plan and the body does get out of balance, with resultant "dis-ease." Holistic therapies aim to correct imbalances and work with the body to help it to heal and recover.

Holistic therapies can often be used in conjunction with conventional drugs to help strengthen and support the system, and in some cases there is a far greater response when the two treatments are combined. Modern pharmaceutical drugs are often necessary in cases where there is a severe imbalance, as in a life-threatening situation, as the stronger chemicals can act quickly to effect a dramatic change.

In any case of "dis-ease," nutrition plays a large part in recovery. Using specific foods can help speed the recovery process, assisting the body to do what it needs to heal itself, by providing energy and essential nutrients.

When choosing a specific therapy it is obviously important to have a sound diagnosis—you can't pull out a specific tool from your toolbox until you know what it is for and why it is necessary. Diagnosing the problem is what your veterinarian is trained to do, and it is important to have your pet checked by a vet when something does not seem right. The problem can be assessed, a diagnosis made and a therapy suggested. This may be a particular drug or procedure, or perhaps one of the complementary medical treatments.

Following is a brief outline of each of the main therapies used in complementary medicine and how they work. While it takes learning and often many years of practice to be proficient in a particular modality, there are some simple procedures that can be used safely in the home, and examples of these are included.

Acupuncture

Acupuncture is probably one of the most "accepted" modalities (forms of treatment) of all the complementary therapies, and many "conventional" veterinarians now recommend and use it. Acupuncture is a part of the large world of traditional Chinese medicine (TCM) that also includes Chinese herbs, exercises, massage and food as forms of therapy. The key underlying idea in TCM is the flow of qi energy through the body in a balanced and even manner, resulting in a state of balance and health. When this qi flow goes too fast, or slows and stagnates in the body, an imbalance arises and illness follows. All the TCM therapies, including acupuncture, aim to regulate this qi flow, returning it to normal and therefore restoring balance and health.

The concept of an energy flow is not a New Age idea, but rather a universal law of nature that is found in all healing systems and is an intrinsic part of all our lives. One can feel energetic (a plentiful flow of energy) or lethargic and slow (a slowing of energy), feel stiffness and pain (stagnation of energy in an area) or flexibility (smooth flow of energy). Even our homes and environment have a flow of energy through them; you can walk into some houses and they "feel" right or not so right, welcoming or not, and this is related to the way energy flows through them.

The qi energy flows through the body along designated highways called meridians, which criss-cross the body in very specific lines. The qi energy is highest in each meridian at particular times of the day, which is an important fact when putting together the whole picture of diagnosis and treatment. The acupuncture points are very specific points along the meridians which can be manipulated (by a variety of means such as needles or pressure) to speed up or slow down the flow of energy, and bring the body back into a state of balance.

The other important aspect of TCM is the balance between yin and yang, which are the extreme opposites of all things—yin is dark, yang is light; yin is cold, yang is hot; yin is feminine, yang is masculine—yet within each quality there is a small amount of the opposite aspect. This is symbolized by the yin-yang symbol where the two aspects are represented by black and white, but within the black there is white and within the white there is black (shown by the small circles within each color).

The meridians are divided into mainly yin or mainly yang, with the more yin meridians on the underside of the body and the yang ones on the upper side of the body. Along these meridians there are very specific points that differ markedly from the surrounding tissue; these are known as acupuncture points. These points have more nerve fibers and nerve endings than the surrounding tissues, more blood supply, decreased electrical resistance, and an increased fine lymphatic supply. These special points can be manipulated by inserting needles (acupuncture), pressure from the outside (acupressure), low electrical currents (electroacupuncture), lasers, injecting vitamins or sterile water (aquapuncture), implanting inert materials such as gold beads and burning special herbs on the ends of needles (moxibustion).

Manipulation of the points can speed up or slow down the flow of qi energy, removing stagnation and restoring balance to the system. Pain is simply stagnant qi energy, and when a needle is inserted into a specific acupuncture point this stagnant qi is stimulated to move on, thus dispersing the pain and restoring mobility or function to the area.

The TCM philosophy and approach differs markedly from that of Western medicine. In the latter it is believed that all disease has a cause, usually a singular cause such as a virus or bacteria of some kind, which creates a number of symptoms and conditions that are often not thought to be related to one another. Treatments involve trying to change, control or destroy the *causative* agent. In TCM, everything is interrelated; there is usually not a singular cause (in fact the "cause" is not very important; the emphasis is more on what is happening), and conditions are explained by one system being out of balance with another. The final diagnosis involves bringing together all the symptoms to form a total picture. Treatment aims to restore the body's overall balance, not simply remove the causative agent for a singular symptom. Both systems often achieve a cure, but the paths they take to reach that final cure are very different.

The origins of acupuncture

Traditional Chinese medicine has developed over many hundreds of years through observation, critical thinking, extensive clinical testing and practice. There is evidence suggesting acupuncture was used in India over five thousand years ago, although it is generally believed to have originated in China. Veterinary acupuncture is also known to have been performed, but it was not until 430 BC that Shun Yang became the first full-time practitioner of Chinese veterinary medicine.

Acupuncture was brought to the West by the Jesuits who served the Chinese courts in the late seventeenth and early eighteenth centuries. In the 1970s acupuncture received a burst of publicity in the West during President Richard Nixon's famous visit to China, which included demonstrations of acupuncture being used for anesthesia during surgery. In recent years veterinary acupuncture has spread widely and there are now teaching courses run all over the world, often under the auspices of the International Veterinary Acupuncture Society (IVAS).

Acupuncture in veterinary medicine

Acupuncture can be used to treat a wide range of ailments. In Western veterinary medicine its main applications are in the treatment of:
- Musculoskeletal problems such as arthritis and hip dysplasia;
- Spinal problems such as slipped discs, spondylosis and muscular back pain;
- Lameness in general, especially muscular or ligament and tendon problems;
- Gastrointestinal problems such as vomiting and diarrhea;
- Epilepsy and other neurological problems;
- Reproductive problems such as infertility, to help increase the chance of conception, support pregnancy and help in difficult births;
- Mastitis and lameness in large animals such as cows. Horses in particular respond well to acupuncture, especially for muscular problems. I have seen an amazing response to acupuncture in a horse with severe back pain, which kicked out at anyone who went near it, and was unable to be handled or have any of its legs picked up. When just one or two needles were used in spe-

cific points (carefully, since the horse was very grumpy) the whole back muscle spasm relaxed and the horse became docile and able to be handled within the space of ten minutes;

- Urinary incontinence in bitches;
- Resuscitation in emergencies.

A typical treatment program starts with an initial consultation to examine the animal, look at blood tests or x-rays, and decide on the best course of action. Each acupuncture treatment involves inserting the small needles at specific acupuncture points, depending on the condition; subsequent sessions may involve a change of needle combination, depending on how the clinical signs change. The needles are inserted and stay in the points for approximately 20 minutes each session, during which time the animal needs to stay as still as possible so the needles are not dislodged. This can be difficult in young or highly active dogs that hate sitting in one place for too long, as well as some cats, and it may be necessary to sedate them while the needles are in place.

The choice of acupuncture points depends not only on the initial problem but also on the quality of the animal's pulse. In TCM, pulse diagnosis does not just mean counting the number of beats per minute, it involves a complex reading of the quality of the pulse, i.e., the rate, rhythm, shape and force. This is a complex art and it requires much practice and training to interpret the meanings of each pulse accurately, but a skilled practitioner can determine the differences between systems, such as whether the liver is overactive and the gallbladder underactive, or if the energy in the kidney is low and needs nourishment. Herbs or acupuncture are then recommended to rebalance these systems well before serious clinical disease develops.

In Western medicine the tendency is to wait until there is clinical disease before any treatment is started, although there are moves toward more use of preventive medicine. The beauty of TCM and pulse diagnosis is its wonderful subtlety, and the advantage of correcting problems while they are still minor, thus reducing stress on the other body systems and working toward overall health.

How acupuncture works

When a needle is inserted into a specific acupuncture point a small amount of damage occurs at the needle site, which stimulates the qi energy to move faster or slow down, depending on the point and the method of needle insertion and manipulation. There is often a tingling or sharp jolt in the area as more often than not the qi is stagnant and the insertion of the needle stimulates it to speed up and move on through the meridians. Pain in an area is simply "stuck qi," and when its movement is stimulated the pain goes.

This is why acupuncture is so useful for painful conditions such as arthritis, in which there is pain over an animal's joint area. Often, a few minutes into an acupuncture session the animal will simply lie down and relax or go to sleep. This is usually due to the release of "happy hormones" known as endorphins, which are often increased when acupuncture is performed. The endorphins also help with pain relief and aid the healing process. It is not uncommon for the patient to be sleepy for several hours after an acupuncture treatment, and this is a good sign, showing that the healing process has begun.

Many animals are a little suspicious at the first acupuncture treatment, but they will often be very happy to come back for subsequent treatments, with some even racing into the room and demanding to be put onto the work table! I find animals often know what is helping them, and they love the attention as well. Not many animals find the procedure painful or uncomfortable, but occasionally they may need light sedation, or the use of specific sedation points, to ensure they sit still for the 20 minutes that the needles need to stay in place, so they receive the maximum benefit from the treatment.

The overall aim of an acupuncture session is to rebalance the system, and you will find that the presenting symptoms will go away as this balance is restored.

Does it hurt?

Most animals tolerate acupuncture extremely well, as most points are non-painful. There are some points that tend to be a little more tender than others, and this also depends on how "stuck" the qi energy is in that area. There is usually a slight pricking sensation as the needle goes through the skin, but there are techniques of insertion that can minimize this. If the needles are pushed in a little too deep it can be slightly uncomfortable, but this is easily remedied by moving them slightly. Overall, the pain of the actual needle insertion is minor, and once the needle is in there is usually little or no sensation or pain.

How many treatments are necessary?

In chronic (long-standing) conditions, I generally recommend an initial course of four treatments at weekly intervals and assess the response after this initial course. More often than not there is a dramatic improvement in the condition and further treatments are only necessary if there is a relapse.

In acute conditions, such as a spinal disc prolapse (or "slipped disc"), or acute vomiting, it may be necessary to repeat treatments daily or even several times a day. Some long-standing problems can take quite some time to improve, so patience is required; it takes time for the body to let go of the old pattern of imbalance and re-establish a new pattern of being in balance.

Acupressure, massage and other methods of point manipulation

It is not always necessary to insert needles in acupuncture points for them to be stimulated. There are many ways to manipulate an acupuncture point, such as injecting sterile water or vitamins, using laser light on the point and implanting gold beads (for permanent stimulation, as with a specific ear point used in the treatment of epilepsy). Another method is by direct pressure or massage, which is called acupressure. There is a whole medical system known as shiatsu which uses acupressure to stimulate the specific pressure points in the body. Direct pressure from fingertips in various ways can often work as well as inserting needles into these points. It's useful where a patient may be needle-shy, and can be done safely at home by the pet's owner. (For more on acupressure techniques see Chapter 6.)

TCM massage is another very useful method of manipulating the flow of qi energy—it is designed to have maximum effect on the qi as it moves through the meridians. There is also a method of getting heat into the meridians by a process of moxibustion, or burning of the herb mugwort, which is rolled into a tight stick and lit, providing intense heat at its point. The lit roll is held over a specific acupuncture point for 10 to 15 seconds (making sure the fur is not singed) and helps to warm the body. This is useful in "cold" animals such as older animals that are continually seeking warm places in which to sit, or may become stiff in the colder weather.

Useful acupuncture points

There are several very important acupuncture points that can safely be manipulated at home to tone up or calm down pets, and even help resuscitate them in an emergency. Get used to finding these points on your pet; every animal's anatomy is different and a point that is easy to find on one animal may be difficult on another. A prime example of this is "stomach 36," an important point on the hind leg (see below). This point is quite easy to find on long-boned, long-legged slim dogs, but much more difficult on a short, bent-legged dog like a corgi. Just persevere and get to know your own pet's acupuncture points.

Point names refer to the meridian they are on, e.g., ST = stomach meridian, GV = governing vessel meridian.

For general health

Stomach 36

Stomach 36 (ST 36; known as "Three Mile Run")

This is one of the major points in the body for stimulating health and well-being by strengthening the flow of qi energy. Acupuncture or acupressure at this point has been shown to stimulate the immune system, reduce fever, heal gastrointestinal disorders, and treat pain in the stifle (knee) and the hock. It is the major point for the digestive system, and is effective in cases of anorexia and lethargy as it stimulates the general qi of the body.

Location and manipulation

On the outside of the hind leg just below the knee, to the side of the prominent bone at the front of the area below the knee (the tibial crest). Just to the side of this is a muscle, and the point lies in the middle of the muscle belly. Use the tips of your fingers and apply steady pressure or a circular motion on the point.

Resuscitation

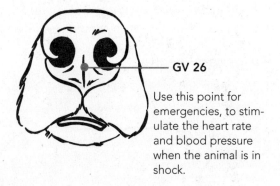

GV 26

Use this point for emergencies, to stimulate the heart rate and blood pressure when the animal is in shock.

Governing vessel 26 (GV 26)

This is a major resuscitation point, useful for stimulating heart rate, blood pressure and pulse rate. Manipulation of this point can be useful in emergencies where the breathing or heart has stopped. It can be used in anesthetic emergencies or severe trauma and is a critical point to know as part of your first aid "kit."

Location and manipulation

On the midline just below the nostrils. Use your thumbnail or the pointed cap of a pen and apply strong pressure to the area.

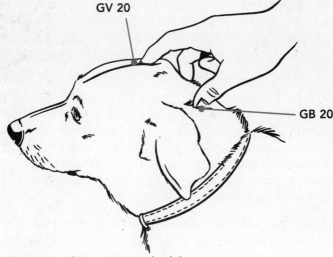

GV 20

GB 20

Calming—three-point hold

Three-point hold—gallbladder 20 (GB 20; "Wind Pond") using both sides, and governing vessel 20 (GV 20; "Meeting Point of One Hundred Points")

This combination of points is very useful to calm an animal that is upset or agitated.

Location and manipulation

Gallbladder 20 is just below the back of the head at the nape of the neck, halfway between the spine and the base of the ear. Governing vessel 20 is on the midline in the notch just in front of the bony lump on the top of the head (the external occipital protuberance). Use light pressure to begin with, which can be increased as the animal relaxes.

TCM daily massage to promote a healthy qi flow through the meridians

The following information has been adapted from Cheryl Schwartz's *Four Paws, Five Directions*[1]. The massage can be done daily to keep the qi flow in the body in optimum condition. It can be relaxing both for the owner and for the pet, as often the giver receives as much as the receiver.

1. Choose a warm, quiet place where you will not be interrupted. Make sure both you and your pet are in comfortable positions, with the animal either sitting up or lying down on its side.

2. Start by running your hands down the animal's neck and spine using gentle strokes. If the animal accepts this (which it will indicate by moving closer to you), you can increase the pressure. This will stimulate the bladder meridian, which starts at the corner of the eye, runs over the head then parallel to the spine and down the back of the hind legs to finish on the side of the outside toe.

3. Using small circular movements, move up under the chin, toward the ears and the corners of the mouth, pulling the lips up as you go. This stimulates the stomach meridian and some of the large intestine and small intestine meridians.

4. Now massage the ears from the base to the end of the ear flap, pulling gently at the base and using small circular movements over the flap. The triple-heater meridian circles the ear flap and coordinates the movement of energy through the three main body areas.

5. Move down the sides of the neck, over the shoulders and back down the spine, using small circular movements with the middle three fingers, and moderate pressure levels. When you get to the lower back area spend some time gently massaging the hips and the backs of the hind legs.

6. Leave this area and move up to the front legs. Begin by massaging down the outside of the front legs with long, stroking movements. This will stimulate the large intestine, small intestine and triple-heater meridians. If your pet is sitting up see if it will lie down now, and do the same to the inside of the front legs, gently pulling each leg forward and up to access this area. This will massage the heart, lung and pericardium meridians. Try and massage the pads of the feet, and gently pinch the web between the toes, as this helps bring the circulation to the tips of the toes before it returns to the heart. In TCM this is where yin and yang meet and

change into each other, and it can also be used to stimulate respiration and circulation in an emergency.

7. Some animals will let you massage their underbelly; if so, use long strokes or small circular movements. This will stimulate the liver, spleen, stomach, kidney and conception-vessel meridians, which will help aid digestion and bowel movement.

8. Return to the hind legs and begin by massaging the thigh area, working firmly into the large muscles on the outside of each leg using long strokes or large circles. You will probably need to stabilize the leg with the other hand just in front of the rump area. This stimulates the gallbladder meridian.

9. Moving down to the knee joint, massage both front and back of the knee, cupping the front while you massage the back. The stomach meridian crosses the knee here, and the bladder meridian runs down the back of the leg. Moving down the leg to the hock area, massage the thin area in front of the Achilles tendon; this feels like rubbing two pieces of skin together. This is a special meeting place for meridians. It is sometimes called the "aspirin point," because it helps relieve joint pain through the entire body. Finish the rest of the leg, ending with some pressure between the toes in the web area.

10. Go and have a cup of tea and a lie down! (This is my suggestion and isn't from Cheryl's book!)

The use of acupuncture in cats

Because of their often very sensitive and active personalities, it can be difficult to insert acupuncture needles into cats. I tend to use the very short, sharp Japanese acupuncture needles, which puncture the skin more easily than the Chinese needles and can be inserted quickly. I tend to adopt the "stab and jump" technique with cats, as they can be very quick with their claws if they don't like something that is being done to them! It is not that the process of acupuncture is very painful—often quite the reverse—but cats can be very sensitive to any form of touch, and a cat often has a large personal space.

I often recommend acupressure or laser in cats, or give a very mild sedative so the treatment runs smoothly and causes minimal distress to the cat. Sometimes I ask the owner to hold the cat while the needles are being inserted and for the following 20 minutes, or I admit the cat and get one of the veterinary nurses to hold it— sometimes cats are better behaved when they are away from their owners!

The use of acupuncture in dogs

Dogs are usually more laid back about having acupuncture than cats are. After the first few needles they tend to relax, and they often just lie down and go to sleep as the endorphins are released. If there is a lot of movement after the needles have been inserted they can fall out, so it is important to try and keep the dog as still as possible, which can be difficult with very fidgety or excitable dogs. If the dog is really wiggly, I may give it a mild sedative. Often, however, just asking one of the veterinary nurses to hold the dog and sending the owner out of the room is sufficient—like cats, dogs sometimes behave better when they are away from their owners.

Very fat or hairy dogs can be a real challenge to acupuncture as the bony landmarks (which help you find an acupuncture point) may be well disguised or simply not there because there is so much fat in the area. It is interesting, however, that even when you aren't 100 percent sure you have the point, but insert the needle in the approximate area, there is almost always a positive response to the use of acupuncture.

Treating trigger points with acupuncture

Trigger points are hard, knotted areas in the belly of muscles that are a result of recurring strain in that muscle. They are a little like repetitive strain injury (RSI) in the muscle. Over time these areas can become thickened and scarred, often resulting in lameness that is unresponsive to many pain-relief therapies.

Many working or show dogs develop these trigger points as a result of hard training and lots of jumping and jarring of the body, or sometimes an old injury in the muscle. Often nothing shows on x-rays or with joint manipulation, and it is only when a careful palpation of the muscle belly is done that a hard, knotted area is detected. When pressed, this "knot" is hard and painful, as is the immediate area around it, as there is referred pain from the original site of injury or stress. Massage can help a little, but acupuncture excels at treating these trigger points, often with miraculous results very early on in the treatment.

One example of this was in a working dog I saw in my vet clinic that had a recurrent lameness in its foreleg, unrelated to a joint problem, which resulted in an obvious limp and pain. The dog had been like this for six months, and was unable to work. X-rays had not shown any abnormalities, and anti-inflammatories had not helped. When I examined the dog I detected a hard, pea-like area in the triceps muscle (at the back of the upper front leg) which was very painful when pressed. We decided to do a course of acupuncture to resolve this trigger point and rebalance the body. After just two sessions a week apart, the dog was completely sound, and the area of very stuck qi (the trigger point) had disappeared. We carried out two more weekly treatments and the problem never occurred again.

It is also possible to inject vitamins or even sterile water into these points, in addition or as an alternative to acupuncture; the vitamins act continuously, stimulating and resolving the trigger points.

Commonly used acupuncture points

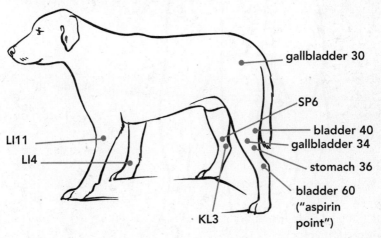

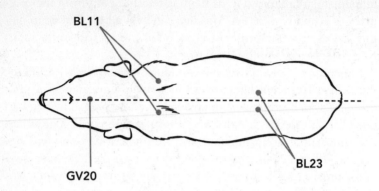

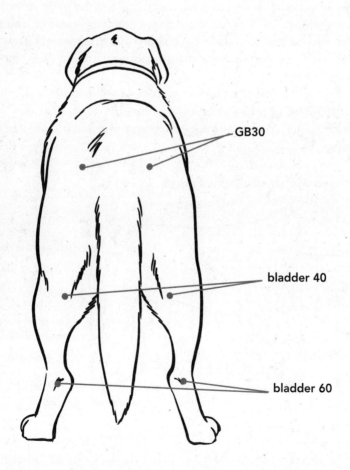

Homeopathy

What is homeopathy?

Homeopathy is the art of treating a problem by using a substance that in its undiluted state will cause symptoms similar to those already present. The central law of homeopathy is that "like cures like." It is based on the observation of various symptoms and treating those symptoms as a whole, rather than a specifically named disease, as in conventional medicine. For example, if one has vomiting and diarrhea, often simultaneously, that is worse after midnight, worse in cold and wet periods, and better in warm ones, then a highly diluted, homeopathically prepared mix of arsenic (Arsenicum album) is indicated to treat the problem. If a non-fatal solution of undiluted arsenic was given the same symptoms would be seen, but by giving the homeopathic preparation, the symptoms can be resolved.

History of homeopathy

The system of astute observation and testing of undiluted and diluted substances on humans was initiated by a German doctor, Samuel Hahnemann, in the late eighteenth and early nineteenth centuries. Hahnemann became disillusioned with the theory behind medicine at the time, and by the way it was being performed, and he began to develop ideas around the homeopathic theory of diluting and prescribing. He tested many substances on himself, one of the earliest and most famous cases being his testing (or "proving," as it is known) of cinchona bark, which was used at the time to treat malaria. When Hahnemann, a healthy person without malaria, took cinchona bark, the classic symptoms of the disease appeared; when the cinchona bark was discontinued, the symptoms went away. This got him thinking about the core theory of "like cures like," and he went on to prove many other substances on himself, his friends and family members.

Hahnemann also developed the theory of minimal dose, which is the multiple diluting of substances to a point where they do not cause the symptoms anymore, but actually cure them. He found that the more dilute he made the remedies, the more potent they were, which is contrary to most thinking. The initial substance was diluted to varying levels, being shaken (or succussed) between each dilution, which transferred the crucial healing energy of the initial substance into the water molecules. This meant that each time a dilution occurred and was succussed correctly, the more concentrated the energy became, and the more potent the remedy. As a general rule, lower dilutions (and therefore potencies) are used for more chronic or long-standing problems, while the remedies that are diluted the most (the most potent) are used for more acute or life-threatening problems.

These remedies are made in a quite specific way and under very exacting conditions, so it is best to purchase them pre-made, to ensure their potency. Many pharmacies and most health food shops carry a range of remedies, particularly those that are used more frequently. There are also specific homeopathic pharmacies that can supply most remedies, or will make them for you; some of these are listed in the suppliers list on page 272.

Choosing a remedy

Since there are many different conditions, all presenting particular patterns of symptoms, choosing a remedy (from thousands) can be difficult. Consulting a well-trained and experienced homeopath is essential. Ideally, work with a vet who uses homeopathy or a homeopath who works alongside a vet. A vet should always be involved.

Homeopathic prescribing can be done in two ways. Constitutional prescribing is more for chronic (long-standing) problems, and fits the particular personality types and symptoms. First aid prescribing is more for acute, emergency situations.

Constitutional prescribing

Constitutional prescribing relies on in-depth consultation and examination, including consideration of the patient's personality, preferences, symptoms, behavior, temperament, habits and when and how things are done in their life. This can be time-consuming, as it may take an hour or more to fully understand the whole "picture" of a patient's life and the presenting problem.

Once this had been done the remedy will be *reperterized* by the homeopath. This means the homeopath will go through a large book called the *Repertory* and find the best remedy for the unique picture shown by that individual patient. Because there are over

7,000 different remedies this can be a very involved process, although a skilled homeopath can often build this picture and decide on a remedy without extensive consultation with the book, since scenarios tend to repeat themselves very frequently.

Skilled homeopaths use this method to find a constitutional remedy that is unique to a particular individual. It will rebalance the body, and many of the presenting symptoms disappear rapidly as the whole system is realigned.

First aid prescribing

The other way homeopathy is used is through "first aid prescribing" for acute situations. Certain remedies are very useful for particular scenarios, and if there are at least three presenting symptoms, then there is a good chance you have the correct remedy.

This by no means replaces the excellent advice that can be given by a qualified homeopath or veterinarian, and I urge you to see one if possible, but this "first aid prescribing" can be useful as it can be done at home in acute situations where there is not time to see a homeopath.

For long-standing or chronic problems or recurring problems my advice is to see a qualified homeopathic vet, as the picture is often complicated, and you are far more likely to get the best results with a constitutional prescription.

How remedies are used

The general rule for dosing with homeopathic remedies is to give a dose initially, then if there is an improvement in symptoms, give another dose when the symptoms begin to return (i.e., after the first dose has worn off). In practice this can be anywhere from every ten minutes to every hour in acute cases, to several days or even months in chronic conditions. In most chronic conditions, the usual practice is to take the dose once or twice daily for a few days, wait until an effect is seen, then repeat the doses once the positive effect begins to wane. It is important not to overdose by treating too frequently, as a "proving" may occur, where the symptoms the remedy is supposed to reverse appear in the animal. If this does occur it can be reversed by simply discontinuing the remedy.

Homeopathic remedies need to be given to animals onto

mucous membranes such as in the mouth, and ideally without food or water half an hour before and after administration. The small pills can be crushed between two clean teaspoons then flicked into the mouth and onto the gums, or crushed and funneled down a small cone made from paper (see page 245 for diagram). It is very important not to handle the pills directly with your hands as your energy will interfere with that of the remedy, which is intended for the animal's use.

I find the liquid remedies the easiest to use in animals as they can be either dropped directly onto the animal's gums or put in a small sterile syringe and syringed into the mouth. These remedies contain some alcohol to preserve them, and cats in particular sometimes dislike the taste of the alcohol, so I use the lower-alcohol remedies, which are much more well-tolerated.

The number after the name of a remedy refers to the level of potency. Each substance is diluted 1 part to 9 parts distilled water (1:10), succussed, diluted again, then succussed again. When a substance is diluted 1:10, three times, the potency is referred to as 3x (from the Roman numeral X, meaning 10); when it is diluted 1:100 three times it is referred to as 3c (C meaning 100). Generally, lower potencies are used for more chronic problems, and higher potencies for more acute problems. I tend to use the 30c potency most often, and most recommendations in this book are for this potency.

Learning through experience

It is important to store the remedies correctly, in which case they will pretty much last indefinitely. However, as we are dealing with an energetic type of medicine, remedies can be affected by other forms of energy. Correct storage means away from direct sunlight, not near electrical appliances (i.e., not on top of the fridge or microwave), away from strong smells (not near the curry powder or garlic!) and out of direct sunlight. I recommend getting a small kit of the most commonly used remedies for first aid (see list on pages 94–97), storing it correctly, getting to know what the remedies are used for and the prescribing symptoms, and then *using* them. This is the best way to learn about the different remedies, and the results are often astounding.

As a veterinarian, handling sore, scared and often angry cats every day, you are at constant risk of being bitten. Before I learned about homeopathy, every time I got a cat bite on the hand it would swell up, be very painful, and often become very infected. I would have to take an antibiotic the moment I was bitten just to stop the bite from becoming infected, but it would still be very sore for several days. As a vet you need to use your fingers and hands every minute of the work day, so this sort of thing puts you out of action for a while. I learned about a homeopathic remedy called *Ledum palustre*, which is very good for treating puncture wounds, and tried it the next time I was bitten. I found that not only did the pain go away immediately, but the bite never swelled or became infected, and I never needed to take antibiotics again for any cat bite—I always simply used ledum. The amazing thing was the almost instantaneous improvement in the symptoms, especially the pain, which can be quite intense with a cat bite.

After that I often tried out a new remedy or treatment on myself before I tried it on my animal friends. In this way I could identify what response was achieved, and go on to use the remedy in the vet clinic. I needed to be convinced that a particular treatment worked and consistently achieved the results I desired, because I didn't want to waste my time on something that was ineffective or inconsistent. Over the years I have found the use of homeopathic remedies to be very effective and very consistent, often achieving miraculous results very quickly and without side effects. Often the cure was long-lasting and very deep, not only treating the physical problem but also any emotional and mental imbalances.

Use of homeopathy in the home

I recommend the use of first aid homeopathic remedies in the home for minor health problems like small cuts, minor bruises and low-grade bites and scratches. For anything more significant than this, if the animal does not respond to the remedy, or if it has stopped eating or is unwell for more than 24 hours, it is very important to contact your veterinarian. As mentioned earlier, getting a diagnosis is very important before deciding on a treatment. If a problem progresses quickly or has unusual or very pronounced symptoms, then your vet is the person best qualified to interpret these symptoms and decide on an appropriate treatment regime.

First aid kit

Try these remedies for your home kit. Use the 30c dilution in most cases.

Apis mellifera

Made from actual bees, *Apis mellifera* can be used for most insect bites where there is swelling, puffiness and edema, and which will "pit" on pressure, often around the face, mouth or eyelids, or in the throat. Will treat many edematous conditions that are worse with heat or touch, where the animal has no thirst, and the symptoms are better with cold applications and moving around in the open air.

Arnica

The injury remedy. Useful in bruising and injury especially where the skin is unbroken and there is a fear of being touched. Reduces shock, helps with recovery from surgery, especially dental extraction, as well as birthing, and can help reduce the chance of a difficult labor. Can be used internally (pills and liquids) as well as externally in creams and lotions.

Arsenicum album

Useful for vomiting and diarrhea (as in food poisoning) which is worse toward and after midnight, when the animal is thirsty for small sips of water, and is very restless, frequently changing its position. Symptoms are improved by warmth and elevating the head.

Belladonna

Useful for "hot" conditions like a fever, as well as inflammation such as mastitis, heatstroke, conjunctivitis and ear inflammation, and where there is a full, bounding pulse, sudden onset, restlessness, redness and heat.

Bryonia

Useful to treat arthritis when symptoms are worse with movement and warmth (note, the opposite symptoms to *Rhus tox*).

Cantharis (Spanish fly)

Useful for cystitis where there is frequent, burning urination, passing small and frequent amounts, and straining to urinate, often with blood. Symptoms are worse for touch, better from gentle massage. Burns and scalds respond to this remedy.

Carbo vegetabilis (Carbo veg)

"The great reviver," used for all cases of shock and collapse, whatever the cause. Used when the condition is worse in evenings and with warmth, better with fanning and cold.

Fragaria vesca

Helps prevent the deposition of tartar on the teeth. Can be given to dogs and cats at regular intervals after they have reached two years old. Use as 6c, a few doses every two months.

Hepar sulphuris (Hepar sulph)

Treats many conditions, especially those involving some kind of discharge or suppuration, usually thick and offensive. Useful for treating ear and eye infections, as well as skin sores such as abscesses, boils and moist, exudative conditions. The lower potencies, for example 1x–3x, promote the flow of these discharges (useful in treating boils and abscesses), while higher potencies, such as 200c, stop or slow the exudative process (useful for treating infected ears or skin). Used for conditions that are worse in drafts and cold, when the animal is very sensitive mentally and physically, and better with warmth, eating and being wrapped up.

Hypericum

Very useful for treating lacerated wounds where nerve endings are damaged, such as wounds on the ends of toes and feet, around the head and at the base of the tail. There are usually excellent results with spinal injuries, especially at the base of the tail. The tinctures can be used as a 1:10 diluted lotion externally (often mixed with calendula as "Hypercal," or wound-healing, lotion), to reduce the pain of open wounds as well as speeding the healing and draining of wounds.

Ignatia

Useful for grief and grieving in animals, such as a bitch that has lost her pups, animals that have been separated from their companions or when a much-loved owner has gone.

Ledum palustre

The main remedy to consider with puncture wounds, and given with Hypericum it helps prevent tetanus. I have used this remedy successfully to treat tetanus in a dog, as well as on myself for numerous cat bites over the years. I often recommend it for treating cat bite abscesses, or for owners to use on their cats as soon as possible after a cat fight, as it will often prevent the formation of an abscess. It is also very good for bee stings.

Nux vomica

A very useful remedy for abdominal and digestive disorders, such as colic in horses, and overindulgence of food in small animals. The patient often wakes between 3 a.m. and 4 a.m., is worse in the morning, better in the evening, after a long nap and with warmth.

Rhus toxicodendron (Rhus tox)

Known as the "rusty gate" remedy, since it is very useful for the classic arthritic animal that is worse after resting, stiff and slow on rising, and improves as it moves around; i.e., better with warmth and massage, worse in the cold. Also used for skin rashes that show redness and blistering of the skin.

Ruta graveolens (Ruta grav)

Useful for sprains and strains on tendons, as well as "bruised" bones where the periosteum is damaged. Also useful for red, hot eyes with aversion to light.

Sulfur

A useful remedy for treating skin conditions, especially if they are musty and foul smelling, involve redness and itching, often with a moist discharge which is worse with heat, and with washing and scratching. Adding sulfur can also increase the effectiveness of other remedies.

Symphytum

Very useful for speeding the healing of fractures and broken bones, especially in delayed union or non-healing fractures. Use with arnica for injuries. Also useful for eye injuries, especially when blunt trauma is involved. Use *after* bones have set, not before.

Flower essences

Now to one of my favorite treatment options, the flower essences. I have used these remedies for over fifteen years, both on myself and on my animal patients, with many incredible successes. There have also been many happy stories of cases that were so improved one would never have believed there was a serious problem to begin with.

The flower essences work on the emotional part of the body to rebalance and correct emotional upsets. They are known as energetic medicines, in that they work on rebalancing the body's energies to achieve balance in the emotional body, resulting in resolution of physical symptoms.

The Bach range

The use of flower essences to heal emotional imbalances is based on the work done by Edward Bach, an English doctor who lived in the early part of the 20th century. Bach studied medicine at University College Hospital, London, where he was also a house surgeon. He later worked in general practice, having a set of consulting rooms on the famous Harley Street in London, and as a bacteriologist and later a pathologist he worked on vaccines and a set of homeopathic nosodes that are still known as the seven Bach nosodes. (Nosodes are homeopathic remedies made using a disease product from the affected part of the system, and used to prevent as well as to treat that particular condition.)

Despite the success of his work with orthodox medicine Bach felt dissatisfied with the way doctors were expected to concentrate on diseases and ignore the people who were suffering them. While he was inspired by his work with homeopathy, he also wanted to find remedies that would be purer and less reliant on the products of disease. In 1930 he gave up his lucrative Harley Street practice and left London, determined to devote the rest of his life to the new system of medicine that he was sure could be found in nature. Being a very intuitive man, Bach would get a sense of the different plants and note what emotions they brought out in him, and he developed a method of preparing the plants that maximized the energy of this emotion. The plants were gathered at the height of their energy, in the mornings when the flowers were freshest and the dew was still present. They were floated on spring water in full sun, then filtered and preserved with brandy (alcohol) for stability, to produce the "mother" tincture. This mother tincture was then diluted 1:10 or 1:100 to produce the actual treatment.

In this way Bach developed the traditional flower essence range of 38 different English flowers from the countryside surrounding the village where he lived. From this work other ranges of essences have been developed, such as the Perelandra flower essences from the United States, the Living Essences of Australia range from Western Australia, the New Zealand flower essences and Hawaiian flower essences. There are many different flower essence ranges available, but I mostly use the traditional Bach range, which is what I will discuss here.

The effect of the emotions

Dr. Bach felt that negative emotional states suppressed the healing process, and that this emotional imbalance was actually the primary cause of physical disease. When these emotional problems were treated, he reasoned, the physical symptoms would go. He identified 12 pathological emotional states which, left untreated, would ultimately lead to physical disease.

The 12 pathological emotional states

1. Fear

2. Terror

3. Mental torture or worry

4. Indecision

5. Indifference or boredom

6. Doubt or discouragement

7. Over-concern

8. Weakness

9. Self-distrust

10. Impatience

11. Over-enthusiasm

12. Pride or aloofness

There is a growing recognition today of the effect the mind has on the body (mind/body medicine). Different thoughts or emotional states can affect the release of neurotransmitters, digestion, the immune system, and many other body systems. The effect of the emotions in producing stress is well known, and the flower essences provide a very real treatment option for balancing the emotions and ultimately balancing the physical body.

Dr. Bach's theory that "there is no true healing unless there is a change of outlook, peace of mind, and inner happiness" and his belief that "disease is a consolidation of a mental attitude" are as applicable to animals as to humans.

Animals can become stressed by many things, resulting in all sorts of bizarre behaviors. Fear is often the underlying emotion that produces stress responses. This may be the result of a lack of socialization when young, unclear hierarchies (pecking order), unclear behavioral boundaries, territorial disputes (very common in cats) or a general emotionally unstable environment (stressed owners often result in stressed animals). Understanding and managing the situations that lead to these fears is as important as treating the fear itself (for more on this see the section on behavioral problems in Chapter 5). Flower essences can help alleviate these fears and markedly increase the effect of management changes, thus producing a much better result in the overall treatment of the behavioral problem.

How flower essences work

The flower essences work to resolve the negative emotional

response so that the emotions are rebalanced and normalized. This is in contrast to many psychoactive drugs, which tend to mask symptoms rather than resolve them, so that the problem may return once the drugs are discontinued.

Flower essences are not homeopathic or herbal remedies. They are only diluted 1:10 or 1:100, they are not prescribed according to the "like cures like" theory, and their actions have not been determined by proving. Neither are they strictly herbal remedies, since they do not have the pharmaceutical activity that concentrated herbal preparations have. Herbal preparations tend to work mainly on the physical body, rather than the emotional, and require a certain level of knowledge and skill because they can be toxic at certain concentrations. In contrast, flower essences are very safe at all concentrations, and are no more toxic than pure water. When they are prepared correctly, the amount of alcohol that is added (purely as a preservative) is negligible, and the benefits of the remedy far outweigh the tiny amount of ingested alcohol.

Choosing a remedy

The flower essences are prescribed according to the emotional state of the animal rather than physical symptoms. While the latter are taken into account, the primary focus is on the emotions; remembering the words of Dr. Bach, problems with the emotions can result in physical disease.

Does the animal show fear or aggression, anxiety or resentment resulting in destruction of things such as furniture or car seats? Does it appear depressed or is it hyperactive, with a very short attention span? Is the animal afraid of sudden loud noises, does it hide under furniture when rain beats on the roof?

What about possible environmental stressors—has there been a major change in the animal's life such as moving house or changing owners, is it expected to perform at shows around strange people and animals? Is the animal kept tied up all day and is it bored, resulting in self-mutilation, or does it suffer separation anxiety because it is left alone all day and does not see its owner enough?

All these are important key indicators that may suggest one remedy over another. However, if you find the remedy you try isn't the "right" one to help the animal, nothing adverse happens, other than not achieving the desired result. You may find that if you select a group of remedies and treat the animal, removal of the "uppermost" problems may release other emotional problems. It may then be necessary to "tweak" the mix to include a new remedy that suits the changed picture better. I tend not to put more than seven remedies together in one treatment bottle, and if one of the remedies chosen is Rescue Remedy (or Five Flower Formula), which contains five essences, then I add no more than five other remedies.

The other interesting thing to take into consideration when choosing a remedy is that animals often reflect their owners' behavioral tendencies. When pet owners realize their behavior is having an impact on that of their animal, they often ask about using the flower essences themselves. There are many flower essence practitioners who prescribe for humans, and many of my clients have gone and gotten some flower essences for their own emotional problems after seeing how well their animals respond to these remedies.

✹ Rescue Remedy (Five Flower Formula)

Rescue Remedy is made by the Bach Centre in the U.K. (which was Dr. Bach's home and workplace during the last few years of his life) and is a mix of five of the 38 flower essences in Dr. Bach's range. Five Flower Formula uses the same recipe and is prepared in the same way as Rescue Remedy, but it is made by a different company, hence the different name.

Rescue Remedy is used to treat stress, distress, shock, panic and terror, and restores calm, reassurance and relaxation. The essences in it are Cherry Plum, Clematis, Impatiens, Rock Rose and Star of Bethlehem.

How are the remedies used?

Each of the 38 different Bach flower remedies, as well as the pre-mixed Rescue Remedy, comes as a "mother tincture," or stock bottle. These are sold in 10 ml bottles, and can be bought individually or as a complete boxed kit. If you only want one treatment bottle at a time, or do not use the flower essences very often, it is probably best to take your recipe to a health food shop or an outlet that has the complete kit and ask them to make up the treatment remedy for you.

To use the flower essences, it is first necessary to make up a treatment bottle. For all remedies in the Bach flower range except Rescue Remedy, two drops of the mother tincture are dropped into a 30-ml dropper bottle filled with three parts spring water to one part alcohol (brandy or vodka). For Rescue Remedy, four drops are used. It is this mixture that is used for giving doses, not the concentrated mother tincture.

Dosage

With giving doses, it is the frequency rather than the amount that is important. The usual dose for most long-standing or chronic problems is four drops four times a day for four weeks. For acute emergencies or sudden shocks, you can dose with three to four drops every 15 minutes until the condition stabilizes, then repeat as necessary.

Administering remedies to your pet

The flower essences can be administered orally, onto the lips or gums, but be careful not to let the animal bite the end of the glass dropper. They can also be put into food or water, or even onto an animal's fur. I often suggest applying the drops to the acupuncture point GV 20 (on top of the head midway between the ears); this is an easily accessible point and it doesn't stress the animal as much as trying to get the drops into the mouth. If the animal is very timid, you can even drop the mixture onto your hands then rub or stroke it onto the coat. It is enough for them to be on the animal— they don't necessarily need to be *in* the mouth or *in* the body. One suggestion is to put the remedy in a small glass vial and suspend it from the animal's collar, so it is working constantly.

You can also mix the essences in a spray bottle and spray them in stables, rooms, kennels, cages, food bowls, etc., or even add them to a bucket of water and sponge them on. (Use 1 dropperful from the treatment bottle to any volume of water.) Veterinary clinics by their nature have animals in various emotional states of fear, anxiety and apprehension (as well as owners!) so to reduce this I have regularly sprayed my veterinary clinic consultation rooms, surgery and recovery hospital with a mix of Rescue

Remedy (for shock, panic and terror), aspen (for unknown fears) and walnut (which helps protect the patient during any state of change). This helps the animals and their owners to relax, as well since keeping the general "feeling" of the rooms in a healthy state, as many negative emotions tend to linger in rooms even after the actual experience is over. Owners often comment on how nice the place feels and how happily their pets come into the clinic, when they usually try to run away at the door of vet clinics! I also have aromatherapy essential oils (such as lavender or lemongrass) on a light-bulb ring (which sits on the light bulb so that, as it heats, the oils vaporize into the air) in the waiting room. This makes the place smell wonderful, in contrast to the smell of disinfectant mixed with dog and cat urine that greets you when you walk into some veterinary clinics.

Use in the home

There are many different scenarios for the use of flower essences. Most behavioral problems will respond to the use of the essences when they are combined with commonsense management procedures. No treatment is 100 percent effective all the time, however, and sometimes it will be necessary to reassess the mixture or your management procedure, or even go to another form of treatment. On the whole, though, the responses I have gotten with these remedies have been very, very good.

One of the most common treatment scenarios is the cat that sprays urine inside the house or has inappropriate bathroom habits. Often this is the result of territory or stress issues. If the urine has been checked by your veterinarian for infection or crystals, and that is not the problem, stress may be the cause. It is possible the patient is being harassed or attacked by other cats, or perhaps there is stress in the house such as building renovations or lots of visitors. Often these are animals that are very timid and fearful, or they may be small or elderly or just a little nervous. In these cases I usually recommend a mix of aspen (for unknown fears), mimulus (for known fears), larch (to increase confidence), willow (for resentment, if this is an issue) and Rescue Remedy (for stress, panic and terror).

Another very common problem is the fear of loud noises. This is common on New Year's Eve but can also be a reaction to such things as airplanes overhead, loud rain on the roof or cars back-firing. The animal may hide under furniture, howl, shake and shiver, and be generally distressed. I have treated this problem very successfully with a mix of aspen, mimulus, larch and Rescue Remedy.

One of the most memorable stories about this mix concerned a farmer who, when he brought his house dog into the clinic for a checkup, mentioned that every time it rained heavily on their iron roof the dog became extremely upset and hid under the furniture. I suggested he try a mix of flower essences, which he obviously thought sounded a bit New Age and highly unlikely to be of any use. But I convinced him to at least try them. To his credit, he did, and the next time I saw him he burst into the room loudly expounding its virtues: "That mimulus—MARRRVELLOUS stuff!" He had given the remedy to the dog the next time it had rained, and instead of becoming distressed, as it had done for the last ten years, the dog had simply curled up and gone to sleep, much to the farmer's amazement. Interestingly, he had given the dog the remedy a couple more times when it had rained and had never needed to do it again after that.

I also prescribed this mix for a similar situation, where a dog became very distressed every time an airplane went overhead. Since the house it lived in was on a major flight path, this happened several times a day. Again, as soon as the animal received the mix it simply curled up, relaxed and went to sleep. The remedies are not sedative in action at all, but they normalize and rebalance the emotions, so the negative behavior is discontinued.

Choosing a remedy mix

Once you know how to prepare the remedies, what they are and where to put them, the next thing is to decide on the appropriate mix. If you are going to use remedy mixes regularly I suggest you familiarize yourself with the description of each remedy so that the knowledge becomes automatic, then you will start thinking of remedies that may be of use with every animal (or human!) you meet.

The descriptions of each remedy that are given later in this Chapter are highly abridged from the initial descriptions given by Dr. Bach. The list is designed to be a ready-reference tool, one that can be referred to quickly when you are confronted with a particular problem, or will get you started without having to go through volumes of descriptions, most of which are related to human emotions. I find that if it is too hard to find the tools you need, you tend not to use them!

The flower essences are so safe and easy to use that, with a little practice and sensitivity to the various presenting emotional signs, practically anyone can pick up the list and choose a remedy mix. The key is to just do it! I have a laminated list in my consultation room that I refer to when checking if I have the correct mix for a particular individual, even though I have been using the remedies for fifteen years or more. Remember, if you get the "wrong" remedy, it doesn't really matter—it just means the mix will not be as effective as it could be and you will need to revisit the list for a more suitable remedy.

My theory on most emotional and behavioral problems is that the animal is either fearful and needs "building up," or is aggressive or overbearing and needs "calming down." The flower essences tend to fall loosely into one of these two categories, with some remedies useful for in-between states. These remedies fit perfectly with our holistic principles of aiming to achieve balance by bringing the emotions, and therefore the physical symptoms, back to a state of harmony—flower essences do this beautifully.

To start you thinking about combinations, I have listed some common problems and the remedies I might choose. Remember that you need to fit the remedy to the animal and not the animal to the remedy, so choose the ones that best suit the picture you have of the problem. I have listed possible mixes, but it is up to the prescriber to decide if the remedy is the best one for a particular situation.

Some helpful combinations for common problems

Note: I refer to Rescue Remedy in these recommendations but, as mentioned above, Five Flower is essentially the same product, made by a different company.

Accidents and trauma

Rescue Remedy, walnut, possibly olive, gentian

Animals that don't get along
Chestnut bud, holly, beech, walnut, Rescue Remedy

Anxiety at events (e.g., shows)
Elm, impatiens (can be used alone, but is also in the Rescue Remedy formula), Rescue Remedy, aspen, mimulus, sweet chestnut

Car sickness
Rescue Remedy, scleranthus, mimulus, walnut

Cystitis (fear-related)
Aspen, chestnut bud, walnut, mimulus, Rescue Remedy

Excessive barking
Chestnut bud, cerato, heather, vervain

Exhaustion
Hornbeam, oak, olive, sweet chestnut, wild rose

Grieving
Rescue Remedy, walnut, honeysuckle, gentian, water violet

Jealousy
Beech, chestnut bud, chicory, holly, willow (if the animal seems resentful)

Leaving pets in catteries or kennels
Walnut, honeysuckle, Rescue Remedy, gentian, aspen

Loss of a body function (e.g., a limb, eliminative function)
Oak, olive, scleranthus, Rescue Remedy, walnut

New animals in the house
Walnut, Rescue Remedy, beech (especially if there is another pet already there), rock water

Overdominance
Chicory, holly, chestnut bud, vine, walnut, beech

Overgrooming
Aspen, mimulus, crab apple, Rescue Remedy, walnut, willow

Paralysis
Walnut, gentian, olive, scleranthus, star of Bethlehem

Recovery from illness
Clematis, crab apple, gentian, gorse, mustard, oak, olive, walnut

Self-mutilation (as opposed to overgrooming)
Sweet chestnut, cherry plum, willow, Rescue Remedy

Separation anxiety
Wild oat, agrimony, aspen, mimulus, red chestnut, rock rose, honeysuckle, star of Bethlehem, Rescue Remedy

Skin problems or infections
Rescue Remedy, crab apple, walnut, chestnut bud

Training
Chestnut bud, clematis, walnut, white chestnut, vine

Travel
Aspen, mimulus, Rescue Remedy, walnut, scleranthus

Trips to the vet
Elm, aspen, mimulus, Rescue Remedy

Vestibular problems (impaired balance)
Walnut, scleranthus, olive, cherry plum, star of Bethlehem, chestnut bud

Vomiting
Rescue Remedy, walnut, crab apple, olive

> **Things to bear in mind**
>
> - Several physical problems have been listed here, and although the remedies work initially on the emotions, there are often remarkable and very quick physical improvements.
> - Always check with your veterinarian if symptoms are any more than very minor—there could be something else going on that only a trained professional can diagnose. I do not in any way suggest you substitute these remedies for a professional evaluation; they are possible tools to use in the appropriate situations.
> - There are several remedies under each heading. I suggest picking the most appropriate for the individual, by cross-referencing with the essence descriptions that follow.

Flower essences and their applications

Because the individual emotional descriptions are derived from the descriptions of human emotions, it can be a bit of a leap of faith to compare them with animal emotions. There are similarities, but care needs to be taken not to anthropomorphize too much (giving human attributes and behaviors to animals). Keep the overall picture and desired outcome in mind, and don't get too bogged down in the tiny detail of the descriptions. If it mostly fits, it's probably the right one! Try it anyway, because the flower essences usually work to some degree even if the one you use is not the ideal choice.

Note that the flower essences are one of the few treatment options you can do this with; most others have to be pretty exact or there can be nasty consequences.

The table beginning on page 110 covers the main flower essences, with the emotional states and related conditions they are best suited to treating. Flower essences marked with * are in the Rescue Remedy formula. The descriptions are from Dr. Bach's original descriptions as well as from sources listed on page 275.

Treating allergies

One very frustrating problem in veterinary practice is the common occurrence of allergies and the trauma that results from itching and scratching. Many a pet owner has spent sleepless nights listening to their dog scratch and chew away at itself, only to have a red, moist patch or worse on its skin in the morning. They may have had creams and steroids to treat the symptoms, but as soon as the dose drops or the drugs are stopped, the symptoms often come right back. To understand why it is so difficult to identify what is causing an allergy, and to treat it effectively and permanently, you need to have some background on what is going on in the first place.

What are allergies?

The word "allergy" comes from the Greek words *allos*, meaning "altered," and *ergion*, meaning "action" or "reactivity." Thus, allergy literally means "altered reactivity"—in other words, when something that in average amounts and normal circumstances is innocuous in most bodies produces a biological sensitivity in others. Therefore, allergy can be defined as an unusual sensitivity to certain substances (known as "allergens"). The reason there is an unusual reaction or sensitivity in the first place is that the immune system is not in balance and is producing symptoms in the body that simply would not appear if it was completely healthy.

Each body seems to "do allergy" in a different way—some have itchy skins, some have diarrhea or vomiting, and some have breathing problems such as asthma. In severe cases, in sensitive animals the immune reaction to a substance, for example bee venom, can be almost fatal.

To holistic veterinarians, allergies are an obvious sign that all is not well in the body. They reflect a need not only to treat the actual allergies, but to improve the overall health of the animal and allow the immune system to rebalance itself, so that it does not produce annoying and potentially harmful symptoms. Unfortunately, in conventional veterinary medicine these symptoms are controlled with drugs that suppress the immune system. This means that often important underlying issues are not addressed—things such as improving the nutrition of the animal, perhaps adding specific nutritional supplements, improving its mental and emotional health with exercise, grooming and attention to the home life, and possibly addressing emotional upsets with flower essences.

Flower Essence	Emotional state	Indications and effects
Agrimony	Concealed distress	• Sensitive; anxious to please; never complains, even when in pain. • Often has a stoic appearance. • Doesn't like to be alone, often restless. • May develop skin problems, arthritis, digestive upsets, urinary incontinence when stressed. • Restores inner peace.
Aspen	Fear of unknown things	• Spooks easily, becomes nervous for no obvious reason. • Panics at new things. • A good remedy to give before storms, thunder, firecrackers, travel, shows, etc. • Good for separation anxiety and animals that urinate through fear. • Restores courage.

Flower Essence	Emotional state	Indications and effects	
Beech	Intolerance	• Grumpy, easily irritated and annoyed. • Doesn't like other animals or people. • Generally tense and rigid, can develop arthritic conditions as the animal gets older.	• Helps reduce territorial aggression. • Good for animals that are sensitive to their environment, develop allergies and are sensitive to heat and cold. • Restores tolerance and flexibility.
Centaury	Lack of assertiveness	• Weak-willed. • Subservient, eager to please. • Catches infections easily and has no resistance.	• Good for dogs that are fearful of other dogs, submissive urination, the runt of the litter. • Restores assertiveness and resistance.
Cerato	Lack (not loss) of confidence	• Easily distracted, especially during training. • Vocal, restless, may have discipline problems.	• Useful for chronic barkers. • Restores confidence.
Cherry plum*	Extreme fear, fear of losing control	• Uncontrollable behavior, compulsiveness, unpredictability. • Fear aggression, self-mutilation, incontinence when excited. • Seem to know they have misbehaved after biting and scratching.	• Restores control.

Flower Essence	Emotional state	Indications and effects
Chestnut bud	Failure to learn from experience	• Accident-prone. • Has recurrent sickness, is not responding to treatment.	• Helps animals break bad habits and learn basic skills. • Useful in training, or any form of behavior modification. • Restores ability to learn.
Chicory	Dominance, jealousy	• Thinks it owns the house and everything in it! • Demands attention and food. • Overly possessive, attention-seeking, can be jealous. • Constantly underfoot or in the owner's lap, overly protective of litter.	• Can become destructive when the owner leaves it. • Restores normal caring and protectiveness.
Clematis*	Absentmindedness	• Distracted, indifferent, lacks interest in present circumstances, scattered thoughts. • Provides focus during training, increases attention span.	• Good for guard and seeing-eye dogs. • Speeds up recovery time after surgery or trauma. • Useful for boredom, restores alertness. • Useful in drug overdoses, exhaustion from giving birth, vestibular disease when the patient is weak, shock, especially if cold to touch.

Flower Essence	Emotional state	Indications and effects	
Crab apple	Cleansing remedy	• Grooms excessively, over-fastidious. • Abused by people and other animals. • Left abandoned to die. • Distressed because they have soiled themselves. • Has a heavily matted coat.	• Useful for "toxic" states; i.e., infections, discharges, wounds, unhealthy coats, poisoning. • Restores cleanliness and dignity.
Elm	Overwhelmed, feeling inadequate	• Feels overwhelmed by a demanding situation, e.g., travel, shows, house renovations, constant stress. • Develops the same disorders as its owners. • Naturally high-strung.	• Useful for anxiety at shows, trips to the vet or groomer, for mothers overwhelmed by the demands of a big litter. • Restores competence.
Gentian	Discouragement, depression	• Run down, discouraged or depressed emotionally or physically. • "Gives up," especially when ill, after stillborn litters. • After the loss of a friend, chronic disease, rehabilitation, a bad experience.	• Useful for detoxifying animals to help the healing process. • Restores perseverance.

Flower Essence	Emotional state	Indications and effects
Gorse	Hopelessness	• Utter despondency and hopelessness, despair. • Doesn't respond to encouragement. • Very slow to recover from an illness, refuses food. • Mothers that have lost their offspring. • Helps encourage healing and recovery, and restores endurance.
Heather	Excessive attention-getting behavior	• Attention-seeking due to loneliness. • Needs to be the center of attention, demanding. • Vocalizes constantly, worse when left alone, can be destructive. • Often friendly to the point of being obnoxious. • Inattentive to the commands of its owner. • Restores a quiet composure.
Holly	The prickly personality	• Tends to bite and anger easily, but can also be loving, tolerant, happy. • Needs more love, or has been abused or neglected (e.g., dogs kept outside/chained up). • Malicious one minute, really nice the next. • Can be used to treat animals that are aggressive, jealous and suspicious. • Good for most cases of aggression.

Flower Essence	Emotional state	Indications and effects
Honeysuckle	Homesickness	• Anxious, especially due to separation. • Has difficulty adjusting to new circumstances. • Separated from home and family, i.e., during kennel and cattery stays, hospitalization. • May exhibit grief with illness, inability to cope with present circumstances. • Restores the ability to adjust to present circumstances.
Hornbeam	Weakness	• Mental and physical exhaustion. • Lost interest in life, a show animal that has lost interest, appears tired. • A good pick-me-up after illness. • Restores vitality.
Impatiens*	Impatience	• Irritable, uptight, does not cooperate. • A show animal that is anxious and nervous. • Restless, excitable, cannot sit still, in too much of a hurry to learn when in training. • Used in neurological conditions where there is nervousness, shaking, seizures made worse by excitement. • May help relieve pain.

Flower Essence	Emotional state	Indications and effects
Larch	Loss (not lack) of confidence, hesitancy	• Fearful, has a victim mentality. • Fears failure. • Cowers in submission.	• Useful for abused animals. • Increases confidence.
Mimulus	Fear of known things	• Has specific fears that can be identified. • Has a fear of visitors, thunder, lightning, heavy rain on the roof, other animals, certain noises, planes overhead, judges in shows.	• Gives courage, reduces nervousness. • May become aggressive if cornered. • Shy, timid, easily dominated.
Mustard	Depression for no reason	• Sudden depression, prefers solitude, chronic illness where the animal has apparently given up hope of recovery. • Deep depression, especially associated with hormonal problems, i.e., when in season or during gestation. • Likes to be alone, especially if an older animal; gets cranky.	• Owners feel something is wrong but don't know what. • Restores serenity.

Flower Essence	Emotional state	Indications and effects
Oak	Lack of resistance in normally strong animals	• Persists in spite of adversity, a hard worker but seems overburdened. • Struggling to overcome a disability. • Helps rebuild strength after a physically stressful situation.	• Good for endurance races where stamina is required. • Good for loss of a body function, i.e., loss of a limb, loss of eliminative functions. • Restores resilience.
Olive	Mental and physical exhaustion	• Worn down from chronic illness. • Useful for detoxification when weak, gives support during the cleansing process.	• Enhances stamina in endurance competitions. • Useful for animals with anemia, any loss of function or coming out of hibernation. • Restores strength.
Pine	Guilt, victim mentality	• Devoted to its owners despite poor treatment, abused, feels rejected. • An animal that has been given away or left behind in the pound. • May cower when upset. • Tries constantly to please its owners.	• Restores a positive attitude.

Flower Essence	Emotional state	Indications and effects	
Red chestnut	Over-protectiveness, over-anxiety	• Has excessive fear and anxiety for others. • Over-protective of offspring or owner. • Doesn't tolerate separation well.	• Useful if an animal needs to be separated from its owner. • Restores confidence and trust.
Rock rose*	Terror	• Suffers terror, panic phobias, extreme fear. • Displays extreme escape behavior.	• Has sunstroke, heatstroke, destroys the house out of fear when left alone during thunder, storms, fireworks, loud noises. • Restores courage and calm.
Rock water	Rigidity, tightness, repression	• An inflexible, rigid, intractable nature. • Stubborn, resists breaking old habits, a picky eater. • Has difficulty adapting to changes in routine. • Shows mental and physical inflexibility.	• Sometimes useful for degenerative arthritis, dominant behavior. • Useful when a new pet moves into a household. • Restores flexibility and spontaneity.
Scleranthus	Loss of balance	• Lacks coordination, any neurological conditions. • May have severe mood swings, uncertain temperament.	• Useful for strokes, paralysis, travel sickness with vomiting, vestibular disease. • Restores stability and balance.

Flower Essence	Emotional state	Indications and effects
Star of Bethlehem*	Mental, emotional or physical shock	• Animal becomes withdrawn. • Useful where trauma (physical, mental or emotional) appears to cause paralysis or loss of function in a body system.	• Good for change, i.e., when moving house, staying in kennels. • Possibly useful for separation anxiety if an animal appears shocked by the change. • Restores calm on mental, emotional and physical levels.
Sweet chestnut	Extreme mental and physical distress	• Hopelessness and despair, feels it has reached the limits of its endurance. • A wild animal that paces in captivity. • May refuse to eat after separation from owners, to the point of death.	• Self-mutilation due to distress (not necessarily boredom). • Very high-strung. • Restores endurance qualities.
Vervain	Over-enthusiastic, impulsive	• High-strung, hyperactive and intense. • May pace, jump and bark all the time.	• May help tendency to roam and escape. • May help calm animals that can't get enough exercise

Flower Essence	Emotional state	Indications and effects	
Vine	Dominant, inflexible	• Strong-willed, difficult to train. • Bullying, very territorial.	• Restores positive leadership qualities.
Walnut 	Transition	• Any life change, such as teething, coming into heat for the first time, a new mother. • After surgery such as neutering and spaying.	• Helps with any changes such as a new home, travel, surgery, loss of a body part. • Aids in the healing process. • Useful in training. • Useful prior to euthanasia. • Restores adaptability and ability to cope with change.
Water violet	Aloofness	• Tends to withdraw and wants to be alone when sick or if grieving. • Often antisocial with other animals and people.	• Good remedy for cats as they are often aloof and indifferent to others around them. • Restores social contact.
White chestnut	Anxiety, preoccupation	• Sleeplessness, restlessness due to anxiety. • Obsessive behavior.	• Helps focus during training, and improves ability to abandon old behaviors. • Restores the ability to rest.

Flower Essence	Emotional state	Indications and effects
Wild oat	Boredom, lack of direction	• Seems depressed as a result of boredom. • Not performing to its capacity. • Animals that retire from an occupation they have been bred to do. • May show signs of separation anxiety, such as chewing, house destruction. • Restores direction and meaning to life.
Wild rose	Apathy, resignation	• Lacks energy and motivation. • Shows no enjoyment of life. • Overly serious and tense. • Can be used during long debilitating illnesses, for animals chained up in a small area, grouchy older animals. • Restores the will to live.
Willow	Resentment, maliciousness	• Exhibits destructive behavior where resentment is the underlying cause. • May urinate or defecate in the house because the owner "did" something. • May destroy the house out of resentment. • Restores a good temper.

When an animal with allergies comes into my consultation room, I talk at length with its owner about its diet, what nutritional supplements it receives, what sort of life it has and what health problems it may have had in the past. The latter provides a very important clue as to why the animal may have the allergies, which can result from repeated exposure to a particularly strong or toxic agent that can overwhelm the body's defenses, or a long-standing and debilitating disease that can weaken the immune system.

Genetics also play a large part in the formation of allergies, although while the tendency to have allergies is often inherited, sensitivity to a specific irritant is rarely passed on. In other words, if you have an allergy to, say, peanuts, then your children may have a tendency to have allergies, but not necessarily to peanuts. The age of onset of an allergic condition often depends on the degree of inheritance—the stronger the genetic factor, the earlier the probable onset.

What can be done for allergies?

Diet

While we cannot do much about the genes we have inherited, or the diseases or toxic insults that have happened in the past, there are definitely things that can be done to improve an animal's overall health to try and bring the immune system back into balance. Diet and nutrition is a very important place to start, as we have discussed in Chapter 3 (see also Chapter 5, "Common problems and their treatments"). An appropriate diet for your pet, with the correct supplements for the presenting condition, is crucial.

Relieving the symptoms

Once diet is addressed, we can also attend to the presenting secondary symptoms, correcting the effects of the allergies while the body is rebalancing. In the case of skin allergies, things like soothing creams, special shampoos, possibly a course of antibiotics or even some kind of anti-inflammatory may be necessary to calm the symptoms down in the short term while we work on long term improvement of the health of the immune system. It is no good having the animal rip itself to pieces by scratching and biting, because this puts further stress on the system, so judicial use of drugs is sometimes necessary in this early treatment phase.

What I do not recommend is the long-term use of strong medications such as steroids and antibiotics. They may have a place in acute and short term treatments, but repeated long-term medication with these drugs can harm the health of the animal (as well as being very expensive). Other things like homeopathic remedies, herbs and even acupuncture also help in treating these symptoms and rebalancing the body.

Determining the cause

The next thing is to determine what substances may be causing the allergies. This is not so that the animal can be kept away from these substances (which is one of the focuses of conventional treatment regimes), but so we can directly treat these things via the immune system, correcting its "over the top" reaction and stopping the body producing symptoms.

How do we do this, you may ask. Well, I asked myself the very same question many times, becoming more and more disillusioned as many allergy-related cases simply did not respond enough with diet changes, supplementation of essential fatty acids, and various herbal and homeopathic remedies. I needed something else that was not only going to tell me what caused the problem, but something that treated it as well. My search ended when I went to a veterinary course on a special kind of allergy treatment known as "Nambudripad's Allergy Elimination Technique," or NAET.

Nambudripad's Allergy Elimination Technique (NAET)

This technique involves using kinesiology, or muscle testing, to determine what is causing the weakness or allergy in the body, then treating it using a form of acupressure.

After attending the course I treated animals with the most severe skin problems, animals that I had been trying to help for a long time, and they all recovered completely. They went off all medication and had no itchy symptoms, and what's more, they stayed that way. Each year I would see them for their annual check-ups, and not one of them had relapsed, which was extraordinary as they had all been itching and scratching on and off for many years.

That was six years ago and I now use NAET in my practice nearly full time for treating allergies. It gives consistent results and helps most animals, usually with an improvement rate (resolution of symptoms) of between 85 and 95 percent.

Some animals' immune systems are very reactive and they can become allergic to new things in their lives very quickly. As fast as you remove their existing allergies, their system creates a new one, resulting in symptoms of varying degrees. These are the cases that are challenging, as they need to be seen every six to eight months for a follow-up treatment, but this is still better than being on steroids every day of their lives.

From using this technique, I have formed the theory that each individual body and immune system can create allergies, which form over time as layers, like onion rings, right from birth (or maybe even before birth). As the animal creates more allergies or layers (becomes reactive to more allergens) it reaches a critical threshold when physical symptoms such as scratching and itching will occur. It is at this point that many owners state that their pet is allergic to a particular substance (for example, beef, grass, a certain plant) because every time the animal goes near that substance, the symptoms start up. In fact, this may be just the latest allergy that has formed, but it is the one that has tipped the body over the edge, to the point where it has begun producing obvious symptoms. When I say "obvious," I mean scratching or itching, or perhaps vomiting, however that particular body "does allergy." However, to the very observant person, that particular body may have had other more subtle symptoms for some time, such as a lack of energy or a slowing down, behavioral problems such as being hyperactive or a bit aggressive, sleeping more, or being slower to get moving in the morning. These signs are often put down to aging or laziness, or just "their nature," but what I have frequently found is that when animals come in to be treated with NAET for the obvious things like the itching and scratching, many of these subtle signs also disappear.

A classic example of this is a young Airedale terrier that was brought to me with a chronic skin problem, with itching and scratching. We decided to start the NAET treatment, and after the first treatment the owner called me to say that the dog had almost changed its personality overnight. Formerly it used to rush and bark loudly at all visitors to the house, leaping up and creating havoc whenever anyone new arrived. In fact, it had done this all its life, to the point where it was put into another room when anyone came to visit. After just the first NAET treatment this behavior suddenly stopped, and the dog now greeted visitors in a relaxed and friendly manner. What's more, it never went back to its old behavior.

Many animals that have been sluggish and slow gain a noticeable amount of energy with NAET, as if the body is correcting an imbalance and getting back to a more balanced state. As the different "layers" of allergies are removed there can be a variety of symptom changes, and not just in the obvious presenting symptoms. I see things like a thicker, more lustrous coat; the breath is often sweeter, eyes seem clearer, and even things like stiffness in the joints can be reduced. All this illustrates how debilitating allergies can be to the body, and how achieving a state of balance can allow our animal friends to be more healthy and enjoy their lives more.

As with any form of treatment, NAET does not completely resolve all problems, but in 95 percent of the cases I have treated there is a significant improvement. Sometimes disease processes are too far advanced or too deeply entrenched in the body for a complete "cure" to be possible. The body has a finite life, and when the imbalances are too great correcting them can sometimes be impossible.

So what is NAET?

Nambudripad's Allergy Elimination Technique is a system that identifies the substances that are creating a weakness in the body (the allergens) using muscle testing, or kinesiology. It rebalances the immune system using acupressure for those specific substances, so the immune system does not react abnormally to them any more.

In other words, if an animal has an allergy to beef, the muscle testing will detect this and the beef allergy can be treated via acupressure. If the animal eats beef after being treated, it won't create allergic symptoms. The allergy has been removed from the body by rebalancing the immune response to beef, so that rather than treating beef as something to be reactive to and making itchy skin lesions, the immune system accepts it in a normal way.

NAET is a truly unique system in that it identifies and treats allergies to eliminate them, rather than simply identifying them so that particular substances that trigger the allergy can be avoided. The conventional patch testing used in both veterinary and human medicine involves injecting many different substances into the skin and monitoring the reaction. The limitation of this technique is that generic substances such as dust mites are injected. With NAET, the substance is simply held on the body and the body's response is noted, so one can test many things very quickly and in their whole state—for example, vacuum cleaner dust, which does contain dust mites, but also a variety of other household substances, such as dead skin cells from all family members, hair, dust, etc. You cannot compare vacuum cleaner dust samples from different households, as each sample is unique to a particular household. Even food samples such as breads, or meat raised in a certain way, may contain compounds that don't appear in every sample.

The NAET muscle-testing technique can test for smells, sounds, even emotions that may be causing a weakness in the body. This is not possible with injectable patch testing. Testing with NAET is also non-invasive. It does not involve sedation or uncomfortable reactions in the skin, and because many substances can be tested quickly treatment can start immediately, without having to wait for a period of time for a certain skin reaction to occur. Depending on how many allergens are detected, treatment and recovery from the symptoms can happen in just a few sessions.

Diagnosis using muscle testing (kinesiology)

The muscle-testing technique used as a diagnostic tool in NAET has been employed for many years by naturopaths, chiropractors and other natural health practitioners. It is not a mystical procedure requiring supernatural powers, but a very commonsense, non-invasive and quick way to gather feedback information from individuals, and anyone can learn to do it.

It uses the body's feedback mechanisms, allowing the tester to ask questions and get a strong or weak muscle response, denoting a positive or a negative answer to the question. (For more information on kinesiology and NAET see *www.naet.com*.)

Treatment using acupressure

Once muscle testing has determined what is causing the allergies, treatment involves acupressure of the main bladder meridian points down either side of the spine. This stimulates the entire nervous system to "reprogram" itself so that it does not recognize the substance you are treating as being foreign to the body, and thus worthy of mounting an immune response to. In other words, it desensitizes the body to that substance, creating a normal reaction to it when it is in or on the body.

NAET is the coordination of these techniques into a very specific procedural method, and it requires professional training and practice to perfect the technique. It will, I believe, become a very useful mainstream tool for veterinarians, as the results are so spectacular, but I suspect it will take the rather conservative veterinary fraternity some time to embrace it. The reason I have discussed this at length is that I believe the more people who know about these techniques, and the greater the demand for them, the more people will train and learn to use them as mainstream tools for treatment.

Herbal medicine

Herbal medicines have been used for many centuries, and until the advent of modern drugs such as penicillin and steroids, they were often the main healing tools people had to work with. Many modern drugs are derived from active ingredients found in plants, and scientists are still finding new drugs from previously undiscovered plant material.

Herbal medicine involves using plant material to produce remedies to:

• Cleanse;
• Support the body in its healing processes;
• Help keep the body healthy by supporting various body systems to prevent illness.

The plants can be used fresh, dried, or made into creams or tinctures (preserved in alcohol). They can be taken chopped or ground up (macerated) as infusions with boiling water, as tablets or capsules, or in food.

Since some herbs can be toxic at certain levels, it is very important to use herbal remedies that are pre-prepared, and follow the instructions carefully, or get specific training in herbalism if you want to prepare your own remedies. Having said this, there are many very safe herbs available for treatments, a number of which are commonly found in gardens or in the countryside. If you are gathering your own herbs it is important that they are spray free, and ideally organically grown, and not gathered from the side of the road because car fumes can pollute the plants, making them toxic to ingest. Probably all medicines have the potential to be toxic at certain levels, even the "safe" ones—it's the dose rate that determines if a substance will be toxic to the body or not, so make sure you know the correct dose of each herb before you use it!

Herbs are used extensively in Ayurvedic medicine and in traditional Chinese medicine (probably even more than acupuncture), where they are prescribed to rebalance the organ systems, as determined by pulse diagnosis. The following individual descriptions are taken from several references and adapted for use in this book. (See references page 273.)

 ## Some commonly used, safe herbs

Alfalfa

- Contains many vitamins and minerals, used as a tonic and cleanser of the system.
- A kidney cleanser, and alkalinizer of the whole system.
- Contains estrogenic compounds and may be of use to stimulate milk in nursing mothers.
- Avoid large doses.

Aloe vera

- Antibacterial and antifungal, also a blood cleanser.
- Very useful externally as a wound and especially a burn treatment; use the gel directly from a freshly cut leaf.
- Used internally as a laxative as well as soothing the digestive tract and helping to normalize its function. Said to improve digestion.
- Use the diluted gel or the dried juice.
- Has immunostimulant ingredients; has been used in cats with feline leukemia with positive results.
- Do not overuse.

Angelica
- Useful for all digestive problems including colic and heart-burn.
- Soothes the stomach.
- Use the seeds as a mild tea.

Barley
- Calms the digestive tract.
- Used in convalescence and for colitis and diarrhea.
- A general nutritive food and nerve tonic.
- Good for the bladder and kidneys.
- Boil barley grains and sieve to make barley water; the soaked grains can also be eaten raw—soak them for two days, preferably exposed to sunlight.

Basil
- A powerful tonic, stimulant and nerve remedy.
- Relieves nausea and severe vomiting, useful for indigestion.
- Can be applied externally as an insecticide.

Blackberry
- An astringent tonic, which contains between 8 and 14% tannin.
- The leaves and root bark are used in teas to treat diarrhea.
- Useful for general debility as a tonic.

Calendula
- The flowers are a very valuable anti-inflammatory and antiseptic.
- Excellent for treating and healing wounds, especially when combined with Hypericum (St. John's wort).
- Used on bruises, burns, cuts, sore nipples, slow-healing wounds, bedsores and abscesses.
- Can be used as a mouthwash or to treat sores in the mouth.

- The flowers contain lycopene, a proven antioxidant helpful for preventing many degenerative disease processes.
- Not to be used during pregnancy.

Chickweed
- Soothing and healing for the digestive tract.
- Used to treat ulcers in the stomach, colitis.
- Used externally as an anti-inflammatory and for all types of skin sores.

Clover (red)
- Very valuable as a tonic and for cleansing the blood.
- Promotes sleep.
- Used in cancer therapy.
- An antispasmodic and expectorant.

Comfrey
- Astringent and anti-inflammatory.
- Can help with bone and ligament healing.
- Used externally as a poultice for boils, burns and infected wounds.

Dandelion
- A blood cleanser, and a general tonic.
- Stimulates bile flow and liver secretions.
- Good for liver and bile problems, as well as kidney problems.
- Anti-inflammatory and diuretic.
- Use the roots as a tea or the leaves raw.
- Very safe.

Echinacea
- A non-specific immunostimulant, especially good for colds, flu and other infectious problems.

- Reduces inflammation and stimulates wound healing when used topically as a poultice.
- Very safe.

Elder
- Contains antiviral compounds.
- All parts of the plant are used—flowers, berries, leaves and roots.
- Roots are used for kidney problems, as a diuretic.
- Flowers are anti-inflammatory, antiviral, analgesic, antioxidant, anti-tumor activity.
- Leaves are used to treat eczema and ringworm.

Eucalyptus
- Eucalyptus oil is an antiseptic, and useful for colds and coughs.
- Leaves are used as an expectorant and cough remedy, and also act as an antiseptic.

Fennel
- Anti-inflammatory, calmative, good for upset stomachs and colic.
- Helps liver regeneration.
- Fennel oil is antiseptic and bactericidal.
- May act as a cancer preventative.

Five-mushroom
- Extracts from five medicinal mushrooms, used as a tincture.
- Highly immune-stimulating, activates the killer T-cells as part of the immune response.
- Very useful for viral infections, especially upper respiratory infections.
- An important mix for treating any infection by stimulating immunity.
- Used in holistic cancer therapy.

Garlic

- Used for asthma, as an antibiotic and fungicide.
- May help with diabetes, by increasing the amount of free insulin.
- Helps prevent blood agglutination (clumping).
- Excellent for the cardiovascular system as it reduces blood cholesterol and lipid levels, helps prevent atherosclerosis, reduces blood pressure.
- Effective against certain intestinal parasites.
- Useful for colds, flu and other infectious diseases.
- In folklore is said to be able to be used to treat most things!
- Avoid large doses and long-term use (may cause a certain type of anemia).

Ginger

- A digestive tonic.
- Helps settle an upset stomach.
- Useful for travel sickness.
- Antispasmodic, calms the intestines.
- Used for pain relief and as an anti-inflammatory.
- Helps protect the liver.
- Avoid large doses; use in small doses during pregnancy.

Ginkgo

- Useful for many geriatric conditions such as cold extremities, poor circulation, memory loss, tinnitus and vertigo.
- Improves mental performance in geriatrics.
- Helps increase brain blood circulation.
- Has low toxicity.

Hawthorn

- A gentle tonic for the heart.
- Improves blood pressure, coronary flow and heart rate.
- Improves cardiac function, breathing problems and fluid swellings related to heart problems.

- Has low toxicity, BUT if it is used with digitalis, use only half the dose of each herb.

Lavender
- Antidepressant, calming.
- Can act as a tonic.
- The essential oil is useful in treating burns, acts as an antiseptic.
- Used extensively in aromatherapy.

Licorice
- Very valuable as an anti-inflammatory, good for gastric ulcers and reducing intestinal spasms.
- Contains GLA (gamma-linolenic acid), which reduces prostaglandin production and increases glucocorticoid concentration in responsive tissues.
- Can be used for itchy skin conditions.
- Stimulates the adrenal glands, helpful in treating Addison's disease.
- Useful in chronic stress and tiredness related to adrenal exhaustion.
- Useful for treating coughs and colds.
- Antioxidant.
- Helps improve liver function, clears jaundice, reduces vomiting and diarrhea.
- Stimulates the immune system.
- May help with depression.
- Not for long term or excessive use; use for four to six weeks only at a time.

Manuka oil
- The New Zealand version of tea tree (see page 134).
- Similar action to tea tree oil but said to be more powerful.
- An excellent antibacterial and antifungal; also a good drying agent with topical use.

Parsley
- Antihistamine and anti-inflammatory.
- Can act as a diuretic, and reduces stomach spasms.
- Good for kidney function.

Red raspberry
- Very useful in birthing (made into a tea) and pregnancy as a tonic.
- Can help expel retained afterbirth.
- Can also be used for diabetes, diarrhea, sores in the mouth.
- Very safe.

St. John's wort (Hypericum)
- Has proven antidepressant and anxiety-reducing actions.
- Anti-inflammatory.
- Used for colds, coughs and insomnia.
- Used topically for bruises and arthritis.
- Often combined with calendula to make wound-healing lotions.
- Overuse can lead to light sensitivity (photosensitivity).
- May be of use in treating AIDS and other viruses.

Tea tree
- As an essential oil is very useful as a strong antiseptic and antifungal agent.
- Very useful in wounds, skin infections and fungal skin problems.
- Dries out the wound, tastes awful so discourages animals from licking the area.
- Can be used for toothache, colds and headaches.
- Good for abscesses, bites and burns.
- Do not use internally or in high doses.

How to use herbs

Teas

Often the doses are not high enough to act in a medicinal way, but teas are an easy way to prepare herbs for low level and long term effects. They can be broadly divided into infusions and decoctions.

Infusions

Use the leaves, young stems and flower petals, either finely chopped or powdered and dried. Pour boiling water over them and let stand for about ten minutes. Use about two teaspoons of dried herbs to a cup of water. Can be stored in a cool place for up to 48 hours.

Decoctions

Use the woody stems, barks, berries and roots. Can use cold or hot water, but it takes longer to prepare than an infusion. Put sliced or chopped herbs in a saucepan, pour over cold water and bring to the boil, then simmer slowly for 20 to 40 minutes. Reduce the volume by one-third to a half. Remove from the heat, strain and store in a cool place for up to 48 hours.

Macerations

These are cold infusions or decoctions used when the active ingredient is sensitive to heat (e.g., valerian, parsley). Use cold water and the herb (chopped or sliced) in a 6:1 ratio. Leave to stand in a cool place for approximately 12 hours, then strain. It will keep for up to 48 hours.

Pills and capsules

This is probably the easiest way to get herbs into animals. The taste is not as strong as with alcohol-based tinctures, and it also concentrates the herbs so less volume is needed.

Extracts

Herbs can be made up in alcohol (as a tincture), water or glycerine. The benefit of this is that dosages can be more exact, so the results are more consistent. The downside is that they can taste quite strong, so getting them into animals' mouths can be a challenge. Tinctures can be heated to remove the alcohol first, which reduces the taste slightly.

Topical use as poultices and compresses

A poultice is applied to the skin, typically to draw the infected material from wounds or abscesses. Comfrey is a particularly useful herb for drawing abscesses, and I have used this with a lot of success in abscesses where the infection has tracked along under the skin and gone deeper into tissues. Boil the fresh or dried herb for five minutes, allow it to cool until it is just able to be applied without burning the skin, wrap in muslin and bandage the affected area. The herb and the heat work very well in helping to drain the wound. Leave the poultice on for as long as possible, usually about a half-hour to an hour, and do not allow the animal to lick or chew it. Be very careful it is not so hot that it is uncomfortable or burns the skin. The animal must be held or confined while the poultice is on, as they can be bulky and come off quite easily.

A compress is where cloth or muslin is soaked in an extract of the herbal preparation (which can be a decoction, tincture or infusion) and applied to the skin. Instead of the actual herb being wrapped in the fabric, there is just an extract of the herb. This is useful for situations like deep bruising or trauma, where the heat and the extract can help soothe the affected area.

Creams and ointments

Herbs and their extracts can be made into ointments and creams that can be applied to the skin or affected areas. The problem with any topical application is that the animal can either lick or chew the medication, and while it is not often toxic, this will reduce the intended action on the skin. Cats especially are extremely fastidious about anything unusual on their coats and skin, and will almost always try to remove a topical application. If creams and ointments are to be used on a cat it is usually necessary to put an Elizabethan collar on them, which means they are unable to lick the affected area (see Chapter 6 for how to make an Elizabethan collar). In dogs, one suggestion is to apply the cream then take the dog for a long walk, feed or play with it, or otherwise distract its attention so the cream can do its job and stay on the skin for as long as possible.

Fresh herbs

Herbs can be picked fresh and used raw as a supplement in food, e.g., dandelion leaves or parsley. The volume of herb needed to achieve an effective medicinal dose is usually prohibitively high, so using fresh herbs is usually reserved for daily supplementation in a preventive or overall health sense. There are many herbs that taste good and will be accepted when chopped into an animal's food, but there are as many herbs that don't taste so great, especially the bitter herbs that are often highly beneficial for digestion and liver health. You may need to add other more strong-tasting foods to disguise the taste. Often dried powdered herbs can be tucked into foods without too many problems.

Dosages for herbs

Unfortunately there are no standard, well-researched veterinary dosing values available for herbs so giving doses can be a bit hit and miss, since veterinarians tend to use human dosages and extrapolate them for their animal patients. It is normal to start with a lowish amount for a particular animal's weight and size,

Herb doses for cats and dogs

Preparation	Cats (10 lbs.)	Dogs (25 lbs.)
Decoction	5ml 2 x daily	10ml 3 x daily
Extract powder capsule (100 mg)	125mg 2 x daily	250mg 2–3 x daily
Extract tablet (250 mg)	125mg 2 x daily	250mg 2–3 x daily
Freeze-dried granules (100 mg capsules)	100mg 2 x daily	200mg 3 x daily
Loose granules	0.25 tsp 2 x daily	0.5 tsp 3 x daily
Syrups (crush extract tablet, or use granules mixed with hot honey)	0.25 tsp 2 x daily	0.5 tsp 3 x daily
Tinctures (remove alcohol by heating first)	5 drops 3 x daily	10 drops 3 x daily
Chinese patent medicines (pills)	10% of human dose	25% of human dose

Note: These doses will vary with the kind of herb and problem. Stronger herbs are given for shorter periods (3–7 days); milder herbs for 10–14 days; supplemental herbs for 1–3 months (or maybe for the lifetime, i.e., for cancer).

observe the responses, and adjust the dose as necessary. It can also take a while for the beneficial effects of a herb to be seen, so patience is required. This is why it is important for anyone using herbs to have some knowledge of what they are doing, and unless the very safe herbs are being used, apply sensible caution—even supposedly "safe" herbs can be toxic in large amounts.

The preceding table has been printed with the permission of Dr. Ihor Basko. It is taken from a presentation at the American Holistic Veterinary Medical Association Annual Conference in 1995, and updated in 2006.

Learning about herbs

If you are interested in using herbal remedies, my suggestion is to get to know ten to twenty different herbs really well, research their use and find a workable dose rate for them. Once you are very familiar with these remedies try learning about another ten or so, and build up your knowledge in this way.

Unlike other modalities such as acupuncture and homeopathy where the use of each point or remedy is very well-documented and tried, herbal medicine in veterinary use is still an emerging science. Most of the literature, particularly with regard to dosages and results, deals with use in humans.

Chiropractic medicine

Chiropractic medicine has been defined as "the science and art which uses the inherent recuperative powers of the body and deals with the relationship between the nervous system and the spinal column, including its immediate articulations, and the role of this relationship in the restoration and maintenance of health."[3]

Basically, it is the manipulation of the spine to realign the bones and ligaments to allow the nervous system (i.e., the brain, spinal cord and nerves) to function without any physical hindrances. As noted earlier, the nervous system has far-reaching effects on many other systems, since it is the control center of the body, telling other systems what and when to do things. It is directly related to the immune system, which is a major focus in holistic thinking.

The nerves and spinal cord are covered with special protective layers, and very slight changes in the way spinal bones (vertebrae) move and articulate together can put pressure on these coverings and affect the underlying nerve function. Even a tiny movement in the bones can result in varying amounts of pressure being put on the nerves, while a large movement can result in extreme pain or even paralysis. Chiropractic medicine works by detecting which bones are even slightly misaligned and easing them back into their correct position. The spinal bones can get out of place through everyday wear and tear, trauma or excessive exercise. Long-term results of this misalignment can range from localized pain in muscles to low-grade chronic illness. When the spinal bones are realigned, the nerves are enabled to function normally and the indirect effect to the rest of the body results in improved overall health.

Chiropractic manipulations must be performed by a trained chiropractor. Theirs is a specialized skill, not only to detect what is out of place, but to realign and replace the affected vertebrae. In animals with large muscle groups and long, large vertebral columns such as horses, this can be quite a big job.

Aromatherapy

Aromatherapy involves the use of essential (volatile) oils from various plants in a medicinal way to effect a physical or emotional response. These oils can be inhaled, rubbed onto the skin or applied to wounds, depending on the oil and the problem.

Therapeutically, essential oils can be used as antiseptic and antifungal agents, for repelling external parasites, and to treat burns and gastrointestinal upsets. This is an area in veterinary medicine that needs more research, because most studies have been done for human use, and animals have a much keener sense of smell than humans. They also have different smell preferences, if the way dogs appear to enjoy the smell of feces and other revolting smells is anything to go by!

All essential oils need to be diluted before being applied to the skin, since they are very concentrated. Use a carrier oil such as almond oil or, with wounds and burns, use wheat germ oil which contains vitamin E and will help heal the skin.

Essential oils

Here are a few essential oils I have used with success in my practice:

Lavender oil
- Has an antidepressant and calming action.
- Useful in treating burns and skin lesions (dilute in almond or wheat germ oil, which is high in vitamin E).
- Richard Pitcairn, the co-author of *Dr. Pitcairn's Complete Guide to Natural Health for Dogs and Cats*, has used it in the treatment of mange in dogs.

Thyme oil
- Has a strong antibacterial effect.
- Is an antioxidant.
- Also an excellent antifungal agent, but acts as an irritant on the skin and should not be used at concentrations over 1%; dilute in almond or wheat germ oil.

Tea tree oil
- An excellent antiseptic and disinfectant, and a selective antifungal agent.
- Can act as an irritant if used undiluted on skin.

Pennyroyal oil
- Pennyroyal oil is very toxic and can be fatal if ingested in its undiluted state. Don't use *at all* in cats as they are regularly grooming and licking, so ingestion at high levels is likely.
- Pennyroyal oil can also cause abortions in pregnant animals if used incorrectly.
- If used correctly and carefully, it can be used as a flea and insect repellent.

Recipes for essential oil use

The following recipes are from *Control of Fleas in Pets Using Essential Oils*, by Tonia Werchon[4].

For washing dogs

To 10 ounces of any gentle shampoo or Castile soap add up to 30 drops of mixed essential oils. Try:
10 drops lavender
5 drops eucalyptus
5 drops rosemary
5 drops cajeput

For washing cats

To 10 ounces of any gentle shampoo or Castile soap add up to 20 drops of essential oils. Try:
15 drops lavender
5 drops orange
Note: do not use pennyroyal or citronella essential oils—they are toxic in cats.

Flea repellent

Mix 10 ml grape seed or almond oil with:
10 drops lavender
5 drops cedar wood or geranium
Use sparingly! Use one or two drops only, massaging into the coat twice a week.

To repel fleas in carpets

Mix 50 drops of lavender, eucalyptus or eucalyptus citriodora in 1¼ cups of water in a spray bottle. Shake the bottle well to disperse the oils and mist the carpet before vacuuming. Vacuum once a week.

To repel fleas on polished wooden floors

Make up an emulsion with:
¼ cup lemon juice
¼ cup olive oil
30 drops lavender oil
Mop the floor with a damp mop dipped into this emulsion.

Chapter 5

Common problems and their treatments

In this Chapter some of the more common health problems are discussed, and there is advice on helpful complementary therapy for recovery. If your animal friend is otherwise fit, healthy and well, but has a minor problem, you may want to try some of the suggestions that follow. But remember these are for simple problems—I always advise getting a firm diagnosis from your veterinarian first, and perhaps running some of the following therapies past the vet to see if they suit the situation.

To a professional, even apparently simple problems may be recognized as key symptoms of a much deeper problem. If any of the symptoms listed below are seen, especially if your pet is very young, very old, or hasn't been "right" for more than a day or so, then it is highly advisable to contact your vet and get his or her advice. Even a very experienced veterinarian finds it difficult to do a consultation over the phone, as subtle but important symptoms may not be obvious; nothing can replace a hands-on examination.

As holistic veterinarians we are constantly looking at the bigger picture, relating early warning signs or symptoms to the whole animal. An example of this is the very common occurrence of cats fighting and being bitten. The bite itself can be treated with several very useful remedies, but it is always necessary to ask why the cat was bitten in the first place. Was the culprit a bully cat in the neighborhood; is your cat going out looking to increase its territory and starting the fights, or is it getting older and more frail and being picked on? By asking these questions, we can treat a simple bite wound as an early warning sign and look at management measures to control the situation—to repel the neighboring bully, for example, or to increase your cat's confidence by using a flower essence. By addressing these issues early on it is often possible to avoid further problems and stress for your animal friend. If not dealt with, these issues could lead to overgrooming, improper bathroom habits and spraying urine inside, which can be much harder to deal with. As always, it is necessary to think in a "whole" way, considering not just the presenting physical sign but also the emotional and mental impact of the symptom.

In the section below on common problems I have suggested questions to ask regarding the animal's management and diet, any underlying problems, and possible consequences if these are not addressed.

! Potentially serious symptoms that need immediate veterinary attention

- The pet has stopped eating for more than 24–36 hours.
- Vomiting more than two or three times in 24 hours; sooner if there is blood, it is very black or if the animal is very unwell.
- Diarrhea for longer than 24 hours or if it contains blood, is extremely liquid, or the animal is very unwell.
- Wounds that are large, deep or will not stop bleeding.
- The pet is very depressed, lethargic, very floppy or very unwell.
- Convulsions and fits.
- Straining to urinate or defecate but nothing is coming out.
- Breathing is distressed or labored.
- Excessive drinking of water, especially with weight and appetite loss.
- The animal has been hit by a car.
- It has eaten any toxic or caustic agent.
- It is having difficulty giving birth.
- It is not putting a leg or foot to the ground, i.e., has a severe limp, or a mild limp that is still present after 24 hours.
- Any other symptom where there is pain, discomfort or anxiety.
- Sudden loss of weight and/or appetite.
- Basically use your common sense—if at all worried, *call your vet!*

How real healing occurs

After much observation and experience, many healers and doctors have observed patterns on how the body heals itself. In homeopathy these patterns were formalized as "Hering's Law of Cure," named after Constantine Hering, a famous American homeopathic physician. These laws described the way a body will try to rebalance and heal itself, if given the chance and the right environment. According to Hering's Law, the body will try to:

1. Localize the problem to prevent spread, i.e., with inflammation;
2. Keep the problem near the surface of the body, i.e., the skin, rather than let it go deep into the internal organs;
3. Keep the problem on the limbs and away from the main trunk area;
4. Keep the problem on a physical rather than an emotional or mental level, which would seriously affect the animal's overall functioning;
5. Keep the condition at the lower end of the body away from the head (the brain and major sensory organs).[2]

An important sign that healing is happening is the appearance of some kind of discharge, whether it is pus, oozy skin lesions, possibly smelly dark diarrhea, a vomit or two, or smelly dark urine. These may be very temporary symptoms, and they can be alarming, but careful monitoring and providing the proper supportive care (not unnecessarily eliminating the symptom) can allow the body to expel the waste and heal more quickly and completely. This is where you need to be under the guidance of an experienced holistic veterinary practitioner, who can assess the severity of the symptoms and their effect on the animal, and advise proper supportive care while the body recovers.

For example, if an animal has a lung infection (a deep-seated problem in a vital organ) and a certain therapy is started (which supports the body, rather than working against it), there may be an initial worsening of the symptoms, such as more coughing. After a couple of days, however, this will lessen and the animal will be less depressed, more active and generally happier in itself, even though the cough is still present. Then, as the cough goes, there may be a worsening of a skin condition, with itchiness and perhaps some oozing sores. This is actually a very important positive "improvement" as the disease process is moving from the deep internal organs to an external organ, i.e., the skin. With proper supportive care, and allowing the symptoms to be expressed without too much trauma (using topical soothing agents, supplementation of a well-balanced diet with essential fatty acids, antioxidants and vitamin C, for example), the skin condition may move from the trunk to the legs and feet (again, a positive improvement) then disappear altogether. Usually, by the time this happens the animal has regained full health, is energetic and happy, and the problem is unlikely to recur because it has been allowed to be expressed fully and be resolved.

Unfortunately, the tendency to demand instant results is often applied to our health and that of our pets, so we give the animal strong drugs that suppress the symptoms (such as corticosteroids) which may result in a quick improvement, but long term does not provide the body with the opportunity to go through the normal healing processes. This is why, once these strong drugs are stopped, the symptoms often return as the body tries to start the healing process all over again.

Now I don't advocate the non-use of drugs, since they can be lifesaving in acute situations. However, in the long-term management of overall illness there are far better options, such as improving the animal's diet, adding nutritional supplements, and the use of homeopathy, acupuncture, allergy treatments, herbs and flower essences. In many situations these measures allow the body to be supported and ease the animal (and its anxious owner) through the healing process.

It is really important to keep this in mind when looking at ways to treat a problem, especially chronic, recurring health problems, which can be quite complex. This is why it is important to work alongside a skilled holistic veterinary practitioner if possible— their skill lies in teasing out the main issues and addressing them properly before moving on to the next issue. I always ask my clients to think about how long a health issue has been present, and warn them that it may take at least half this time, if not more, for the animal to regain full health. If the disease process is too far gone and deeply entrenched in the body, a full recovery may not be possible, but with partial healing the animal may be well enough to live a reasonable life.

Common problems and their treatments

✵ **Note:** For information on how to administer pills, liquids and other remedies, and how to apply acupressure, see Chapter 6. Where acupuncture or acupressure is recommended, unless you have had training in the insertion of acupuncture needles, I recommend acupressure only.

Abscesses

Causes

Generally abscesses are the result of some form of injury where the skin has been broken and bacteria has invaded. The body mounts a response, fighting the infection, localizing it and then expelling the debris. Pus forms, comprised of dead white blood cells (which the body uses to fight the infection), dead bacteria and other debris resulting from the infection. This is why some pus is very smelly, because some bacteria cause more local damage than others, and there is literally rotten tissue that needs to be expelled from the body.

In cats the most common reasons for abscesses are fight wounds such as scratches and bites. The teeth and mouth often contain really nasty bacteria, and a bite deep into the tissues can inject these bacteria under the skin, usually resulting in an infection and abscess. There may even be broken off teeth or claws left in the wound, as well as other foreign matter such as soil. Grass seeds can sometimes work their way along under the skin and there can be a discharging hole that never heals, and will not do so unless the foreign body (i.e., the seed) is removed.

What you may see

There may be limping, scabs or a little blood after a fight; your cat may act in a strange manner, hiding or acting scared, or it may smell really bad (the result of anal gland material on the coat from the stress of the fight) and be muddy and wet from rolling around. This may progress to an often painful swelling under the skin; the hair will often drop out in the area, and the swelling often comes to a head and bursts, ejecting pus and dead tissue. The animal may become unwell and stop eating, or it may act as if nothing is wrong. In all cases, if pus is present, it needs to drain out from the body in some way.

Treatment

Drainage is the most important principle with abscesses. It may be necessary to help the body eliminate the toxic matter, in which case a decent-sized drainage hole must be made and kept open until all the pus and debris has gone. Your vet may need to open the abscess under sedation, or it may burst of its own accord. Once it is open, it is useful to bathe it twice daily with a wound-healing lotion such as Nelsons Cuts & Scrapes Cream (a mix of Hypericum and calendula). This cream is antiseptic, stimulates wound healing and assists with local pain.

Be ruthless about removing any crust or scab that forms over the hole in the first week or so. After this, you will notice a "healthy" scab forming where the underlying tissue is a light pink, clean, and there is no more discharge. The abscess will heal from the inside out, with the skin hole being the last thing to heal fully. If it closes over too soon, the abscess may re-form and the process will start all over again.

The system can be supported through this healing time in the following ways:

- With a **good-quality diet**, although if the animal is not eating, respect its need to fast for 24 hours or so.
- **Provide a quiet, warm place** in which your pet can sleep and recover.
- **Increase vitamin C** to 500 mg a day for cats and small dogs (up to 18 pounds in weight), 1000 mg for medium dogs (18–55 pounds) or 1500 mg for large dogs (over 55 pounds).
- **Increase antioxidants** (Nature's Life ACE Antioxidant complex is an option).
- **Give the animal five-mushroom mix** (into the mouth) until it is better (at a dose of approximately 1 drop for every 11 pounds per day).
- **Homeopathic remedies**:
  - ❖ *Ledum 30c* for a fresh bite; if given in the first hour or so after a bite it can often prevent an abscess forming, as well as markedly reduce the pain involved (from personal experience!).

❖ *Silica 30c* to help push out pus and increase drainage (don't use this if your pet has an internal bone pin, wires or microchip).

❖ *Hepar sulph 30c* for a very painful abscess or one that is highly sensitive to the touch; the lower potencies (1x to 30c) will encourage the flow of pus, whereas the high potencies (200c) will stop the pus, which is not recommended in this situation.

• **A hot compress of comfrey** (make sure it is not so hot that it burns or is uncomfortable) is an excellent way of softening and drawing an abscess. It can be a bit clumsy to use in a cat, but very useful in larger animals where you can bandage it to the area.

• **Use a Bach flower remedy** to address the emotional stress. If your pet is very timid and scared after a fight and the subsequent treatment, try aspen, mimulus, crab apple, walnut and Rescue Remedy (use more frequently at the beginning when the pet may be very stressed, then as necessary, possibly two to four times a day).

❓ Questions to consider

Was the abscess the result of a fight injury?
Why did your pet get into the fight in the first place? Is it being picked on? Is it looking for trouble? (If a male, has it been neutered? It is very important to get your cat desexed, as unneutered males get into far more fights, as well as fathering many offspring.) If your pet is being attacked, you may need to help it defend its territory by squirting the marauder with a water pistol, not leaving food out to attract other cats, and providing your cat with a safe place to retreat to.

What is the cost of your cat getting into a fight?
This does not only include vet costs such as possible sedation, surgery and drugs; cat bites can spread viral infections such as Feline Immunodeficiency Virus (FIV) which can lead to the condition known as AIDS (Acquired Immune Deficiency Syndrome). There is also often a huge emotional cost to your cat; in addition to the obvious pain of the bite and resulting

abscess, there is the trauma of being beaten up, being ill, and a possible trip to the vet and ongoing treatment to consider.

If this stress is recurring it can result in undesirable behaviors such as overgrooming (pulling out the hair) and even spraying urine or defecating inside the house (if one of the underlying reasons is that they are being picked on by other cats).

Until you remove or rectify the underlying reasons for something it will generally never be resolved; repeatedly treating the symptoms is often just a Band Aid approach.

What else can I do to prevent recurrence?
As well as the suggestions above (neutering, scaring off the aggressor), if your cat is very timid you can look at increasing its confidence with a flower essence (try aspen, larch, mimulus and Rescue Remedy, four drops four times a day for four weeks).

In addition, the healthier an animal is, the less likely it is that a bite will progress to an abscess, because its immune system will be able to effectively deal with the problem.

Allergies

For more on the background of allergies see "Allergies and their treatments" in Chapter 4. Here are some further ideas.

Causes

When allergies occur, basically the immune system is out of balance and is reacting to everyday things in the environment. This imbalance may be caused by general illness , genetics, toxins in the environment, an unbalanced diet, over-vaccinating or stress (emotional, mental or physical). Sometimes even otherwise healthy animals develop allergies.

What you may see

The symptoms vary depending on which body system is reacting. There may be skin-related problems such as itching, redness, crusting and scabs; loss of hair; recurring ear problems, or other signs such as occasional vomiting, diarrhea or recurring cystitis (bladder inflammation).

The problem may start with licking and chewing at the feet, and over time may progress to the trunk of the animal, then up to the head area. If we look at the progressive nature of illness, then movement in this direction is not a good sign—it means the condition is not being resolved but is advancing. If the symptoms then go to an internal organ this is an even worse sign, as the disease process or imbalance is being driven deeper into the body and not moving away from it.

Treatment

- **A good-quality diet** appropriate to the presenting problem and to the age and size of the animal. With a stressed immune system there is no room for poor, highly processed foods such as those found in many of the cheaper dog treats and canned foods. Some of the commercial diets available from veterinary clinics seem to work quite well for skin problems, but they are often dried, which adds heat to an often already "hot" system. There are also prescription diets for most problems, and they can also be very useful. My preference is for a fresh, well-made, wholefood diet, but it is vital to make sure all the recommended supplements are used (see Chapter 3). Other useful additives include:

  ✤ Extra essential fatty acids, especially a plant-based omega fatty acid supplement such as evening primrose oil, combined with a fish oil, which can act as a natural anti-inflammatory (GNC offers a variety of evening primrose and fish oil capsules). Dose is related to animal size and severity of symptoms. Take care not to overdo the dose of fish oil in cats, as it can be quite high in vitamin A which in large doses over an extended period can cause joint problems. My suggestion for cats and small dogs up to 18 pounds is a quarter capsule daily for a couple of weeks, then three times a week; for dogs 18-55 pounds half a capsule, and for dogs over 55 pounds a whole capsule. Always check with your vet if you are giving doses long term, but once symptoms improve I tend to switch to using flaxseed oil daily (which is very safe) and use the fish oil product if symptoms recur.

  ✤ Other important supplements include extra vitamin C (500 mg for cats and small dogs to up to 18 pounds;

1000 mg for dogs 18–55 pounds, and 1500 mg for dogs over 55 pounds); if your pet develops diarrhea on this dose, reduce it. Use the low-acid chelated formula. Also consider a well-balanced antioxidant mix.

✤ If you are not using cat or dog powder (see Chapter 3), the addition of kelp to the diet is very useful. This supplies many trace elements that are vital for good health.

✤ Add ground pumpkin seeds to the daily diet; these are high in zinc, which is critical for skin health among many other things.

- **NAET** (Nambudripad's Allergy Elimination Technique)—in my practice, I routinely improve the diet and aim to rebalance the immune system with the NAET procedure (see Chapter 4). There are an almost infinite number of things an animal may be reacting to, and NAET pinpoints exactly what these are and corrects the body's response to them.

- **Secondary symptoms such as excess oil and smell** (secondary seborrhea) can be treated with commercial medicated shampoos, or try manuka oil washes (mix 1 tsp manuka oil with warm water and sponge down the skin daily until the smell and greasiness goes). Topical use of calming creams, such as PetAlive's Wound Dr., will also help. This cream contains many substances that are useful for inflammation, such as tea tree oil and rosemary, and other herbs that are soothing and healing. In very itchy cases where the animal is biting and scratching, causing massive self-trauma, I sometimes resort to a very short course of antihistamines or low-dose steroids, or perhaps a short course of antibiotics for very smelly seborrhea, which reduces the self-damage while the other treatments are starting to work behind the scenes. I stop these as soon as possible, once the deeper-acting remedies and treatments start to take effect. Although I do not generally advocate the use of strong drugs to remove superficial symptoms, in this case they can prevent massive self-damage that may take ages to heal. When the immune system is so overactive that it causes these symptoms, the drugs can act quickly to calm it down, while the complementary therapies will rebalance, fine-tune and act in the longer term to keep it healthy. The animal's quality of life is paramount, and there is no reason not to take the best from both medical systems—conventional and complementary—to provide the best treatment option for each individual.

- **You might want to restrict vaccinations** to the minimal essentials at the greatest intervals, because certain vaccines come up all the time in NAET testing as causing a problem. While it is possible to rebalance the system with NAET, vaccines still affect the immune system to some degree (which is how they work!).

- **Flower essences** can be useful to calm and relax animals with bad allergies. Try Rescue Remedy, walnut, crab apple and chestnut bud, four drops four times a day for four weeks, if it is a chronic problem.

- **Herbs** that can have a useful anti-inflammatory and anti-infection effect are licorice, tea tree and manuka oil, St. John's wort, parsley, lavender oil, fennel, dandelion, chickweed and calendula.

- **Homeopathic remedies** can be very useful, but you will need to see a trained homeopath since many skin problems can be complex and difficult to treat.

- **Acupuncture/acupressure**—to rebalance the immune system, use points GB 20, LI 11, SP 6, ST 36 and LU 7.

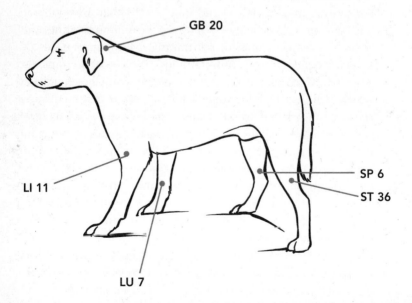

? *Questions to consider*

Was the animal's diet a good quality one right from birth?
Or was it highly processed and of a poor quality?

Has the animal had a toxic insult, serious accident or significant illness in the past?
Any of these can greatly affect the immune system, to the point that allergies can become evident later on.

Has the animal been on strong drugs such as steroids and antibiotics for an extended period
(the animal may have become allergic to these drugs)?

How is its emotional and mental health?
There may be a flower essence that can improve these, and aid the overall health of the body (see Chapter 4).

Is the animal in a high-stress environment?
This will adversely affect the immune system and increase the chance of allergies. Make any management changes that will reduce stress, and use a flower remedy (see the list in Chapter 4).

If skin conditions are not treated in an appropriate way, by correcting the underlying imbalances in the body, there is a very real risk of the disease processes being driven deeper into the body and resulting in a more serious condition at a later date. A classic example of this is the eczema/asthma complex, where individuals starting out with eczema often develop asthma as the condition goes deeper into the body. As the asthma improves, the eczema often reappears, as the disease process moves to a more external part of the body. Once the eczema goes, the individual is much healthier.

Anal gland problems
The anal glands are two small sacs that sit right beside the anal opening, just under the skin. A duct, or thin tube, connects the

inside of each gland to the surface of the anal opening. The function of the glands is to produce a fishy-smelling secretion that covers the fecal lump as it passes through the anal opening, and helps mark the animal's territory. These glands are also discharged when the animal is very frightened, such as during a fight or an accident, and sometimes, if the glands are very full, small drops of the extremely potent secretion may leak out of the duct and sit around the anal area or be wiped onto furniture or blankets.

Causes

Normally, the anal glands are emptied daily, each time the animal defecates. A lack of regular exercise can lead to irregular defecation. So too can stress or an inability to relax enough to empty the bowels, which can occur when there are too many animals in a confined area (raising territory issues) or the animal does not have a private area to go to defecate. If the animal has been constipated or has diarrhea, or if there is not sufficient bulk in its diet to produce a good-sized fecal lump, the glands may not be properly emptied (because the fecal lump is not firm enough to squeeze the glands as it passes through the anal area). The secretions may become very thick and dry out, and are not squeezed out down the narrow duct to the outside.

Sometimes the duct can become blocked with residual sac material, or become inflamed due to a minor infection, reducing its ability to drain. This can lead to the formation of abscesses.

What you may see

I sometimes have clients who complain of a very smelly dog, and on checking find that the ears, mouth and coat are fine, but the anal glands are semi-blocked and overfull. A tiny amount of the secretion leaks out, leaving a very powerful smell. The animal may also scoot along carpet or even gravel, as the overfull gland puts pressure on the anal area; the scooting, or sometimes excessive licking in the area, means they are trying to relieve the discomfort.

If the animal develops an anal gland abscess, this will usually burst out through the skin beside the anus. Before it bursts, the area is extremely painful, and often the animal is very sick and depressed.

Dogs seem to be affected by anal gland problems far more often than cats; in the latter they usually occur in overweight cats that can't get around to lick and clean their anal areas.

Treatment

- **Provide regular exercise**, plenty of space and somewhere private for the animal to go to the bathroom.
- **Correct constipation or diarrhea problems**, or if the fecal lump is always too small, add fiber to the diet. I often advise considering a homemade diet, but if people don't want to do this then adding oat bran to the diet can be useful (1 tsp twice daily for cats and small dogs; up to several tablespoons twice daily for larger dogs). It is also useful to add more raw vegetables and fruit to the diet, like grated carrot, chopped greens or apple with the skin on. Whole grains and brown rice (all cooked) are good at bulking up the feces. There are also commercial veterinary prescription diets designed to increase bulk in the feces that can be used.
- **Manual emptying of the glands**—if the animal is scooting its bottom along the ground, then get the glands checked. They may need to be manually expressed by your veterinarian, who can also check there are no other problems, such as an abscess, a tumor (cancer) in the glands or even an allergic reaction or infection in the anal area.

    Regular manual emptying is not the aim here—this should be just a temporary measure. It is crucial that the underlying reasons for the blockages are addressed and a preventive approach adopted. If all else fails, the anal glands can always be surgically removed, but this is a final solution that is only appropriate if the animal's quality of life is severely impaired.
- **For abscesses**—clean the area twice daily with a lotion such as Nelsons Cuts & Scrapes Cream, or flush the gland with it, using a syringe, ensuring proper drainage of infective material while the glands heal. Give five-mushroom, echinacea and vitamin C, but remember if your pet is very unwell, it needs to be seen by your veterinarian. Hot comfrey compresses can help draw material from the infected area.

? Questions to consider

Is the animal getting enough exercise, fiber in its diet, and is it defecating regularly (at least once or twice a day)?

Does it have other health problems, such as skin problems or general bad health?
A problem with the anal glands may just be one more indicator of a poorly functioning system.

Is the problem recurring?
If so, *always* get the area checked as there could be other problems such as tumors or fistulas (infected sinuses to the skin).

Arthritis

Causes

Arthritis is an inflammation in the joints, which often leads to disintegration of the joint structure to some degree (degenerative joint disease), damage to the cartilage that lines the joint, and frequently, new bone forming in the area and restricting joint movement. All this can add up to stiffness, soreness and reluctance to move or jump up, for example into the car or onto the couch.

Arthritis is often an aging problem but even young dogs can develop arthritic changes if a joint has been damaged due to trauma, or if there is a high genetic predisposition in that breed. Rapidly growing, large breed dogs are susceptible to joint damage in the first year of life, because they are growing so fast. If the diet is not supplying crucial minerals such as calcium and phosphorus at the correct levels, or the diet is too energy-dense, or there is a genetic predisposition combined with too much vigorous exercise (especially from three to ten months of age), or a combination of these, the joint may be damaged.

Hip dysplasia, which can lead to arthritis, is a heritable condition more common in the larger breeds such as Labradors and German shepherds. Hip dysplasia is where the hip joint is not firmly held by the ligaments in the hip socket, and over time the hip structure degenerates due to the laxity and damage that occurs. The smooth ball at the top of the long thigh bone (the femur) becomes squared off and the cartilage lining on this ball wears away, reducing the production of synovial fluid, which is crucial for joint lubrication. As the body tries to stabilize this laxity, extra new bone is formed, leading to a lowered range of movement in a joint that needs to be able to swing in a wide arc to function correctly. This is why there is often stiffness and lameness with arthritis and degenerative joint disease.

Other common sites for arthritis to form are the shoulder, elbow and lower back, especially at the junction of the ribs and the lower spine and again at the junction of the lower spine with the pelvic bones, as these areas have a lot of movement and rotation and are not well supported by ribs or the pelvis. The kneecaps, or patellas, can also be lax in some animals and pop in and out of the correct position, often resulting in degenerative changes in the joint surface.

In all these cases, the smooth and continuous cartilage lining is damaged in some way. Because this crucial lining makes the lubricating fluid called synovial fluid, which keeps the joint moving correctly, any damage can result in a dry, grating joint that becomes inflamed, swollen and often painful.

The immune system can also cause joint damage if it decides to attack the joint surfaces, as in some rheumatic diseases. This creates severe inflammation and pain, and unless it is checked and settled it can lead to degenerative joint disease.

Treatment

Prevention

- **Try not to breed** from animals that have a history of joint problems, as it tends to be passed on to their offspring.
- **Ensure that through pregnancy the mother has an excellent diet**, rich in the minerals and vitamins crucial for overall health.
- **Ensure the growing puppy or kitten has the correct growth diet**, as outlined in Chapter 3. Feed a high-quality diet containing the appropriate supplements, which will provide nutrients and protective compounds (antioxidants) to the

whole body, including the joints, decreasing the likelihood of degenerative diseases over time.

- **Do not exercise puppies for more than 20 minutes a day** until they are one year old. Let them run around the garden, but outside exercise like long walks and runs should be kept to a minimum until this time, when the bones and joints have passed their excessive growth phase. This applies particularly to larger breeds of dog (55-pound adult weight and above) but smaller dogs will also benefit from not overdoing things in that crucial first year. While it is important for developing puppies to get positive growth experiences, and get used to traffic, cars and the other things you see on walks, the rule is moderate, not excessive, exercise. Take it easy during that rapid growth phase, allowing everything to mature in its own time.

- **Add extra vitamin C** to the growing animal's diet—approximately 200 mg per day for small dogs and cats, up to 1500 mg per day in the large breeds of dog. There is some disagreement about whether this has any noticeable beneficial action, but because an animal's own production levels can be low as their bodies are developing, I believe supplementation is important at this time because it helps with healing and protects developing tissues. Use the buffered, low-acid version of vitamin C.

- **Don't let your animal friend become overweight**—this increases the likelihood of joint disease due to extra wear and tear. Make sure it has regular exercise to keep the weight at a correct level, as well as keeping all systems in the body working well.

- **Ensure the emotional health of your pet**—emotional and mental rigidity (animals with a hard, intractable nature, for example, or stubborn animals that resist breaking old habits) may lead to physical rigidity. Rock water, a Bach remedy, can be helpful for this.

If your pet already has arthritis

- **Feed a well-balanced diet** that contains carrots, celery and beet, as well as kelp (see Chapter 3 for sample recipes).

- **Add an evening primrose and fish oil essential fatty acid supplement.** (With cats take care not to overdo the fish oil levels; I suggest three times a week for cats. For dogs, try daily initially then every two to three days once the condition is under control. Flaxseed oil can also be used daily in the food on an ongoing basis to help reduce inflammation; use 1 tsp daily for cats and small dogs, up to 2–3 tbsp for larger dogs.

- **Include a nutritional supplement** containing green mussel extract, glucosamine and bovine cartilage (remember to give your dog the gristle off the ends of chicken bones as well, but not the actual bones), as well as minerals such as boron (for bone health), calcium, phosphorus and herbs. Another option is to try Arthritis/Joint Relief, an herbal supplement with anti-inflammatory and antioxidant properties. You can order it online from Only Natural Pet Store (see page 271 for info). Use it three times per day, and lessen with improvement.

- **Acupuncture and acupressure** usually give excellent results, with positive relief from stiffness and pain. Try doing acupressure at home twice a week if your animal friend is showing moderate symptoms, or once a week as a follow-up to keep the symptoms at a low level. Use points BL 60, GB 34, BL 40, GB 30, ST 36, LI 11, BL 11 or local joint points, depending on which joint is involved.

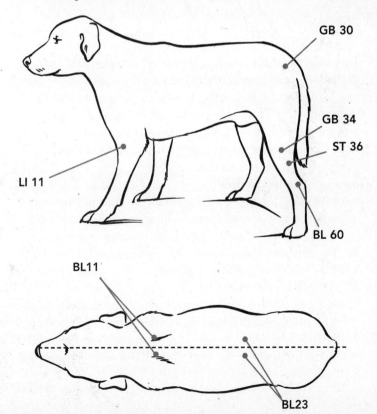

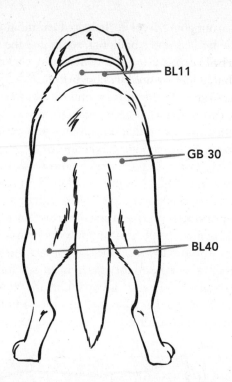

- **Injectable products** such as Rimadyl® or Adequan®, which are available from your vet, help improve the health of the cartilage in the joint, thus helping to produce more synovial fluid of better quality. These are worthwhile drugs as they improve the overall health of the joint in the long term, with few side effects. I recommend a course as part of an overall approach to management of joint disease.
- **Homeopathic remedies**:
  - ❖ Use *Rhus tox 30c* if the animal's symptoms are worse when it gets up but improve as it moves around; worse when it is cold, better when the weather is warm, and better when the affected area is massaged or rubbed. Use it daily for about a month, and if some improvement has occurred continue using it for as long as it is helping, possibly up to several months. There are many other homeopathic remedies to fit different symptomatic presentations of arthritis—for example, if your animal is better with rest, worse with movement, a possible

remedy may be *Bryonia*. Consult a homeopath or a homeopathic book to learn about the various remedies.

- **Herbal remedy** —Devil's Claw is a useful anti-inflammatory herb that can be used with arthritis.
- **Massage** over the hips or other areas that may be stiff and sore can be very beneficial, as often the animal will lie in one position for some time, not easily able to move due to the joint stiffness. Massage can encourage blood circulation and help stiff muscles. Use long strokes down the hind legs and small circular movements over the joint area, taking extra care if this area is sore.
- **Keep exercising your pet**, gently if it is stiff and sore, but movement is important to prevent things from seizing up. Forget the jumping and jerking from catching balls or Frisbees. Instead take regular, slow walks over flatter areas for as long as is possible for the individual. This is very important not only for its physical health but for its mental and emotional health.
- **Make sure your pet is not overweight**, since extra weight adds extra stress to sore joints.
- If the condition is very painful, **short term use of anti-inflammatories** and pain relief drugs may be necessary. These drugs can also help slow the degeneration in the joint, and pain control is very important to ensure your pet's quality of life, but I prefer to try all the above suggestions before considering the long-term use of these drugs. I have found that I rarely need to use long-term pain relief drugs, as the other options have worked so well. I tend to use pain relief and anti-inflammatory drugs if the animal has an acutely inflamed joint, until the pain has subsided, then often the other remedies are sufficient. Bear in mind that often once a joint has established arthritic changes it will tend to be damaged from time to time if, for example, your animal friend jumps off the couch too fast or dashes up the hall to answer the doorbell. This re-inflames the existing condition, and the joint can be acutely sore for a few days. Rest is very important in these cases, and this is where a low dose of pain relief may be useful. The problem is that if you relieve the pain too much the animal will think it is fully recovered and will not rest the affected joint and allow it to settle down!

? *Questions to consider*

What was the condition of the parents' joints and their arthritis history?

Was the puppy fed correctly and did it have appropriate exercise levels in the first year of life?

Is the animal overweight? Does it get appropriate exercise?
Has it been expected to do a lot of jumping and sharp turns throughout its life (as with many working dogs), or repetitive actions over a long period of time? These all put strain on joints.

Has the diet been of a good quality and well-balanced throughout its life?

Has there been any trauma such as accidents, ligament and tendon damage, strains and sprains?

What breed is the animal?
Is it a high risk breed for arthritis, or are there genetically predisposed joint problems? (For example, West Highland White terriers can be prone to a femoral head (hip joint) degenerative disease; German shepherds can be prone to hip dysplasia).

Behavioral problems

Behavioral problems can be very complex, and every case is unique to the individual. When dealing with any behavioral problem I spend a good hour talking with an animal's owners about its personality, lifestyle, diet, environment, upbringing, any traumatic experiences and even its breeding. Certain breeds of cat and dog can be more prone to behavioral problems than others, and even an animal's genetic make-up can affect its behavior. My theory is that most behavioral problems arise when owners set unclear behavioral boundaries, or when there are territorial or hierarchy disputes, or stress-related issues, which are usually fear based.

1. Boundary issues

Boundary issues arise when animals are not given clear, consistent reminders about what behavior is allowed and what is not allowed. It is important to decide what an animal is and is not allowed to do, then make sure allowed behaviors are rewarded, and non-allowed behaviors are firmly and clearly denied. This does not mean using violence or force, but instead a consistent reminder using the voice and management techniques to make non-allowed behavior a negative experience so the animal clearly knows it is unacceptable.

Violence such as hitting or smacking generally makes matters worse, especially if the animal is timid or shy to begin with. However, a well-timed "Bah" in a loudish voice, along with holding up a hand as if to say "No," can be quite effective. Obviously if you do this all the time its effectiveness decreases markedly, so reserve a specific negative sound solely for this job, so the animal associates the sound with doing something wrong. If even doing this stresses the animal, consider a less forceful noise or action, but something that still sends a clear message that what they are doing is wrong. Make sure everyone who is around the animal regularly also acts in the same way; everyone must know what behaviors are and are not allowed, and provide the same rewards or disciplinary action.

Rewards for good behavior can be food tidbits such as small pieces of dried liver flakes, a small biscuit or a pellet of dried food. Follow this up with a pat or an encouraging tone of voice. Again, if you are consistent in what you do and say in response to specific behaviors, the animal will know a positive from a negative behavior and stay within these boundaries. An animal that clearly knows what it can and cannot do is usually a far more relaxed and happy animal, as it is not worrying about getting things wrong and displeasing its owners.

2. Territory or hierarchy disputes

Some behavioral "problems" are related to the struggle a dog or cat is having in determining or maintaining its territory, or in multi-animal households, where it fits into the pecking order. Dogs and cats go around their territory boundaries and spray urine to mark the particular area as theirs, so other animals will smell their unique scent and know there is another animal in that area. Dogs take this to the next level and many will pee against every lamp-post and upright structure on their walks, to cover other urine smells and add their own to the mix.

Cats also use urine spraying, and it can become a problem if they start to spray inside the house. If a cat is afraid to go outside because of an aggressive neighboring cat, or if it is very stressed in its home environment, it may feel powerless to control its environment and start spraying inside as a response to this stress. Multi-animal households are more likely to have "inappropriate toileting" problems, especially when there are more than three cats in a house. A mini-hierarchy will often begin to form when there are three or more animals, with the least dominant member at the bottom of the family group. Getting to the top, and staying there, may involve confrontation or the apparently dominant "top cat" may just passively display dominant behavior.

Sometimes, problems arise when a dog decides the hierarchy within the family unit is not clearly defined. It may use growling and even biting of other family members, both animal and human, to reinforce its position. Although some dogs may show dominant behaviors (such as intimidation) and try to be at the top of the family pack, they may not necessarily always show aggressive behaviors (such as biting or growling). One scenario is where the dog recognizes the man in the household as "top dog" (as he is often larger, has a deeper and more forceful voice) but not the woman or children (who are usually smaller in stature). A struggle then begins as the dog tries to position itself between the woman and the man. The dog may growl or show its teeth when the woman wants it to get off the couch or move away from a particular area, or it may snap to get its own way. This is potentially a very serious situation and I always recommend professional help if there is aggression or biting. This help is crucial to train not only the dog but everyone else in the household. If the dog is simply being pushy, without obvious aggression such as growling or biting, try the following:

- The "authority" figure (often the man of the household) should stay away from the dog, and the person toward whom the bad behavior is directed (frequently the woman) should take over the dog's feeding and walking for a while.
- The dog must be made to sit and "submit" before any treats are given. Things like being made to sit or even lie down

before it gets its food, before the door is opened and before it gets in the car all define the person's dominance over the dog, without any violence or raised voices.

- I don't recommend hitting or yelling as this can either escalate into aggressive reciprocating behavior or go the other way and make the animal frightened, which can result in fear biting.

3. Stress-related behavioral issues

In a stressful environment, some sensitive animal personalities can be affected. Cats especially are very sensitive to change and noise, and they can develop behavioral problems that may seem unrelated to the stress. Common problems are overgrooming (pulling out the fur in clumps or over a large area), spraying urine or defecating inside. Things like moving house, noisy renovations, strangers, parties, disruption to the household and even relationship problems between the humans in the household, resulting in arguments and raised voices, can all be possible stressors for sensitive animals.

Our animal friends all have their own personalities—some are very gregarious, friendly and laid back, while others are antisocial, timid and very rigid in their routines. These are the cats that are most likely to have adverse behavioral responses to stress. Removing the cause of the stress and using a flower essence to rebalance the emotions often corrects the behavior without needing strong behavior-correcting drugs such as Prozac or amitriptyline.

Treatment

Treating behavioral problems can be a very specialized and complicated procedure since the treatment needs to be tailor-made for the particular individual and situation. The following is a basic guide, but it is often necessary to consult a professional for help in retraining your animal friend. With any behavioral problem, it is important to try and get to the bottom of the situation and find out why the animal is behaving in a particular way.

- **Always get a vet to check your pet**. Some behavioral problems may be directly related to physical problems such as cancers, lumps, poisoning, etc.
- **There may be an environmental reason**, such as an aggressive neighboring cat that is causing stress in your cat's life. Getting rid of marauding cats can be a challenge, but there are

simple things you can do, like removing food that may be accessible to other cats, using a magnetic cat collar so only your cat is able to come inside, or scaring off the other cat by squirting it with a water pistol, garden hose or other non-violent means.

In one case I encountered, the cat seemed very frightened of walking on the carpet and would not stay on it for very long, instead walking around the room on the furniture. Before this behavior started, it would roll on the carpet a lot, and after questioning the owner I wondered if the cat was getting minor static electricity shocks from the nylon carpet. It turned out that it had a very dry coat, which developed a build-up of static electricity after the cat had been rolling around, so that when it walked on the carpet it got a little electrical zap. While this is an unusual case, it illustrates the need to examine the situation in detail to look for possible reasons behind the behavior, then to try to do something about the cause. In this case we consulted an electrician, who told us that dampening the dry coat would reduce the build-up of static electricity. We ended up combing a small amount of oil into the coat, which reduced the static build-up and stopped the small shocks, and the cat started walking on the carpet again.

If you are doing renovations, provide a "safe" and quiet place for your cat to go to, such as a box up on top of a wardrobe or behind some furniture, or consider putting it in a cattery for some of the time.

- **Make sure the diet is high-quality** (see Chapter 3). Add extra B vitamins in the form of a supplement that contains all the B-complex vitamins. If you only give one or two of the B vitamins, it creates a deficiency in the others. Use a supplement with 5–20 mg of all the B vitamins.
- **Minimize exposure to common household toxins** such as cleaning products, cigarette smoke, and extra chemicals such as some flea preparations, insecticides, etc.
- **Herbs** such as chamomile, valerian and St. John's wort can be useful to calm and settle the animal.
- **Management** is as important as treatment, so try to identify the problem and remove the cause.
- Use **flower essences** to help rebalance the emotions (see Chapter 4 for advice on choosing the appropriate essences).

For chronic or long-standing problems, use four drops four times a day for four weeks. You may need to change the mix as behaviors change.

- **You may need professional help** with specific problems.
- **Many homeopathic remedies are excellent** for behavioral problems, but a full consultation may be necessary to determine the remedy that best fits the picture. A useful remedy for grief is *Ignatia 30c.*

? Questions to consider

Consider the animal's history—was it adequately socialized as a puppy or kitten, has it been badly treated or neglected? What behavioral problems may be associated with the breed of animal? Has it been traumatized in the past by an accident or event? Is the animal grieving for a lost owner or animal friend?

Is the animal living in a stressful household at the present time?

For example, are there renovations going on, a lot of people coming and going or loud noises (such as airplanes, backfiring cars, firecrackers)?

Is there a person or animal in the household, or a neighbor, that may be aggravating the animal or giving it a hard time?

Does the animal have a predictable routine, a safe place to go to that is away from the household action (especially for feeding and sleeping) and clearly defined behavioral boundaries to follow?

Some animals simply just develop behavioral problems for no apparent reason. Your vet or animal behavioralist is the best person to consult for all these problems.

Bladder problems (see *Urinary tract problems*)

Cancer

Cancer is the unchecked growth of abnormal body cells. It occurs when the body's regulating controls have broken down and the cells multiply and either spread throughout the body, growing in different sites, or stay in a localized site, sometimes causing ulceration, "blocking the pipes" or simply putting pressure on vital organs.

Every day our bodies remove large numbers of old cells and make large numbers of new ones, and if the body is healthy and in balance this all happens in an ordered and systematic way. Among all these new cells, which are forming new linings or new tissues, there are sometimes slight imperfections or disorder. In a healthily functioning body this disorder is immediately recognized and corrected—the abnormal cells are removed and destroyed, or their growth is checked. Your body is constantly recognizing and tidying up the things that, if left unchecked, can become out of control, grow wildly and result in problems such as cancer.

Prevention is the key

Maintaining good health and staying in balance is more than just having energy and feeling good. It means preventing the body getting out of balance, out of control and eventually succumbing to degenerative diseases such as cancer.

The immune system is the critical factor in the body's regulatory systems. Special cells in the immune system circulate constantly, recognizing disorder and correcting the situation. These cells function optimally when the whole body is healthy, but there are a number of possible factors that cause them to become less effective. These include things like increasing age; poor diet; lack of important vitamins, minerals and proteins; stress; high exposure to toxins such as food pesticides or growth hormones (found in some inorganically grown meats); car exhaust fumes, and excessive use of strong drugs. The result may be that cancer begins to grow, unchecked by the weakened immune system.

Prevention is the most important thing, because once a body has cancer it is not easy to correct the imbalance. A good fresh diet, ideally with organically grown ingredients, exercise, TLC (tender loving care), emotional and mental health, fresh air and sunshine all help prevent serious disease, because the immune system stays healthy and its monitoring systems are most efficient.

Dealing with cancer

If cancer is already present, then drastic life changes need to be made to try and reverse the damage to the weakened body and immune system. The reason why "treating" cancer is so complex and difficult is that there are so many types of cancer, with varying levels of malignancy (ability to spread throughout the body), and therefore varying levels of body function destruction. The treatment of cancer can have several outcomes:

- Improving the quality of the animal's life until the cancer advances to the point where this is no longer possible;
- Increasing the expected lifespan;
- A "cure," where cancer is removed from the body or system, or it shrinks to the point where it has no more negative effects on the body.

Each case must be treated individually, as there are so many different types of cancer, and many act differently in different bodies. Determining the type of cancer—through a biopsy, blood tests, x-rays, ultrasound, etc.—helps us to understand its nature, what to expect and how to deal with it. In all cases there are sensible management actions you can take to help support the body as it tries to heal.

Diet is crucial

Get a recipe that is appropriate for your pet's age, size and condition, by talking to your vet or a nutritionist. There is even a commercial prescription cancer diet available.

- **A fresh natural diet** may take a bit of extra effort to prepare, but because you are dealing with a serious body malfunction it is vital to support the healing process. Use organic meats and vegetables, which will reduce the intake of pesticides and provide a greater range of nutrients. Many organic foods are grown in improved soil, using fertilizers that contain trace elements such as selenium, which is an important antioxidant. Use raw foods where appropriate, especially algae such as chlorella, and sprouts, which contain vitamins to help support the body. However, if the animal is very frail and cold, use more warming foods, cook more of the food, and avoid too many sprouts and the algal supplements like spirulina and chlorella, which are very cooling.

- Use the **powders and oils** described in the natural diet recipes (Chapter 3). These contain kelp, which contains crucial minerals and vitamins; brewer's yeast, which supplies B vitamins and other trace minerals, and essential fatty acids, which help with inflammation.
- **Flaxseed oil** can also be used as a supplement, or a mix of fish oil and plant oil, such as evening primrose.
- **Antioxidants such as vitamin A, vitamin C, vitamin E and selenium** are important because they help the body remove toxins and prevent further free-radical damage. Check doses with your vet.
- **Add vitamin C** at 1000 mg/day for every 15 pounds of body weight; if diarrhea occurs, reduce the dose. Use the low-acid version, which is buffered and less likely to cause an upset stomach at this high dose.

Stimulate the immune system

- **Use five-mushroom** to help stimulate the immune system. This mix stimulates the "killer T" cells, a type of immune cell that fights cancer.

Environment

- **Ensure the animal's environment is as free of pesticides, insecticides and other pollutants as possible.** Reduce the use of household cleaners, sprays, flea preparations, fly sprays and washing powders as much as possible, and use the eco-friendly versions which are mostly based on inert and relatively safe ingredients such as baking soda. (See the list of eco-friendly suppliers on page 271, for the sake of your own health as much as your animal's.)
- **Don't walk your dog near car exhausts**, make sure its drinking water is as pure and clean as possible (use spring or filtered water) and stop smoking, because secondhand cigarette smoke is as highly toxic to animals as it is to humans.

> **!** **Do not vaccinate your pet**—the immune system is already on overload and adding to it can be the last straw.

Herbs

- **Use Essiac herbal mix** (or a similar herbal mix). Essiac is a mixture of several herbs that have been used by herbalists for many years as a cancer treatment. (It is named after a nurse, Rene Caisse, who used the mix to treat cancer.) Essiac mix (also known as Sheep Sorrel Mix) can be obtained in capsular form, which is a convenient way of getting it into animals. The mix, which contains burdock root, slippery elm, sheep sorrel and Indian rhubarb, acts by cleansing the system and stimulating immunity. Other similar mixes are also available, such as "Floressence" which in addition to these herbs contains blessed thistle, red clover, kelp and watercress.

- **Mistletoe extract** (the therapeutic extract has the trade name Helixor) has been used in human cancer therapy in Europe, and it can also be used in animals. It can be expensive, as the treatment often continues for many months, and the procedure for using it is rather complicated. It involves injecting the extract at daily intervals and measuring the temperature to see if a fever has been initiated. This can make the animal feel unwell, but it acts to enhance the immune system so that once the fever goes away, there is renewed immunity to fight the cancer. This treatment does not suit everyone, since it involves a very high input from the pet's owner, with most of the treatment being done at home. However, the results for certain tumors have been very encouraging.

Homeopathy

There are some homeopathic remedies that can help with certain tumors, but you need to see a trained homeopath to determine which would be most suitable for your pet. Some examples are:

- *Thuja 30c*—as an antidote to vaccine reactions; use for three to four weeks.

- *Conium 30c*—used in older animals, for hard swellings, muscular weakness in the hind legs, lymphatic swellings, small mammary tumors, and possibly chronic ulcers with a discharge.
- *Natrum muriaticum 30c*—for cats with solid tumors, especially animals that have appetite problems.

Conventional treatment

- **Surgery and/or chemotherapy** are often the main forms of cancer treatment in conventional medicine. In some cases surgical removal may be the best option, but if lifestyle and dietary changes are not made as well then the likelihood of success is much reduced. Again, achieving balance in the body is critical, and it is important to remove as many of the contributing negative factors as possible—i.e., bad diet, toxin load, stress load, etc.
- Conventional cancer treatments often involve harsh drugs that often aim to destroy the cancer cells rather than enhancing the body's defenses and fighting the cancer via the immune system. The decision about which way to go is often a difficult one, and each individual case and body is different. **Some situations do best with conventional treatment and some with other forms of therapy**.
- If the conventional route has been taken, **I highly recommend using as many of the above suggestions as possible to help support the animal's system as it tries to heal**. Some animal owners have come to me after careful consideration, deciding that chemotherapy or surgery was not the path they wanted to take. Through the use of the above therapies it has often been possible to enhance the animal's quality of life to some extent, and the owners have been able to take an active role in trying to help their animal friends. This has often made things easier to accept, especially if euthanasia was necessary further down the track.

> **!** Acupuncture and acupressure are not advised in the treatment of cancer. There are one or two techniques that trained acupuncturists use, but the practice is not generally recommended with most forms of cancer.

Quality of life

The whole point of trying a treatment for cancer (and, in fact, any "dis-ease") is to improve the animal's quality of life. This means enabling the animal to live a reasonable life without pain or suffering, be it physical, emotional or mental. There may be a short initial period when the quality of life is not as good as it could be (such as during recovery from surgery), but there must be some chance of improvement in the longer term to make invasive and painful treatment such as surgery worthwhile.

This can be difficult to assess with cancer as it can be very unpredictable. It is often necessary to take things from day to day, as the situation can often change quickly. This is why it is important to work closely with your veterinarian. Surgery and chemotherapy can be traumatic to an animal, and if there is no real likelihood of improvement it is better not to put the animal through this trauma, but to keep to the non-invasive and non-stressful techniques outlined above. There may be a need for pain relief during this process, and it is important to work with a sympathetic veterinarian so pain levels can be monitored and addressed.

Animals show pain in many ways—some withdraw and become very quiet, some become aggressive and snap at their owners, while others become vocal and restless. Your vet is the person best qualified to determine if your animal is in pain, and where the pain may be, and to do something about it. There is very little quality of life if there is constant pain, and unfortunately many cancers can be quite painful, especially in the liver or the bones. The animal's right to die must also be respected, and as an owner one must examine the motives behind extensive therapy in the face of overwhelming degeneration. Are you treating the animal for yourself, or are you making what time your animal friend has as comfortable and respectful as possible? Chapter 8, "Saying goodbye and letting go," covers this topic in more detail.

? **Questions to consider**

Is the diet supporting the healing of the problem?

What pollutants and environmental toxins is the animal exposed to, and how can I reduce the level while it is being treated?

Is there any pain?
You will need to ask your vet for an appraisal.

What therapies are going to provide the maximum response—invasive or non-invasive?

Do I have my animal's best interests at heart in choosing a particular therapy?

What quality of life does my pet have?

Constipation

Causes

Constipation can result from a lack of exercise to stimulate bowel movement, an unsuitable diet without roughage and fiber, or a generally sluggish elimination system, especially in older animals. Bone chips and fragments can also cause constipation in certain individuals. Pelvic bone injuries (such as healed fractures) which can create a narrowing of the rectal area, or hernias in the pelvic area are other causes.

In cats, a dirty litter box can be a cause; some cats will not use a dirty box.

What you may see

The animal may strain to defecate, with nothing coming out. Alternatively there may be very hard, dry stools, sometimes with streaks of fresh, red blood on the outside (due to the stool scratching the rectal lining or mildly damaging the anal area on the way out). As the bowel can be sore, there is sometimes excessive licking in the anal area or pain when the animal is lifted. The animal may also be depressed and have stopped eating. Sometimes there may even be liquid feces as well, due to the gut trying to push out the hard fecal lump. The liquid squeezes around the lump and leaks out.

Treatment

- Always **get your pet checked by a vet** if it is constipated. The following tips should help with prevention and chronic (long-standing) problems.

- **Diet**—make sure it is high-quality and suitable for the animal. Increase the amount of raw food in the diet (cooking breaks down the cell walls of plant material and this roughage is important to provide bulk and attract water into the bowel). Use high-fiber fruits and vegetables such as apple with the skin on, raw green vegetables, figs and prunes.
  - ❖ Bran adds fiber to the diet, as do most whole grains. Oat bran is especially useful—add $1/_2$ tsp to 1 tbsp to each meal.
  - ❖ Add extra water to the diet to encourage the correct water balance in the body.
  - ❖ Avoid all bones if there are bone fragments in the feces.
- **Powdered psyllium husks** or seeds act as a bulk-forming agent in the bowel and as a laxative; try $1/_4$ to 2 tsp mixed in water once a day.
- **Aloe vera juice** can act as a gentle laxative as well as soothing and healing the lining of the bowel. Note, however, that sodium benzoate or benzoic acid, which is used as a preservative in some forms of aloe vera juice, is poisonous to cats. Make sure you get juice that does not contain this preservative.
- **Exercise** is crucial because movement helps stimulate bowel movements. Make sure your pet has plenty of places to go to the bathroom, especially if it needs privacy to do so. A wide open area will not always suffice—your pet may need bushes to hide behind.
- **Digestive enzymes** (such as papaya extracts) added to the diet can also sometimes help.
- **Aluminum toxicity** can cause chronic constipation. Aluminum can be absorbed into the body from aluminum cans and cooking utensils, tap water, processed cheeses and white flour.
- **Herbs**—senna and cascara can be effective laxatives, and are available in tablet form. Avoid long-term use of laxatives as they can make the bowel "lazy" and worsen the problem.
- **Lactulose**—this is a synthetic sugary liquid that is designed to attract liquid into the bowel. Check with your vet if this is suitable for your pet.
- **Homeopathy**—the choice of a homeopathic remedy depends on what signs are exhibited. Consult a trained homeopath or a reliable book on the subject. Some useful remedies are:

- ❖ *Nux vomica 30c*—use for an irritable animal that is straining but not producing much, or if it is worse after rich foods or emotional upsets.
- ❖ *Bryonia 30c*—use if the stools are large, hard and dry, mucous membranes are dry, or symptoms are worse when the animal moves.
- ❖ *Lycopodium 30c*—for ineffectual straining with small, hard stools, especially if the animal is pregnant.

- **Flower essences**—consider using these if the constipation is related to an emotional upset. A stressed animal is less likely to relax enough to empty its bowels on a regular basis. Remedies to consider are the general fear and stress essences: aspen, mimulus, crab apple (for detoxification) and Rescue Remedy.

- **Acupuncture and acupressure**—constipation reflects a general sluggishness of the whole system, and acupuncture can help with the presenting symptoms and restore balance to the body. Use the points ST 25, SP 6, ST 36 and LI 11.

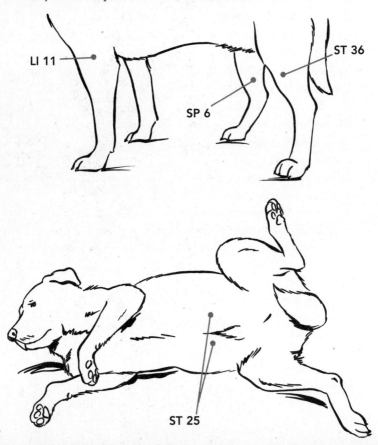

LI 11

ST 36

SP 6

ST 25

? Questions to consider

What is the underlying reason for the constipation?
In chronic constipation, could there be heavy metal toxicity,
dietary or emotional problems, behavioral problems? Is there
a structural problem, e.g., in the pelvic region, the nerves or
the primary intestine, or is the whole body sluggish?

**Has this occurred after the animal has been fed cer-
tain foods, exhibited certain behaviors or gone to
certain places?**

**Is the animal simply too afraid to go outside to defe-
cate due to a stressful situation such as a neighboring cat waiting to attack, loud noises or lack of
privacy?**

Diabetes

Diabetes mellitus (or sugar diabetes) in cats and dogs results in a
lack of insulin in the body. Insulin is a hormone that is produced
in the pancreas, to help use the blood sugar (glucose) that is
released into the bloodstream as part of the digestive process. Glucose is the energy source for the body that drives the muscles and
organs, with any excess being stored as fat for future use. When
there are inadequate levels of insulin in the body the glucose
remains in the blood in abnormally high levels, spilling over into
the urine as the body tries to get rid of the excess blood sugar,
while the rest of the body effectively starves as the glucose doesn't
get to the places it needs to.

Causes

Recent research suggests that diabetes is related to an immune
system disorder in which it attacks the pancreas and interferes with
insulin production. Diets that are high in preservatives, artificial
colorings, sugar and highly processed foods, as well as the animal
being exposed to high levels of stress or shock, can also possibly
lead to diabetes. From my observations it seems certain breeds and
body types are predisposed to diabetes; for example, it seems to be
more prevalent in Burmese cats than in other breeds, and in animals that are overweight and not very active.

What you may see

The animal may have increased thirst and urinate a lot more, as the high sugar levels in the blood remove water from the body, effectively dehydrating it. The animal often loses weight as the body does not get the energy it requires, it may be lethargic, and appetite is often increased. The high sugar levels in the bloodstream also damage tissues such as the eye and internal body linings, which can lead to recurrent infections such as bladder infections. There may be diarrhea and vomiting.

It is crucial to get your animal checked by a veterinarian if it shows any of these symptoms. Long-term elevated blood sugar levels age the body and reduce life expectancy. Even when the insulin is supplemented by injections, degeneration of the body tissues continues, so even with treatment, life expectancy is usually reduced. However, early detection and stabilization can make a huge difference to the longevity of your animal friend.

Treatment

The main aim in treating diabetes is to normalize the blood sugar as much as possible. It is often a case of managing the condition rather than curing it, as once it is established it is unlikely to reverse itself.

- **Diet**—feed the animal two or three times a day rather than once, as this helps keep the blood sugar at an even level. Feed a good-quality, well-balanced natural diet if possible, fresh and raw, as raw foods take longer to digest, which leads to a more even release of blood sugar. Avoid highly processed foods as they often contain high levels of sugar and are assimilated quickly, creating dramatic swings in blood sugar level. Whole grains (these need to be cooked), vegetables and raw meats all break down at a slower rate, and since diabetes is a "hot" and "dry" condition, feeding cooling, uncooked foods with a high water content will help rebalance the system. Also, there are high-quality prescription or commercial diets which can help with management.
  - ❖ Alfalfa sprouts, spirulina, chlorella and barley grass juice all contain chlorophyll, which is a very useful supplement because it helps the body utilize minerals and vitamins more efficiently. Grains such as millet, rice, oats

and corn are good, as are vegetables such as carrots, green beans and spinach, parsley, garlic and avocado. Fresh fruits are fine but have higher sugar levels, so use the more acidic fruits like lemons and grapefruit which can help reduce blood sugar. Banana is the exception, as it aids detoxification.

✤ Reduce most fats in the diet, with the exception of crucial essential fatty acid supplements such as flaxseed oil; this contains GLA (gamma-linolenic acid) which helps to regulate insulin. Concentrated fish oils should be used with care because they can lead to a temporary worsening of the condition, but the actual fish containing these oils is fine since the accompanying proteins and minerals buffer this reaction. Add seaweeds to the diet; they are high in important minerals and vitamins. (This information is taken from Paul Pitchford's very useful book *Healing with Whole Foods[1].*)

✤ Supplementing with important minerals and vitamins is very useful, especially chromium, zinc and manganese to help balance the blood sugar. Discuss the amounts with your veterinarian, as too much of one may cause interactions with other minerals. There is a natural chromium-containing substance found in primary yeast called "glucose tolerance factor" which is very useful in diabetes management; also use the dog and cat powders which contain brewer's yeast and kelp. Add vitamin C (500–3000 mg per day, depending on the size of the animal), use double the usual dose of vitamin E, and ensure all the vitamin B complex is given.

• **Homeopathic remedies:**
   ✤ Try homeopathic *Insulin 6c*;
   ✤ *Iris versicolor 30c* is a good pancreas remedy.

• **Vigorous exercise** helps to lower blood sugar levels, and it also improves circulation which is often poor in diabetics.

• **When diabetes is first diagnosed, use insulin injections** monitored by your veterinarian to bring blood sugar levels into a relatively normal range. As the dietary and management changes listed above take effect the amount of insulin can often be reduced markedly (in consultation with your veterinarian).

- **Acupuncture/acupressure**—try SP 6, BL 13, BL 20, SP 21, CV 12, BL 23 and ST 36.

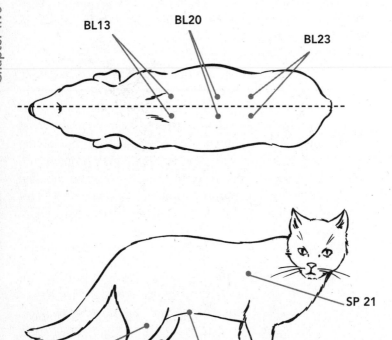

If your animal friend is very weak, only acupressure a couple of points a day; otherwise do weekly acupressure sessions and monitor blood glucose changes.

? Questions to consider

Is your pet overweight?
This is a common predisposing condition for diabetes, so help your pet lose that weight now!

Does your animal friend eat a lot of sugary or highly processed foods?

Has there been a high level of glucocorticoid steroid use in the past?
For example, to treat the itchiness caused by inflammatory skin conditions?

Does your pet get regular vigorous exercise?

Is your animal continuously stressed?
This can lead to constant raised levels of natural steroids in the body, possibly leading to immune dysfunction and maybe on to diabetes.

Diarrhea

Diarrhea is really more a symptom (like vomiting) than a "disease" on its own. When the large or small intestine is irritated, possibly by bacteria, viruses, worms, allergies or a physical irritation like pieces of bone, or in osmotic diarrhea where body fluid is drawn into the bowel due to high sugar levels, then the normal peristalsis (regulated bowel movements) speeds up. The contents of the intestines are shunted along at a much faster rate, so normal removal of fluid from the intestinal content does not happen, leading to diarrhea.

Causes

The most common cause of diarrhea is eating something that may be spoiled or foul—this is particularly likely if the animal has just been to the beach, for example, or it is garbage night and there are bins full of rotten food material on the street. As long as there are not any other symptoms, the diarrhea is minor, and the animal is otherwise bright and well, then it is best to let the body do its job of ejecting the toxic material and allowing the bowel to heal. Normally it does this very quickly, but if the animal is otherwise unwell or the diarrhea continues for more than one to two days, seek veterinary attention immediately.

What you may see

Increased frequency of defecation and liquid feces, often with straining, are commonly seen. Other symptoms depend on where the irritation is. For example, if it is near the beginning of the digestive tract (the small intestine) there is not usually much straining, but if there is blackish tarry diarrhea this may indicate bleeding in the small intestine, which needs immediate veterinary attention. There may also be quite a large buildup of gas, causing bloating, burping or flatulence. When the large intestine is irritated, there is usually more straining to defecate, more mucus (jelly-like lumps) and the diarrhea is usually pushed out with much greater force. Bright red fresh blood indicates bleeding in the large intestine, which also requires immediate attention from the vet.

In most cases the body is trying to flush out the irritant by speeding up the movements and removing the potentially toxic material from the digestive tract. Obviously fluid is lost from the body, so dehydration and electrolyte loss become the biggest worries with diarrhea that lasts more than 24 to 36 hours. Very small or very young animals dehydrate quickly because of their immature systems and smaller size.

Treatment options

- **First off, give the gut a rest** (give it a chance to heal). Stop all solid food for 24 hours, and rest the animal.
  - ❖ Make a broth by boiling up meat, rice and vegetables until they are soft, strain out the solids, and feed the liquid to the animal (little and often, usually every hour or so). The rice and vegetable water is very soothing and replaces some of the lost electrolytes, and the meat gives the broth some taste.
  - ❖ If the diarrhea settles within 24 hours, feed the remaining solids from the broth for a couple of days, starting with a small amount, little and often, then slowly build up over the following few days to normal foods.
- **Give the animal plenty of clean fresh water**, but no milk or other dairy products.
- **Add oat bran to the diet** once the diarrhea has settled and the animal is back on its regular diet, especially if antibiotics have been used. This provides a useful substrate for "good" bacteria to grow on.

- **There are commercial electrolyte replacement formulas**, but these are usually only necessary if the diarrhea is copious and lasts more than 24 hours, or if the animal is small, young or weak.
- **If the animal is vomiting as well**, see your veterinarian immediately.
- In his book *Dr. Pitcairn's Complete Guide to Natural Health for Dogs and Cats*[2], Richard Pitcairn suggests using slippery elm to soothe the gut lining; mix 1 tsp in 1 cup of water, bring to the boil and simmer for 3 minutes, stirring constantly. For cats use 1 tsp of the mixture; for medium-sized dogs 2 tsp to 2 tbsp; for large dogs 3–4 tbsp. Use every four hours, as necessary.
- **Kaopectate solution**, which is made from plant pectin and finely ground earth, soothes the lining of the intestine without affecting the mobility of the digestive tract (which quite a few of the conventional gut-protectant formulas do). Remember, you are trying to work with the body to eject the problem substance, so anything that slows the movement of the digestive tract will allow the causative agent to stay in the body for longer.
- **Homeopathy**—there are many homeopathic remedies that can be used, depending on the presenting signs. Dosages depend on how sudden and acute the problem is. In moderately acute cases, give doses every four hours for a total of three treatments; if there is no change within 24 hours you may need to try another remedy or see your vet. Examples of possible homeopathic remedies include:
  - ✤ *Arsenicum album 30c*—the classic food-poisoning remedy, where there are frequent bowel movements, with a small quantity and with straining, getting worse toward midnight, and with vomiting present. The animal will be thirsty for small, frequent sips of water and seem restless, weak and cold. Symptoms are improved with warmth.
  - ✤ *Mercurius corrosivus 30c*—for frequent bloody stools with a lot of straining that is not relieved by passing the stool.
  - ✤ *Pulsitilla 30c*—where the animal is subdued and timid, with no thirst. A good remedy when the animal has overeaten, or had food that is too rich.
- **Acupuncture or acupressure** can be very helpful for digestive upsets, especially if there are underlying reasons due to a body imbalance. It can be useful in acute diarrhea, but would

definitely be considered where there is chronic diarrhea. Try the points ST 36, SP 6, ST 25, LI 11 and LI 4.

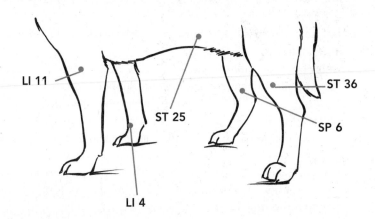

- **NAET** (Nambudripad's Allergy Elimination Technique) is excellent in chronic diarrhea where allergies are causing the problem. Chronic colitis responds exceptionally well to this procedure, and I have used it in several very chronic colitis cases (of three to four years' standing) with a near 100 percent recovery. (See Chapter 4 for more on NAET.)

❓ Questions to consider

Has your pet had access to spoiled food or garbage?

Is the pet very unwell? Is it vomiting? Is there blood in the feces? Has the diarrhea continued for more than 24 hours?
If so, see your vet immediately.

Are there other symptoms such as stomach pain or severe straining, or hard feces then diarrhea?
Your pet may actually be constipated; the body is speeding up the bowel to try and push the fecal lumps out, and the diarrhea oozes around the outside of the fecal lumps.

Has your pet been wormed regularly?

Intestinal parasites can cause diarrhea, mostly in young animals.

With diarrhea, there may be human health issues such as campylobacter or salmonella. Always wash your hands well after attending to your pet, and have a culture analysis done to check for a possible causative organism.

Ear problems

Causes

Dogs with floppy or heavy, hairy ear flaps, such as Cocker Spaniels, are often more predisposed to ear infections than those with ears that stand up, because air circulation and drainage is impaired. Water in the ears after swimming or being bathed can also lead to ear infections, because the skin in the ear canals becomes soft and soggy, making it easier for bacteria and yeasts to multiply and invade.

The underlying reason for chronic ear problems, in particular, is often an imbalance in the immune system. It may be overactive and produce allergies, which show up in the ear or on other parts of the skin (the lining of the ear canal is really a continuation of the skin), or it may be underactive, which shows as recurrent invasions from bacteria and yeasts. It is important to assess the status of the immune system in animals that have recurrent problems.

Ear mites, small external parasites that multiply in the ear, are very irritating and can be quite difficult to eliminate. Although they are more often found in young animals they sometimes appear in adults, usually those with a depressed immune system. Grass seeds and other foreign objects can also lodge down the ear canal and cause discomfort, often producing extremely irritating symptoms. They can be quite problematic as they can perforate the ear drum, enabling infection to develop deeper in the middle ear, which can result in balance problems.

Some dogs have ear problems as a result of anatomical abnormalities, if they are born with problems in the structure of the ear canal, resulting in constriction and poor drainage. Others may have very constricted ear canals as a result of chronic or recurrent ear infections that leave scarring in the ear canal, which reduces its diameter. There may also be growths or polyps which affect drainage.

What you may see

The animal may shake its head, flap its ears, scratch at the ears with its paws, or rub the ears along the ground. There may also be matting of the fur around the ears as a result of rubbing and irritation of the area.

Often there will be a discharge from the ears, which varies depending on the type of infection:

- Yeast infections usually have a musty smell, with a dark brown, oily discharge.
- Bacterial infections usually look green or yellowy, are very smelly, and discharges often run out of the ear or ulcerate the skin in and around the ear. There is usually bleeding as a result of the animal violently scratching at the ears.
- Ear mite infections often have a dry, brown, crumbly discharge, and are very itchy. When your veterinarian looks down the ear canal with the correct instrument (an otoscope) they can see the very small, moving, whitish mites.
- There can be combinations of the above.

Treatment

The main aim of treatment is to make the environment in the outer ear canal unfavorable for yeasts and bacteria to live in. It is also important to increase the animal's overall vitality and bring its system back into balance, particularly if there is an imbalance in the immune system. In either case, following the recommendations below will help to treat the secondary infection (symptoms) and well as the primary cause (the imbalance in the immune system).

- *Always* **get your pet's ears checked by a veterinarian first**. The vet can have a good look down the ear canal and determine if the cause is infection, allergies, growths or foreign bodies. Polyps or small growths inside the ear canal will often need to be surgically removed.
- **A high-quality diet is essential**. Many ear infections show "heat" signs, with hot, smelly, red ears, so a diet that is high in

cooling foods, and as much raw food as possible, will help to cool the body. According to traditional Chinese medicine, head and ear problems are often related to liver heat, as the heat rises from the liver up to the head. If there is moist heat, there is probably a spleen imbalance as well.

To help the liver, avoid processed, overcooked foods as much as possible, especially the cheaper canned foods and treats. Also avoid warming foods such as poultry, venison and lamb—these add to liver heat. Follow a natural diet, including the powders and oils, as well as the diet recommendations for allergies, i.e., essential fatty acids (which act as natural anti-inflammatories), Vitamin C and antioxidants.

- **Remove excess hair down inside the ear canal** by plucking with forceps—you may need to get your veterinarian or groomer to do this because it can be a bit uncomfortable for the animal. This improves drainage and air circulation, allowing the skin to dry out and heal, and making the environment in the ear canal less favorable for the yeasts and bacteria that love to grow in warm, moist places.

- **Clean the debris from the ear canal** with a special ear-cleaning solution such as Epiotic, available from your veterinarian. These solutions are usually acidic, and thus create an environment in the ear which is unfavorable for yeasts and bacteria. Other options are to use apple cider vinegar, hydrogen peroxide or witch hazel.

  Fill the ear canal, massage gently from the outside until you hear a squelching sound (this means the liquid material has been well-washed around inside the ear canal and has loosened the wax and debris) then wipe off the excess material with a cotton ball. You can wrap the cotton ball around your forefinger and firmly wipe down inside the ear canal, but do not use cotton buds as you may poke them down too far and damage the eardrum (see illustration on page 188 for how to hold the ear).

- **Calendula tincture** can also be used; it acts as a healing agent for the inflamed skin inside the ears. Sweet almond oil with garlic oil will act to lift yeasty brown discharges as well as help treat the infection. Your veterinarian may prescribe a

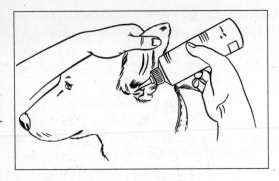

1. Fill ear canal with ear-cleaning solution. Hold the ear flap upright, to straighten the ear canal.

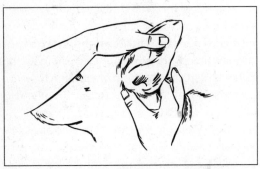

2. Still holding the ear flap up, massage the base of the ear between thumb and forefinger to loosen debris.

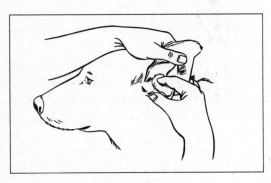

3. Gently wipe away any debris that has come to the top of the ear canal with cotton wool wrapped around your forefinger.

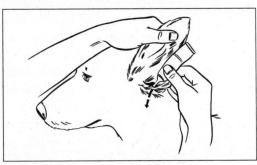

4. Get the ear ointment right down inside the ear canal and massage as in step 2 to work it to the bottom of the ear canal.

mixture of antibiotic, anti-inflammatory and antifungal cream to put in the ear. This can be useful for quick alleviation of symptoms, but unless the ear canal is cleaned as directed, the infection is very likely to recur. For mild problems, cleaning is often all that is necessary. When this is combined with a dietary change, and management of the hair, etc., most chronic ear problems respond well.

> **!** If your dog's ears are normal, *leave them alone!*

- To prevent difficult, long-standing ear infections from recurring, **regular cleaning can be very useful**. I suggest using the cleaning solution before medication every other day for a week, then progressively three times a week, twice a week and weekly, unless very little material is being removed from the ear canal. For ongoing management of chronic problems, I suggest regular cleaning every ten days or so; cleaning is most important over the summer months when the ear canal is warmer and more susceptible to infections. As the ears improve, you can stretch this to every two to three weeks, but increase the frequency if the problem is recurring. After swimming, flush the ear canal with the cleaning solution—this will help prevent recurrent problems.
- **Homeopathic remedies** can be used for ear problems. Try:
    - ❖ *Pulsitilla 30c*—useful if the animal is submissive and pitiful, and wants to be held. Use once every three days, and continue only if it is helping.
    - ❖ *Silicea 30c*—for recurrent ear inflammation with wax and fluid build-up, severe irritation with head shaking and rubbing of the ears. Use three doses, 12 hours apart, then wait for a month. Don't use any other homeopathic remedies during this time.
    - ❖ *Sepia 30c*—can be used for cats, where they have very itchy, waxy, dirty ears, and scratch and react violently when the ears are cleaned.
- **If the outer ear canal is very painful when massaged** there may be a grass seed in it. Visit your vet to have it removed; this may need to be done under sedation if your dog is very sensitive about its ears.

- **Dilute manuka oil** can be used as a wash for treating yeast infections.
- For **ear mites**, proprietary veterinary drops can be used, or Dr. Pitcairn suggests a mix of almond oil and a 400 IU capsule of vitamin E. Use a pin to make a hole in the capsule and add the contents to the almond oil, warm it in water (in a small dropper bottle), and put half a dropper in the ear every other day for six days (i.e., three treatments). The oil will smother the mites and start the healing process. After this add the herb yellow dock (*Rumex crispus*) as an infusion or tincture, putting it into the ear canals every three days for three or four weeks. As the mites lay eggs that hatch every two to three weeks, you need to continue treatment for at least this long to catch the emerging mites. Generally an ear mite infestation indicates a poor state of general health, and usually appears in young animals with immature immune systems.

✸ A note about dog ear anatomy

The eardrum lies at the end of the outer ear canal, which has a vertical and horizontal component. In a dog the size of a Labrador (about 65–90 pounds), the length from the outer ear area (the part you can see) to the eardrum is approximately 1.5 inches. This means you need to make sure the entire length of the outer ear canal is cleaned and has adequate medication inserted to reach to the end of the canal.

- **NAET** can be used to identify and treat underlying allergies, and can be extremely useful in recurrent ear problems, especially if there are other skin problems. It is still necessary to treat the secondary infections, but once the allergies have been eliminated both the ear problems and the skin problems often disappear.
- **Acupressure and acupuncture** can be helpful in addressing the underlying body system imbalances, especially the liver and spleen (in moist conditions). Try the points LI 4, LI 11, TH 17, GB 20, BL 23 and KI 13.

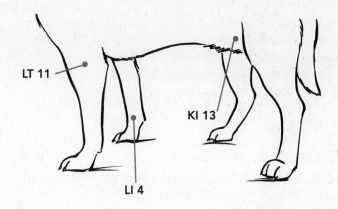

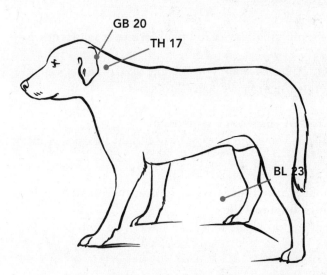

- **In really severe or chronic ear infections** your veterinarian may want to do a culture of the bacteria in the ear, so the correct antibiotic can be used to eliminate the infection. Ear infections can be very uncomfortable, and a dose of antibiotics can provide relief quickly (as can a well-chosen homeopathic remedy) while you move on and address the primary causes (such as allergies, structural ear canal and management problems and immune system imbalances).

✳ Using an antibiotic ear cream will help the secondary symptoms and provide quick relief to a very sore and inflamed ear, but all the underlying reasons for the infection *must* also be addressed, or the infection will almost always return once the antibiotics are stopped.

❓ Questions to consider

Does your animal friend have other allergic conditions?
If so, the ear problems are probably related to a primary allergy of some kind.

Is there a physical ear canal problem that is affecting drainage?
For example, excess hair, constriction of the actual canal, polyps (growths), or heavy, hairy ear flaps?

What kind of discharge is present?
This will give you some clues as to what may be causing the secondary infection.

And most importantly, what is the overall health of your animal friend like?
Recurrent ear problems reflect an underlying imbalance in the body.

Epilepsy

Causes

No one really knows specifically what causes epilepsy, but there are probably many contributing factors. Things like genes (inheritance from the parents), nutrition (especially the mother's nutrition during pregnancy) and toxins in the environment are all possible causes. Anything that affects the brain and nervous system, like heavy metals, viruses, vaccination or poisons, are possible reasons for the electrical impulses in the brain going haywire, which is what happens in epilepsy. The condition is diagnosed by the exclusion of any other diseases, so a thorough examination and full blood tests need to be done to establish whether it really is epilepsy.

What you may see

The animal may have convulsions and seizures, which can vary in length. They usually start with one or two episodes, with long intervals of several weeks or months, then often progress to several times a week. The animal may be disoriented before and especially after the fit. It may lose control of its bladder and bowels, and you may see it salivating, panting, and lying on its side and paddling its legs. Long term, there may be signs of brain damage.

Treatment

Conventional treatment involves sedation to varying degrees, more so during the fits, as well as long-term control using sedative drugs. A holistic approach involves:

- **Diet**—it is recommended to remove all artificial colorings and preservatives from the diet, because these may irritate the nervous system. Make sure the diet is a high-quality one. If you are using a homemade diet, it is recommended to reduce the amount of meat used, especially organ meats such as liver and kidney, because they tend to concentrate toxins. Supplements are essential, such as the powders and oils described in Chapter 3 as well as a multivitamin tablet. The seaweed components provide important antioxidants, vitamins and minerals, while the yeast provides the essential B vitamins. Extra B vitamins in the form of a complete B vitamin supplement are also very helpful, as nerve tissue requires B vitamins, especially when under stress. Vitamin C, zinc and magnesium are also important for the nervous system. Check with your vet for recommended amounts for the size of your dog.
- **Reduce toxins in the environment** as much as possible. Avoid exposure to cigarette smoke, exhaust fumes and household cleaners.
- **Herbs** can be useful—skullcap is a calmative and nervous system repairer; passionflower and valerian are also calmatives.
- **Acupuncture/acupressure**—in traditional Chinese medicine seizures are often related to liver imbalances, and acupuncture can create balance and eliminate the symptoms.

I have had a lot of success with implanting small pieces of gold wire (gold bead implants) into a special acupuncture point in

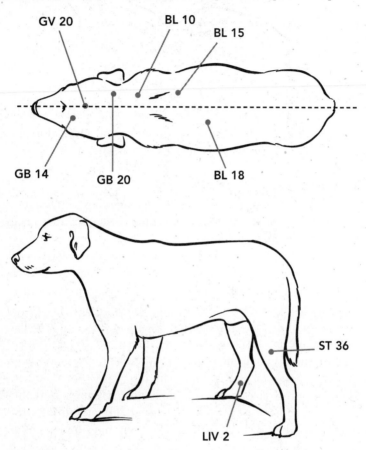

GV 20   BL 10

BL 15

GB 14

GB 20   BL 18

ST 36

LIV 2

the ear flap (see diagram opposite). Acupressure on this point can also reduce the incidence of fits, and there are also temporary pins that can be inserted into this point and work in the same way. The gold bead implants are done under light anesthesia and remain in place permanently, constantly stimulating this point and preventing fits. In several cases where I have implanted the gold beads, medication has been reduced markedly and even stopped, without the fits returning. General points for acupressure are GV 20, GB 14, GB 20, BL 10, BL 15, BL 18, ST 36 and LIV 2.

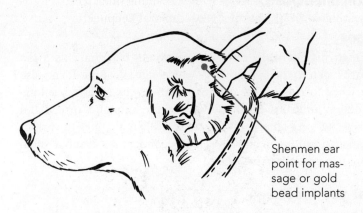

Shenmen ear point for massage or gold bead implants

? Questions to consider

Has there been prior exposure to high levels of toxins?

Do the blood results show any obvious abnormalities? (If not, then fits are probably due to epilepsy.)

Consider the frequency and length of convulsions before using drug therapy; there are several commonsense alternatives, as listed above, which are worth trying first.

Are there pre-existing liver problems? These can lead to fits.

Eye problems

The most common eye problems are:

- Conjunctivitis—inflammation of the inside lining of the eyelids;
- Corneal scratches or ulcers—damage to the surface of the eyeball;
- Eyelid problems—entropion or ectropion.

1. Conjunctivitis

Causes

Conjunctivitis can be the result of infection by bacteria, chlamydia or a virus such as the herpes virus, which causes cat flu. It can also occur when foreign bodies or dust get under the eyelids, resulting in irritation and subsequent rubbing by the animal. Corneal and other eyeball problems can be a cause, as can allergies to various substances, resulting in itchy eyes and secondary self-trauma, often leading to a secondary infection.

What you may see

With bacterial infections there is usually a greenish or yellowish discharge from the eyes, the lids may stick together after sleep, and the eyes are usually very itchy and red.

Foreign bodies such as grass seeds under the third eyelid (the flap of skin that retracts in the middle angle of the eye) can lead to damage to the corneal surface due to the eye movement and self-trauma. In most cases the eye is nearly closed and the animal avoids bright light, because it is uncomfortable. The animal may rub the eye intensely, and there can be redness, a clear and copious discharge (watering) from the eye, or even a nasty secondary bacterial infection.

Itchiness, rubbing, redness and irritation can also indicate an allergy. These often start with a clear discharge, which may change to become pustular and yellowish if there is a secondary bacterial infection.

Viral conjunctivitis due to infection by the herpes virus (which causes cat flu) can become chronic because the virus can trick the body into not noticing it is there. Although the main symptoms of cat flu may be long gone, the virus remains in the lining of the eyelids, often worsening when the animal's immune system is stressed. Usually there is a clear discharge from one or both eyes, but if it becomes secondarily infected by bacteria then the discharge becomes yellow, green or white.

Treatment

- **The first thing is to try to determine the cause**, which usually means a trip to the vet. They will examine the eye and possibly stain it with a special dye to check for corneal scratches, as well as checking under the third eyelid for foreign bodies.

Once a diagnosis has been reached you can try some of the following treatments, but always listen to your veterinarian's advice first.

- **Using a cotton ball, bathe the eyes** with water that has been boiled, had salt added (1 tsp per cup of water) then cooled, removing excess discharge and crusting. Wipe from the middle of the eye to the outside, and use a clean wipe for the second eye so you don't transfer infection between the two eyes. Once the eyes have been cleaned, use euphrasia (the herb eyebright, made from the tincture, and diluted—use five drops tincture to one cup of water) as an eye wash for itchy red eyes, to soothe and aid healing. Some nasty infections require antibiotic creams to reduce the discomfort and remove the bacterial load quickly to speed up healing. For mild conjunctivitis, try bathing the eye with cold black tea, several times a day. The tannin in the tea can act as an anti-inflammatory.
- **If allergies are the primary cause of recurrent conjunctivitis**, NAET will help identify the causative agents and eliminate the abnormal reaction to them.

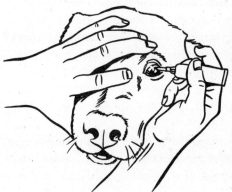

Applying eye ointment. Use the left hand to steady the nose and open the upper and lower eyelids. Hold the nozzle parallel to the surface of the eye so if the animal moves it won't get poked in the eye with the tip. Do not allow the surface of the nozzle to touch the eye.

- **As always, a high-quality diet** is crucial for overall health, especially if viruses or allergies are the primary cause.
- **Five-mushroom extract** (used orally) is useful for stimulating the immune system in viral infections. It acts by stimulating a massive increase in killer T cells, which are important parts of the immune defense system.
- Your veterinarian may give you a **cream or drops** for the irritation or the infection.

2. Corneal scratches

Causes

Trauma is the usual cause of corneal scratches—e.g., a stick, cat claws during a fight or self-trauma secondary to conjunctivitis—or there may be a foreign body under the eyelid. Viral infections such as herpes can result in corneal ulceration.

What you may see

The eye is often partially or completely closed. There may be redness, watering, irritation and soreness, or a whitish area or cloudiness on the surface of the eye. The animal may show photophobia (avoiding bright light), hiding under furniture or going to a dark room.

Treatment

- **Always get your vet to check the eye first**, because if there is a deep ulcer this can potentially be a dangerous situation, resulting in permanent eye damage.
- **The eye will often heal on its own** given the right environment. Viral ulcers can take a very long time to heal, so stimulating the immune system and improving the overall health of the animal with an excellent diet is very important. Consider five-mushroom extract (used orally) if there is a viral ulcer.
- **Homeopathic remedies** can be helpful in trauma situations; for example:
    - ❖ *Symphytum 30c*—for trauma from a blunt object (e.g., for a dog that has been kicked by a horse); this remedy also helps trauma to the orbital area (the area around the eye).
    - ❖ *Ledum 30c*—for a puncture wound to the eye.
- **If there is an ulcer that is very deep** or is not healing within a week or so, your vet may need to scarify the area and create what is known as an "eye flap." This involves stitching the third eyelid to the upper lid, covering the surface of the eye, protecting it from further damage and allowing the cornea to heal without the constant irritation of the eyelid blinking over the top.

3. Eyelid problems

Entropion

This is where the eyelids curl inwards and the eyelashes irritate the surface of the cornea. In some animals this condition is inherited, or it can be temporarily caused by inflammation and swelling of the eyelids from infection or irritation. Trauma from fights or accidents can also result in abnormal eyelid position. If the condition is a permanent one surgery is the best option, removing a thin strip of skin on the affected lid, which enables the eyelashes to sit in the normal place. This surgery is simple and there is usually an excellent outcome. For temporary inflammation, treat the cause, such as infection or a foreign body.

Ectropion

This is where the eyelids turn outwards, resulting in a pocket area where dust and debris can accumulate and cause conjunctivitis. Again, this can be inherited in some breeds of dog, such as Basset Hounds, or it can be caused by trauma or temporary swelling of the eyelids due to infection. Surgery is usually needed in the permanent cases.

 Questions to consider

Is the animal living in a dusty environment?

Does it dig in the sand or the soil?

Are you doing home renovations that are creating dust, or have you been doing any painting and sanding?

Has it been very windy, especially when there is a lot of pollen around?

Has the animal been in a fight lately?

Has the problem been present from birth or just for a short time?
Eyelid disorders can be present from birth; trauma is suspected if the problem has suddenly appeared.

Fleas

The life-cycle of a flea

By understanding the flea's life-cycle, control can occur during the adult phase (on the animal) and during the environment phase (off the animal).

- In optimum conditions (70% humidity), it can take only three to four weeks to complete the flea life-cycle (from egg to adult). It can be as long as five months or more in cold conditions.
- Eggs, which are pearly white, oval and about 0.02 inch long, are laid on the host and fall into the environment.
- Eggs hatch into larvae that are approximately 0.1 inch long and live in bedding and carpets away from light. The larvae feed on dust and the feces of adult fleas. In about a week pupae form in cocoons.
- Adults hatch when stimulated by vibrations caused, for example, by walking and movement in the environment, and are attracted to the host by its body heat.

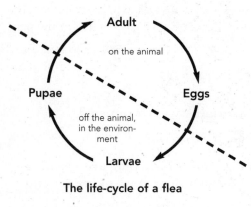

Adult
on the animal

Pupae

Eggs

off the animal, in the environment

Larvae

The life-cycle of a flea

1. Adult: live on the animal
2. Eggs: laid on the animal and fall off into the environment
3. Larvae: live in dark undisturbed places like under furniture, and feed on carpet debris
4. Pupae: lie dormant until environmental vibrations stimulate hatching.

★ **The golden rules of treating fleas**
1. Treat all animals in the household.
2. Treat the environment.

Treating the animal

Treating the animals in your household can take many forms. Some treatments are more toxic than others, so be very careful about what you put onto your animal friend. If the flea load is low, using things like herbal washes, essential oil repellents and the like may be all that is necessary. If flea numbers are very high, try bathing the animal with the wash described in the aromatherapy section of Chapter 3, apply the lemon wash described below, use a flea comb to remove the adult fleas, and institute an intensive flea eradication/repellent program, making sure the environment is treated as well as the animals. Regular repellent sprays will keep the fleas away. You may need to use an effective commercial preparation as well.

Management is very important—treating the environment and all animals in the home will be far more effective than just doing one part of the job in a haphazard manner. It is worth trying the methods described here rather than relying on commercial flea products, some of which are definitely safer than others. Some are downright toxic and should definitely be avoided, especially if an animal's immune system is challenged in any way. Only use products from a veterinary clinic, and not ones that are designed for treating worms at the same time because they are taken into the system in much greater amounts rather than remaining on the outer skin level. Avoid the organophosphate powders and sprays. In general, powder applications are not that effective since they are messy and need to be applied regularly (every three to four days). Some of the commercial insecticide flea powders are potentially very toxic, especially to kittens and cats.

Treating the environment

Treating the environment is crucial—95 percent of the life-cycle of fleas is off the animal and in your carpets, furnishings and dust on the floor. Vacuum at least once a week with a good vacuum cleaner to suck up eggs, larvae and pupae before they hatch into adults. Diatomaceous earth can also be used: put some into a salt shaker bottle and shake it onto carpets, rugs, pet beds and furniture. It can be a bit messy to use, and make sure you don't inhale it as it can irritate the airways slightly. Diatomaceous earth is made up of fossilized freshwater organisms which have been ground into a very fine powder. It is non-toxic and acts by getting under the chitinous plates on the flea, interfering with its moisture control mechanism and causing it to dry out and die. It can also be used on animals as a powder, but care needs to be taken to make sure it isn't inhaled (it can act as an irritant).

If you prefer powders and don't mind the dust, use the following herbal flea powder to repel fleas. It is safe, and can be used in the environment and on animals, although it is best used on the animal or in its sleeping area rather than in the carpet. The recipe for lemon spray, taken from Diane Stein's book *The Natural Remedy Book for Dogs and Cats*, may also be useful, although it may not be sufficient where flea numbers are high.[3]

For additional recipes for flea repellents to use on animals, carpets and wooden floors see Chapter 4 (page 141).

 ### Herbal flea powder[3]

Combine in a shaker finely powdered eucalyptus, rosemary, fennel, yellow dock, wormwood and rue. Apply sparingly to the coat or carpet as needed.

Lemon spray[3]

Add the skins and whole fruit of lemons, oranges and grapefruit to a large pot of water. Boil for about half an hour, until concentrated. Strain out the residue and put the liquid in a sprayer. Use regularly on your animal friend. This mixture will make them and the house smell nice as well as repelling fleas!

? Questions to consider

Do you live in a humid climate, or has it been consistently warm and humid for a few weeks?

The optimal speed of the life cycle is three weeks at 70% humidity.

Have you just moved into a new home where there used to be animals?

If so, there may be high levels of flea eggs and larvae in the carpet.

Do you vacuum the carpet regularly, especially in corners and under furniture?

Does your animal scratch and bite itself suddenly?
This is probably in response to a flea bite!

Is there small black curly or dust-like matter in the fur at the base of your animal's tail and along its spine?
This is probably flea "dirt" or feces.

Are there red, raised areas in the skin, or other skin lesions at the base of the tail and the lower back?
If so, they are probably flea bites.

Kidney problems

The degeneration of kidney function and subsequent kidney failure is one of the more common aging problems, particularly in cats. This is known as "chronic renal failure," where the problem arises slowly over a period of months or even years, and is progressively degenerative, usually causing the animal's death. "Acute renal failure," causing kidney function to be severely disrupted due to factors such as infection and inflammation, can occur at any time in an animal's life. If treated correctly and soon enough, the animal can recover and normal kidney function resumes, however this is an emergency situation and immediate veterinary care is required.

The kidneys are important for keeping the water balance in the body as well as filtering out toxins in the bloodstream, especially breakdown products of protein metabolism, such as urea. Normally urea is filtered by the kidneys and voided in the urine. When the kidneys are not working well, blood urea levels are elevated, which causes nausea (and hence vomiting), increases the chance of infections, and can cause ulcers in the mouth and gut as the body tries to excrete the urea in any way it can.

No one really knows why chronic kidney failure begins, and it can be difficult even to know it is starting as the kidneys are very good at compensating for deficiencies in their function. The kidneys are made up of many "units" called nephrons, that with aging die off a few at a time until only about a third are still functioning. As an animal nears this critical level you often start to see symptoms such as increased thirst, pickiness with food, loss of weight and fur that starts to look clumpy and stick up a bit due to mild dehydration. There may be an increased frequency of urination, and the urine is usually pale since it is dilute. As the degeneration continues, these symptoms become more pronounced, and the animal gradually "fades away" and dies.

Treatment of the condition has two aims: First, to slow this degeneration as much as possible, since once the nephron function is gone, there is no way to get it back; second, to help the remaining nephrons to work better.

What you may see

The animal may show increased thirst—cats don't normally drink much water, because they have adapted to getting most of their fluid from the food they eat. If you see a cat drinking from a water bowl on a regular basis it is probably a sign that things are not as good as they could be. The exception is if they are eating a lot of dry food that doesn't contain much water, since they have to get water from somewhere! (Milk is more of a treat than a thirst quencher; cats may drink milk even if they are not thirsty, so it is not a good indicator of thirst.)

There may also be increased urination of dilute urine, as a result of the increased water intake and the lack of kidney function to concentrate the urine.

There may be reduced appetite and weight loss—cats often become very fussy about their food, only eating small amounts and constantly changing their preferences. This lack of food naturally leads to a reduction in weight.

The animal may have sunken eyes and a rough-looking coat—the coat can stick up and look clumpy and a little oily as a result of dehydration. The coat color can also change from black to a reddish brown. As the degeneration advances, there may be vomiting, smelly breath (due to gum ulceration from increased blood toxins), not eating, disorientation and weakness, eventually leading to death.

Treatment

- **Early veterinary diagnosis** is important—get regular checkups as animals age.

- **Diet** plays an important part in slowing degeneration and allowing the nephrons to work better.

  ❖ A low-protein diet helps reduce the load on the kidneys, slowing the degeneration and reducing the side effects of renal failure. Food needs to be made as palatable as possible, and since the animal does not usually feel like eating much, it needs to be high in calories to keep body weight up. The ideal kidney diet is low in overall protein (but it must be highly usable protein, such as lean meat, eggs, etc., rather than secondary sources like soybeans), high in easily metabolizable energy, and contains higher than normal water-soluble vitamins such as vitamin C and B (which are flushed out of the body faster with the excess drinking). Phosphorus and sodium levels are usually also elevated when the kidneys are not working well, so their intake needs to be watched as well.

  ❖ Prescription renal diets, which are available from veterinary clinics, take the guesswork out of providing different levels of protein, energy and micronutrients. The dried form can add to the dehydration stress on the body, so it is important to ensure adequate water is available. The diets also come in a wet form, which is preferable.

  ❖ Special diets such as those shown in this section are useful, but they need to be followed closely.

  ❖ The most important thing is to get the animal to eat something. If it refuses the special kidney diets you may need to try some favorite foods to stimulate the appetite then gradually get them on to a special diet. Try heating the food, or add some fishy foods like tuna, or even yeast flakes on top.

- **Kidney glandulars** can be an effective adjunct to dietary changes. These are basically powdered kidney tissue with added minerals and vitamins to aid kidney function. They are often quite tasty, and usually easy to get into the animal.

- **Alfalfa** is a useful herb for strengthening the kidney tissue, and it is also quite palatable. It can be added to the food daily in powdered or capsule form, or as a tincture, although animals sometimes find the alcohol in the tincture off-putting. If they will take it, give it to the animal three times a day (two drops for cats and small dogs; four drops for medium-sized dogs, and six drops for large dogs). Add the tincture to some water to dilute the taste. Once you see an improvement reduce to once daily or every other day, as required.

- **Exercise, fresh air, sunshine** (but avoid overheating), daily brushing of the coat to stimulate the blood supply to the skin (which acts as an eliminative organ), and regular baths (as long as these do not stress the animal too much) are all useful.

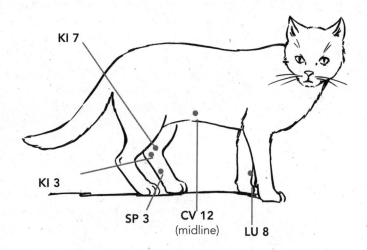

KI 7

KI 3

SP 3

CV 12
(midline)

LU 8

- **Acupuncture or acupressure** can be very useful for building up the kidneys' energy levels (qi), as well as rebalancing overall energy levels. Try the points SP 3, KI 3, LU 8, KI 7 and CV 12.

The following recipes are reprinted with permission from *Dr. Pitcairn's Complete Guide to Natural Health for Dogs and Cats*[2]. They need to be followed closely, with all the additives, to be effective. Check with your veterinarian that they are suitable for your particular animal.

 Cat diet for kidney problems
1 cup ground chicken or lean heart
4 cups cooked white rice
4 eggs
2 tbsp cold-pressed safflower oil

1500 mg calcium
$1/_8$ tsp iodized salt
1 tsp parsley, finely grated carrot or other vegetable (optional)
$1/_8$ tsp potassium chloride (optional, for saltier flavor)
5000 IU vitamin A
taurine and other cat vitamins
50 mg vitamin B complex
2500 mg vitamin C ($1/_2$ tsp sodium ascorbate)

Mix everything together in a large bowl. Serve raw if the cat will accept it. If it will not, before you add the vitamins bake the mixture for about 20 minutes in a moderate oven. Cool, then add the vitamins.

This is enough for five days. Let your cat eat as much as it wants. If it is not eating well make sure it gets the vitamins separately—use 5–10 mg vitamin B complex per day, 250 mg vitamin C, and follow the directions for daily doses of cat vitamins.

 ## Dog diet for kidney problems

$1/_2$ cup ground beef
$2^3/_4$ cups cooked white rice
1 egg
2 tbsp cold-pressed safflower oil
600 mg calcium
$1/_8$ tsp iodized salt

2 tbsp parsley, finely grated carrot or other vegetable (optional)
$1/_2$–1 clove garlic
dog vitamins
20 mg vitamin B complex
5000 IU vitamin A
1000 mg vitamin C

Mix all the ingredients together. Serve raw if your dog will accept it. If not, before adding the vitamins bake in a moderate oven for 20 minutes, cool, then add the vitamins.

Feed the dog as much as it will eat; this recipe should feed a medium-sized dog for a day.

❓ Questions to consider

Is your animal friend drinking more, eating less and losing weight?
If so, get it checked by your vet.

Has it had a previous kidney infection earlier in its life?

Is your cat hyperthyroid (overactive thyroid gland)?
Your vet can diagnose this.

Is your cat's fur looking rough and sticking up?
It may be mildly dehydrated, possibly due to kidney problems.

Is your cat vomiting more than usual and does it have smelly breath?
Again, get it checked by the vet.

Liver problems

Because the liver performs so many functions, any upset can have far-reaching consequences. The liver is closely linked to digestion, blood cleaning and manufacturing, storage of important minerals and vitamins, and a myriad of other critical functions. Even mild imbalances can have obvious effects, such as digestive upsets (e.g., vomiting and diarrhea). There may be behavioral changes when improper blood cleaning leaves toxins in the blood that irritate the brain, and blood sugar and energy levels can be affected. In traditional Chinese medicine, anger is the emotion related to the liver. Often you will see animals become grumpy and angry when their liver isn't working as well as it should.

Causes

Constant stress will seriously affect the liver, because the increase in circulating cortisol damages the liver tissue. Certain drugs such as steroids and anesthetics have a similar effect, as do environmental toxins taken into the body via food, water, breathing and even through the skin. The liver is susceptible to toxins such as pesticides and heavy metals because it has a major role in removing them from the rest of the body. These toxins are often stored in the liver if they are unable to be removed by the kidneys, intestine or skin.

Household cleaners, car exhaust fumes, cigarette smoke, a poor, highly processed diet, and food additives such as colorings and preservatives can all potentially create problems in the liver. Bacterial and viral infections can also cause liver problems.

What you may see

An imbalance in liver function will often result in an overall body imbalance, the most obvious signs being skin problems, recurrent infections, and stomach upsets, with possible vomiting, diarrhea, weight loss and appetite changes. There may also be lethargy and general weakness.

Advanced liver disease can result in fluid accumulation in the abdomen, and jaundice. By the time there is obvious jaundice (when liver function is reduced and byproducts of its filtering action are left in the blood, turning the skin and whites of the eyes yellow) the liver function is seriously impaired and the animal is very unwell. Jaundice can also occur with immune-related diseases where there is a breakdown in blood cells, which is a very serious condition requiring immediate veterinary attention.

Treatment

Assuming the damage is not too advanced, there are things that can be done to help the liver heal itself. The liver has highly regenerative properties, and given the right conditions it can heal itself from quite extensive damage. Make sure your vet examines the animal and diagnoses the problem.

- **Diet is crucial.** Initially, in the acute phase, reduce the food intake to clear chicken broth, or even just filtered water, to reduce the work the liver has to do. Once the condition has stabilized, feed a fresh, homemade diet with all the supplements, but reduce the fat intake. Use lean meat (remove all visible fat) and don't add the oil mix until there is a noticeable improvement; after that reintroduce it slowly, preferably using flaxseed oil as the oil source. Good protein sources are eggs, cottage cheese and lean meats. Commercial prescription diets from your veterinarian are another option.

Divide the feeds into several small ones each day rather than one large one, so the blood sugar remains at an even level and the liver is not overwhelmed by large volumes of food. Use liver-cooling foods such as beet (an excellent liver cleanser), mung beans and their sprouts, seaweeds (especially kelp), lettuce, cucumber, watercress and some fresh liver twice a week. Use as many fresh, organic raw foods as possible (these will have fewer toxic residues), but make sure things like rice and beans are well cooked.

If the animal is very frail and cold, lightly cook some of the food to help the digestive process and warm the animal.

Vitamin C is important as an antioxidant and to aid the healing process, as is a full B complex supplement. Using cat or dog powder that contains brewer's yeast and kelp (seaweed) is very important—if these are not tolerated, it is vital that a multivitamin supplement is used.

- **Herbal remedies**—there are some excellent liver-supporting herbs, and these are very useful in both the healing phase and the ongoing supportive stage. When there has been a major problem with the liver it can take many months to regenerate, and during this time it is very important not only to rectify the situation that caused the damage in the first place (which often involves a major lifestyle change) but to create an appropriate healing environment so that it can recover. Using herbs (as well as diet) in this recovery period can be the main difference between recovery and relapse, so try and include both in the recovery phase.

Useful herbs include the following:

❖ St. Mary's thistle (or milk thistle, *Silybum marianum*) is a powerful antioxidant and liver cleanser, a useful detoxifier, and helps with liver repair.

❖ Parsley is high in vitamin C and other vitamins and minerals, and is very helpful for healing. It acts as a mild diuretic, which helps remove toxins from the body faster. Use it raw, finely chopped, in the food.

- ❖ Burdock root acts as a mild diuretic and aids blood cleansing.
- ❖ Alfalfa helps with liver detoxification, and is a highly nutritive herb.
- ❖ Dandelion root is also very supportive of liver function.
- **Homeopathy** can be a very useful adjunct to the supportive care described above, depending on the symptoms. See a trained homeopathic vet for advice.
- **Reduce environmental toxins**: use eco-friendly, non-toxic household cleaners, organic foods, filtered water, go for walks well away from roads (car exhaust fumes), ensure there is no cigarette smoke or paint fumes in the environment. If your pet has a liver problem, think about what your household toxin levels may be doing to *your* health!
- **Acupuncture or acupressure** can also be excellent for rebalancing the entire system as well as the liver. Treatments can be used either to sedate or to support the system, depending on what is needed. Try points LIV 3, LIV 13, LIV 14, BL 18 and BL 19.

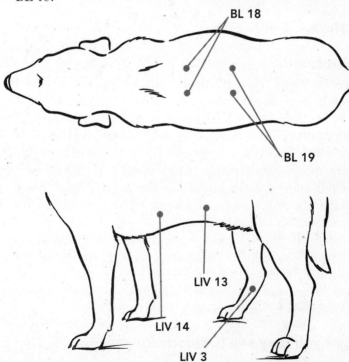

- **Reduce stress in your pet's life** (and yours!). Remember that your animal friend will mirror you in many ways—if you are stressed, they probably are too. Use flower essences to calm and settle your animal friend. Remove possible causes of stress such as aggressive neighborhood cats (using non-violent scare tactics) and provide a "safe" place for your cat to retreat to.

? Questions to consider

Is your pet's diet, lifestyle and toxin exposure level causing the problem?

Are there toxins in your environment that could be affecting you as well as your pet?

Is there an underlying reason for the liver failure, such as cancer?

Mange

Causes

There are two types of mange that occur in dogs and cats. Demodectic mange is relatively common in dogs, and to a much lesser extent in cats. It results from high population levels of the small skin mites known as *Demodex canis* (in dogs) and *Demodex cati* (in cats), which live in the hair follicles.

The other type of mange, which tends to be less common, is sarcoptic mange, caused by the skin mite *Sarcoptes scabeii*. This form is extremely itchy, and it can also be transferred to humans via contact with an infected animal.

Demodectic mange tends to occur mostly in young dogs with undeveloped or unhealthy immune systems. The mites are present in the hair follicles of healthy animals in low levels, and it is only when the immune system is not keeping these levels in check that the mites multiply and spread over the body.

What you may see (Demodectic mange)

Lesions often start on or near the head and eyes, or the feet area, and appear as a thinning and loss of hair. They are not often too itchy, but if the area becomes secondarily infected with normal skin bacteria they can be more itchy and pustular. The skin may develop a "mousy" or "musty" smell, and if the lesions are very active the skin can be thickened and flaky.

Many cases are self-limiting and clear up without treatment by the time the animal is 12 to 14 months of age, as the immune system develops and matures. In severe cases this doesn't happen, and the mange can become generalized over the whole body. This indicates a severely lacking immune system that requires careful management. These cases are also very susceptible to other infections, and treatment starts with the basics of diet and immune system repair, rather than just treating the obvious symptoms.

Treatment

The aim of treatment is to increase the overall health of the animal, especially the immune system, so that the body can mount its own defense. This is much better than having to use the conventional, toxic washes and treatments that are designed to kill the mites. These washes are powerful insecticides and they hammer the animal's already weak system, putting extra pressure especially on the liver and elimination systems. In mild cases, the use of diet, herbs and homeopathic remedies is usually all that is needed.

- **Diet**—use the natural diet, including the supplements, and using organic ingredients if possible. Avoid cheap commercial foods that contain colorings and preservatives. A high-quality commercial diet can also be used, and since this condition often occurs in growing puppies, a growth food is necessary. Add extra vitamin C: 500 mg/day for small dogs; 1000 mg/day for medium dogs and 1500 mg/day for large dogs. Use vitamin A at recommended veterinary doses appropriate for your animal friend. Use an evening primrose oil/fish oil combination and flaxseed oil for essential fatty acid supplementation, following the guidelines provided in the "Allergy" section above.
- **Herbal remedies**:
  ❖ Lavender essential oil is known to kill the mites; it can be diluted 1:10 with a carrier oil such as wheat germ oil and applied daily until the lesions go.[2]
  ❖ Manuka oil or tea tree oil, diluted in the same way as lavender oil, can also be applied.

✤ Black walnut hull tincture can be applied externally.

✤ Internally, use echinacea and goldenseal.

✤ Five-mushroom is useful—use orally, 1 drop per day in small dogs; 3 drops per day in medium-sized dogs, and 6 drops per day in large dogs.

✤ Anecdotally, neem seed oil has been used to treat mange.[4] If the infection is severe, spreading rapidly and there is a secondary bacterial infection (redness, itchiness, pus in the hair follicles) then it is even more important to stimulate the immune system. Use the above suggestions, especially the echinacea, goldenseal and five-mushroom, until the lesions are gone. In severe secondary infections, antibiotics may be necessary.

- As reluctant as I am to use toxic washes, in very severe cases it may be necessary to use them very, very carefully, to slow the spread of mites quickly and relieve the system of the side effects while implementing the dietary and immune stimulative options mentioned above. If you do use these washes only bathe a quarter of the body at a time, once every three days until the whole body has been covered. By then, the herbs, homeopathic remedies and diet will have had time to take effect.

    Be very, very careful when disposing of the wash after use, since it will pollute waterways and kill fish and water organisms. Stand the animal on a gravel path while it is being treated so that some filtering can occur, rather than simply flushing the wash down the drain.

- **External applications of soothing creams** such as Eczema Cream will help the irritation, as well as getting the secondary infection under control.

- **If the skin is severely infected with bacteria**, then a course of antibiotics may also be necessary to help the body to rebalance quickly. These are not, of course, substitutes for the basics of diet, herbs and homeopathy, but rather a short, early treatment option, to try to remove the secondary load from the body, while supporting it with these other crucial essentials. It is very important not to use corticosteroids when your pet has mange, as this will further suppress the immune system.

- **Homeopathic remedies**:

    ✤ *Sulfur 6c* is the classic mange remedy; start with a daily dose until there is an improvement then reduce the frequency as the skin gets better.

❖ *Arsenicum 30c* (if very itchy) or *Psorinum* are others that may be used; again, choosing which remedy to use depends on the presenting symptoms.

• **Acupuncture or acupressure** can be used to stimulate the immune system and help disperse the imbalances associated with the redness and itchiness in the skin. When the overall health of the animal is improved, the immune system is able to keep the mites under control. Try LI 4, LI 11, ST 36, BL 23 and SP 6.

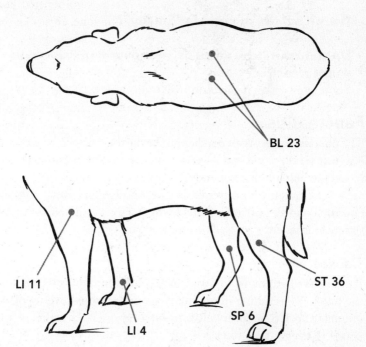

BL 23

LI 11

LI 4

SP 6

ST 36

? Questions to consider

Is your puppy underdeveloped or the runt of the litter?
This can mean it is more likely to have immune system problems.

Does it get infections or become unwell easily?

This may be a reflection of an unbalanced immune system.

Is there thinning of the fur, especially around the eyes, ears and feet?

Are there scabs and scaly areas on its skin? Are there itchy areas?

Does it smell "mousy" or "musty"?

Do you have itchy areas on your own skin, especially your forearms?
Some types of mange can transfer to humans.

Pancreatitis

The pancreas is an organ that lies just below the stomach; it produces enzymes for digestion and hormones that are important in the maintenance of blood glucose levels (insulin). Inflammation of the pancreas (pancreatitis) can result in the leakage of these digestive enzymes and severe irritation of the surrounding tissues in the stomach, liver, etc.

Causes

Pancreatitis is thought to occur when the immune system attacks the pancreas, resulting in an inflammatory response. Many of the animals affected are overweight or on a very rich, fatty diet, which seems to trigger the attacks.

What you may see

Symptoms can range from a mild digestive upset to a severe condition with nasty vomiting and diarrhea, stomach pain, distress and weakness, possibly resulting in shock.

Treatment

Prevention is the best policy, with all the commonsense things like a good-quality diet, keeping your animal friend at the correct weight, and making sure it has plenty of exercise to keep all the body functions working optimally. Sometimes pancreatitis becomes a chronic problem with regular flare-ups, which are usually brought on by overindulging in rich, fatty foods (for example, after the animal has gone through the garbage bags eating rancid, greasy garbage).

Severe acute attacks of pancreatitis require immediate veterinary attention, with emergency IV fluids to help rehydrate and flush the system. Once the animal is stabilized and able to go home, management can be as follows.

- **Diet** is a really important management tool. There are commercial prescription diets specific to pancreatic problems, available from your veterinarian, or you can feed a good-quality natural diet, but reduce the oil and fat content in the food. Feed lean meats (trim off all visible fat), provide fish oils in capsular form, and include vitamin E capsules at recommended doses (this is important as an antioxidant and to help heal the damaged pancreas). Vitamin C is also important to aid healing; use it three times a day, initially 250 mg for cats and small dogs, up to 1000 mg for large dogs; if diarrhea develops, reduce the frequency of the dose. The use of bioflavonoids enhances the vitamin C action. I recommend using the chelated lower acid form.

  ✤ Give the animal several small feeds a day rather than one large feed, avoiding a large influx of food that can be a strain on the digestive system.

  ✤ Stick with simple, bland foods, especially cooling foods such as rice, and raw vegetables such as cabbage.

  ✤ Barley grass or wheat grass are also very cooling and soothing (use them fresh as juice, or dried as a powder, available from health food stores).

- **Homeopathic remedies**:

  ✤ *Iris versicolor 30c*—use if the animal is vomiting repeatedly, with a lot of drooling, lack of appetite and tenderness over the liver/pancreas area.

  ✤ *Pulsitilla 30c*—if the animal has no thirst, seeks cool surfaces to lie on, and is very clingy and whiney.

- **Acupuncture/acupressure**—try GV 14, BL 17, BL 20, BL 21, ST 36 and SP 6.

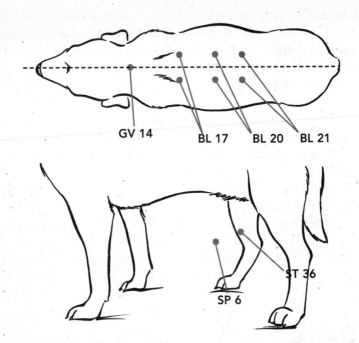

GV 14   BL 17   BL 20   BL 21

ST 36

SP 6

❓ Questions to consider

Is your pet overweight and sluggish?

Does it get sufficient vigorous exercise to stimulate the digestive process?

Does its diet contain rich, fatty foods?

Does it have other immune-related conditions such as skin disease?
This may be an indication that its immune system is out of balance.

Urinary tract problems

The most common urinary tract problems are: **cystitis** (an inflammation of the bladder); and formation of **crystals or stones in the urine** (often leading to cystitis), which may result in obstructions.

Cystitis results from either a physical irritation to the inside lining of the bladder (usually from small stones or gravel produced in the urine when it remains at a certain pH for an extended period); infection by bacteria, or an immune-related problem that results in low-grade inflammation between the cells of the bladder lining. This is known as interstitial cystitis, and it is related to an imbalance in the immune system. Sometimes the bladder lining can become infected, although the current thinking is that this is not as common as once thought, so using antibiotics may not be as useful as previously considered.

The emotions connected to cystitis are "annoyance" or "feeling irritated," so using flower essences to calm the emotional animal and management such as removing the cause of the angst are important.

Causes

There are several theories as to why these problems occur, but no one is really certain about the exact cause. Feeding an animal highly processed commercial foods, especially the cheaper, cereal-based foods, results in a highly alkaline urine, as does frequent small feeds (as when dried food is left out all the time so the animal can graze). The most common types of gravel or stone formation occur with these highly alkaline urine states.

Poor-quality food leads to pressure on the eliminative organs such as the kidneys, digestive tract and skin, as they try and remove the toxic byproducts that are present in higher levels in these foods. The urine is the end product of kidney elimination, so if the urine has a higher load of toxins than usual the bladder lining will almost certainly be affected and irritated, leading to inflammatory problems. Poor diet can also lead to immune dysfunction and a possible immune-related inflammation in the bladder wall (interstitial cystitis). Bacteria are able to adhere more easily to a damaged bladder wall and recurrent infections eventuate.

Long-term lack of access to clean, fresh water can result in mild dehydration and consequent chronic concentration of the urine, making the urine "thicker" and more prone to sand and gravel formation. Retention of the urine for long periods can also lead to the urine becoming concentrated in the bladder. This can occur, for example, when an animal is shut inside for long periods of time, when a cat is afraid to go outside because of the threat of attack from other cats, or when fastidious cats "hold it" rather than using a dirty litter tray. Regular flushing of the bladder is important to keep the bladder lining healthy and reduce irritation from concentrated urine. In addition, regular urination doesn't allow the urine to sit for long periods, thus reducing the likelihood of crystal or stone formation.

What you may see

In both types of urinary tract problems you see straining, passing of small amounts of urine (sometimes bloody), discomfort and often anxiety due to the irritant nature of the condition. The animal may be angry and lash out, or subdued and hide away. Either way, it is a very uncomfortable and distressing condition, and well worth avoiding by preventive measures.

If the gravel or stones become lodged in the urethra (the small tube that leads from the bladder to the outside of the body) and the tube becomes blocked, the straining often becomes severe, and little or no urine is passed. This is an emergency situation as the bladder can become overfull, with tremendous back-pressure up the tubes to the kidneys. If this is left untreated, kidney failure, shock and death can occur in a relatively short time.

Treatment

Generally

- **Diet**—use a high-quality diet as outlined; be sure to include the supplements as directed, if using a homemade diet.
- Check with your vet if these supplements are necessary in your pet's situation:
  - ❖ Vitamin C (250 mg twice daily for cats and small dogs; up to 500 mg twice daily for large dogs) for a month or so, then reduce as improvement occurs.
  - ❖ Vitamin E is important for healing the damaged tissues and to help prevent scarring of the urethra and bladder lining. Use 50 IU per day for cats, 200 IU per day for medium-sized dogs, 400 IU per day for large dogs.
  - ❖ Vitamin A—use 10,000 IU once a week for cats, 2500 IU per day (for small dogs) to 10,000 IU per day (for large dogs) for a month, then reduce as improvement occurs. Note: Cod liver oil in the dog and cat oil will be sufficient to provide this. It also contains vitamin D,

which is important especially if the animal is kept inside all the time and doesn't get any sunlight.

❖ Vitamin B complex to help calm the animal.

Acute cystitis

- **Make sure your pet is examined by a veterinarian** to check if there is a urethral obstruction (blockage of the tube from the bladder to the outside of the body); if so, it will need to be catheterized (which entails passing a catheter up the urethra to unblock it).
- **Try homeopathic *Cantharis 30c*** for cases where there is severe straining, bloodstained urine, the animal cries out in pain and there is a lot of licking in the urethral area.
- **If your pet needs to be catheterized** Dr. Pitcairn recommends *Staphysagria 6c* (one dose every four hours for a total of three treatments) to help with recovery.
- **Give your pet plenty of liquids to drink** to flush the bladder.

Chronic cystitis

Chronic or recurrent cystitis is common with interstitial cystitis, and can be very challenging to treat.

- **Diet is important**. Use a slightly higher meat content than usual, as this will result in a more acidic urine. Reduce the amount of cereal in the diet, but make sure there are raw vegetables, and use the powder and oil supplements. Brown rice and corn, well-cooked adzuki beans and unpeeled potatoes are useful for painful and bloody conditions. The preferred meats are beef and rabbit, and small amounts of chicken. Use the additional vitamin supplements as above. There are also veterinary-only prescription diets that can help in the control of chronic cystitis.
- **Cranberry** has been shown to prevent bacteria attaching to the bladder wall. Add cranberry capsules to the diet, or replace one-third of the pet's drinking water with unsweetened cranberry juice if it will tolerate it. Cranberry also acidifies the urine, preventing triple phosphate crystal formation. Using vitamin C in the form of rose hips will also acidify the urine.
- **Homeopathic remedies**—try one of the following, using a dose every four hours for three treatments. If there is no change within 24 hours of treatment then reassess it.

- *Pulsitilla 30c*—for an animal that prefers to lie in cool places and avoid heat, and passes urine containing blood little and often.
- *Rhus tox 30c*—when the animal is worse with cold (e.g., symptoms are worse after lying on a cold floor or in cold weather), better with warmth; worse after resting, better after moving around.
- *Mercurius solubilis 30c*—much licking after urination, straining, producing just a small amount of urine, thrashing of the tail, very annoyed.

- **Herbal remedies**:
  - Try equisetum, or horsetail grass, which is very high in silica. Use 2 tsp of the herb in $1/2$ cup of hot water; give $1/4$ tsp of the mix three times a day for a week or more.
  - Barberry root can be useful where there are stones—for cats and small dogs use 1 tsp of the root in 1 cup of water, and give three times a day; use up to 2 tbsp for large dogs.
  - Sarsaparilla root can be used as above (but double the amount of herb used in the mixture) if there is gravel in the urine.
  - If there is infection, try echinacea or goldenseal.
  - For triple phosphate crystals use cleavers, red clover or eyebright.
  - For uric acid crystals use celery root, cornsilk and gravel root.

- **Acupuncture or acupressure** are very useful in chronic and acute cystitis to rebalance the underlying system problems (according to traditional Chinese medicine, cystitis is caused by excess heat or damp heat in the body). Try the points Bl 23, CV 4, CV 3, KI 7 and ST 36.

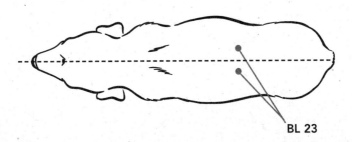

BL 23

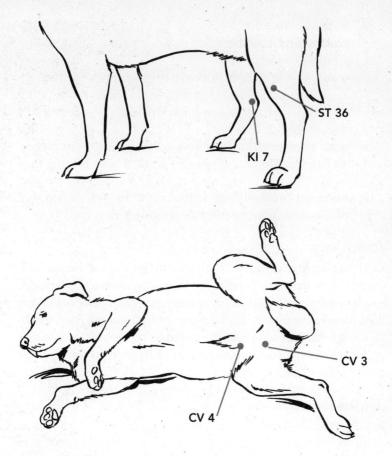

- If the animal is stressed by other cats or loud noises, is generally annoyed and refuses to go outside to urinate, try the **Bach flower essence** mix of aspen, mimulus, walnut, willow and the Rescue Remedy mix. If the animal is very scared, add larch or elm.
- **Consider management carefully.** Make sure litter trays are cleaned regularly to encourage their use, make sure your animal friend can get outside to a safe and quiet area to go to the bathroom, and get rid of unwanted and aggressive neighboring cats by squirting them with water pistols or generally making them very unwelcome.
- **Regular exercise** is important for emotional health, to get the body functions moving efficiently, and to provide regular urination opportunities.

? *Questions to consider*

Is my pet eating a good-quality diet?

Can it get outside to urinate easily?

Is there an emotional reason why it has recurrent bladder problems?

Is there an underlying imbalance in my animal friend's health that needs addressing?

Vomiting

Vomiting, like diarrhea, is a symptom rather than a disease, and features in quite a few conditions. When the stomach is irritated for any reason it will respond by speeding up its movements, which often results in nausea or regurgitation of the stomach contents. In traditional Chinese medicine this is known as "rebellious stomach qi," where the normal downward flow of qi energy with digestion is reversed and goes up instead.

Causes

Spoiled food can result in an infection in the stomach, causing inflammation and subsequent vomiting. Bacterial and viral infections, allergies, overeating, and physical irritations such as bone chips, fur or other indigestible matter in the stomach are other causes. Other digestive organ upsets can result in vomiting, such as pancreatitis, hepatitis, intestinal upsets and kidney problems, as well as middle ear problems and brain irritation (due to infections and inflammation). Emotional stress can also result in vomiting in some instances.

What you may see

Regurgitation of food either immediately after eating or some time afterward. If the vomit is like dark coffee grounds, this indicates that there is bleeding into the stomach and the stomach acid has caused the blood to go brown. This is an emergency situation and requires veterinary attention.

There may be fur or other foreign, indigestible material such as pins, sticks and other garbage that has upset the stomach. It is better for it to come back up rather than carry on down into the intestine and possibly cause an obstruction. If there is obvious bloating of the stomach area, or the vomiting continues for more than 12 hours, then it is important to see your veterinarian.

The animal may be uncomfortable and distressed before vomiting as the stomach contracts and moves, resulting in nausea. Cats and dogs will sometimes eat grass to make them vomit and clean out the stomach if they are feeling nauseous.

Treatment

- **Have your animal friend checked by your veterinarian** to identify the underlying reason for the vomiting. Where there is bloating, surgery is usually necessary and since it is an emergency situation, getting your pet to the vet immediately is important.
- **If the vomiting is related to overeating or eating spoiled food**, the animal may just vomit once or twice and then be fine, but if it is depressed and unwell or the vomiting continues, it is important to see your veterinarian for a thorough examination.
- **Rest the stomach**, and allow it to settle down before giving any food. A fast is important to allow this to happen—nothing in the mouth for at least six hours after the last vomit, then try a few tablespoons of boiled water cooled to body temperature. If this stays down, half an hour later try another few tablespoons of water. Do this for a couple of hours. If there is no more vomiting in this time, allow the animal to drink water freely, making sure it is warm, not chilled.
- **Make a broth** from well-boiled rice, vegetables and meat or bones, sieve out the solids and try offering the liquid portion, a small amount at a time, every 15 to 20 minutes. As long as there is no further vomiting in this time, continue for 24 hours with the liquid broth. The vegetables contain salts and electrolytes that can replace those lost when vomiting. Well-cooked rice water is very soothing and nutritive for the digestive tract and is very useful for any stomach upset. Adding some soy sauce or beef bouillon adds to the flavor as well as the sodium level.

- If all is well after the 24-hour fast, then give a small amount of the well-cooked soup solids every two hours over the following 24 hours, continue this for the next two days, then gradually get back onto the usual diet.
- **Homeopathic remedies**—depending on the symptoms shown, try one of the following:
  - ❖ *Nux vomica 30c*—useful for flatulence and indigestion, also vomiting where the animal has overeaten and is sick, and wants to be on its own. Give every four hours until the symptoms are gone.
  - ❖ *Arsenicum album 30c*—this is very useful for vomiting due to spoiled food. There will be a thirst for small quantities of water, and symptoms tend to be worse toward midnight. Give every four hours until the symptoms are gone.
- **Herbal remedies**—try:
  - ❖ Peppermint—very useful to calm the stomach.
  - ❖ Goldenseal—especially good for any bacterial or infectious stomach upset.
  - ❖ Chamomile—excellent for indigestion and cleansing the liver.
- **Acupuncture/acupressure**—helps to calm the rebellious qi. Try the points ST 36, PE 6, CV 12, CV 14 and BL 21.

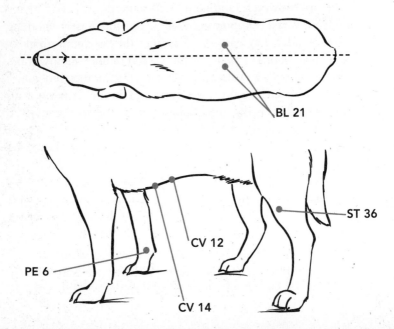

BL 21

ST 36

CV 12

PE 6

CV 14

For chronic stomach upsets (sensitive stomachs)

- *Always* make sure your pet has been thoroughly checked by your veterinarian.
- **Diet is crucial**. Sometimes the food your pet is eating simply doesn't agree with it. It may be too rich, and your pet may be reacting to preservatives and colorings, or it may have a food allergy that results in digestive upsets. Maybe try a natural diet, including the supplements, making the change slowly to allow the stomach to become accustomed to the new food as the body detoxifies. There are also prescription commercial diets that can be used. Usually the stomach settles with the healthy food, but it may also require one or more of the following.
- **Herbal remedies**:
  - ✤ Chamomile tea—very good for indigestion, and emotionally relaxing. If your pet is stressed this will help to calm it and settle its stomach.
  - ✤ Peppermint—calms the stomach.
  - ✤ Slippery elm—helps to heal the stomach.
  - ✤ Garlic—useful for animals that get upset stomachs as a result of diet changes, or are prone to gas and constipation.
  - ✤ Aloe vera juice—soothing and cooling to the stomach and digestive tract linings. Remember not to get the version with benzoic acid or sodium benzoate in it (for cats).
- **If your animal friend is stressed** and emotionally upset and this is affecting the digestion, then the flower essences can be very useful. Try to determine the main reason behind the stress and remove the cause (e.g., aggressive stray cats, loud noises, etc.). Try Rescue Remedy, aspen, mimulus and agrimony—use every 15 minutes until settled, then four drops four times a day for four weeks.

? Questions to consider

Has your cat or dog had access to spoiled or rotten food?

Does it have any other concurrent conditions, i.e., organ problems such as kidney or liver problems?

Do you have a long-haired cat?
The problem could be caused by furballs.

Does your cat or dog gulp down its food without chewing well? Unchewed food can upset the stomach, or can swell (e.g., biscuits) resulting in regurgitation.

Wounds

Wounds can vary from mere grazes to deep gashes, and the treatments vary accordingly. There are some basic principles that need to be followed, and some excellent remedies to assist and speed up healing.

Treatment

The basic principles are:

- **Stop any bleeding**—direct pressure can be applied with a clean towel or bandage, and the animal kept quiet while you get to the vet and have it assessed and possibly stitched. It is ideal to elevate the affected area higher than the animal's head, but this may not be possible with many animals! A pressure bandage may need to be applied (see page 248 for how to do this).
- **Once the bleeding has stopped, clean the wound** and remove any debris, grass, soil, etc., bathing it with cooled boiled water with 1 tsp salt to a cup of water, flushing the area gently so you don't start the bleeding again. A syringe can be useful here, or gauze dressings, but avoid dry cotton wool as it tends to stick to the wound.
- **If it is a large wound, or very open, it may require stitching** by your veterinarian, using a local anesthetic or even light sedation. Your vet will advise if it needs bandage support or is best left open to the air. The stitches are usually removed approximately ten days later.
- During this time the animal may lick and bite at the wound, which can delay healing. The occasional lick is fine, but constant worrying at the wound is not. **You may need to put an Elizabethan collar around the animal's head**, or tape a clean cotton sock above the wound to prevent licking (see page

250 for how to make an Elizabethan collar). The animal will usually leave the wound alone once the stitches are removed, since much of the initial healing has also occurred by then. The return of full strength to the skin takes much longer, depending on how deep the wound was and where it is (areas that move a lot, like elbows and knees, can take longer than, say, the rib area or the back).

Healing

Speed of healing also depends on the health of the immune system; if it is in balance and working well, healing time is very quick. Nasty sores can linger if the immune system is stressed or unhealthy, so keeping the animal healthy with a good diet and all the other preventive measures mentioned earlier such as exercise, fresh air and sunshine, grooming and attention, will help with rapid healing. Other important things to aid healing are:

- **Diet**—fresh, natural, with all the supplements (powders and oils). Also add:
  - ✤ Vitamin C—use the low-acid chelated form (250 mg twice daily for cats and small dogs; 500 mg twice daily for medium dogs, and 1000 mg twice daily for large dogs). If diarrhea develops, lower the dose. Use at this rate until the stitches come out, then give the animal half the dose for a further month.
  - ✤ Vitamin E—this can be taken orally (50 IU daily for cats and small dogs; 200 IU daily for medium dogs, and 400 IU daily for large dogs). Once the stitches are out and the skin has closed over the wound, you can apply vitamin E directly from the capsule (prick it with a pin); this will reduce scarring of the skin. (This is also useful for burns, once the skin has closed over the wound.)
  - ✤ Vitamin B complex—extra B vitamins may be required over and above the powder mix, especially if your animal friend is stressed as a result of being confined and treated.
- **Bathe the wound twice daily** with a wound-healing lotion like Nelsons Cuts & Scrapes Cream. This is an excellent healing stimulant and antiseptic, and can be applied to an open wound safely, speeding up healing time immensely.

- **If there is infection present**, use the herb goldenseal or echinacea (pour boiling water over 1 tsp dried herb, leave to steep for 15 minutes, cool and apply externally three to four times daily). Make sure any infected wounds are checked by a veterinarian, as antibiotics may be required.
- **Homeopathic remedies**—as soon as the wound occurs, use:
  - ✤ *Arnica 30c*—this will help with the trauma and shock.
  - ✤ *Phosphorus 30c*—if there is a lot of bleeding. Use both these remedies every 15 minutes for several doses (usually about three) until the condition has stabilized, then stop.
  - ✤ *Bellis perennis 30c*—where there is deep bruising and muscle damage; use as above.
  - ✤ Once the wound has closed, the area can be bathed with arnica tincture, diluted 1:10, to help with bruising and pain. It should not be used on broken skin.
- **Acupuncture/acupressure** is very useful for non-healing wounds. Use a technique called "ringing the dragon," in which you place acupuncture needles all around the edge of the affected area at 45-degree angles, leave in for 20 minutes, then remove. Do this every three days until healed. This technique is excellent for scars, skin ulcers and non-healing granulomatous lesions.
- **Activated manuka honey** applied to infected wounds and ulcers can stimulate healing; it is now being used with dressings in human medicine.
- **Colloidal silver** in the liquid form can be applied to wounds to stimulate healing.
- **Manuka oil** is a useful antiseptic for minor wounds; it is good to have in the car or first aid kit to wipe over wounds to treat and prevent infection.
- **If your animal friend is stressed** over the accident that resulted in the wound, try using Rescue Remedy from the Bach flower range, at the time of the accident and every 15 minutes after that until the animal is settled. If it remains anxious, try adding aspen, mimulus and walnut to the Rescue mix. Use four times a day for as long as necessary.

? Questions to consider

Does the wound need stitching, i.e., is it long and gaping?

Is it very contaminated with dirt, hair or other matter?
It will need to be cleaned.

Is it bleeding a lot or just a small amount?
It may require a pressure bandage to help stem the bleeding.

Was the wound caused by an accident or is your pet being victimized by other animals?
This may lead to behavioral problems.

Consider the emotional trauma associated with this sort of injury and whether you should be using a flower essence such as Rescue Remedy.

Chapter 6

Holistic first aid and how to medicate animals

It is always best to be prepared for emergencies. Take the time to assemble a first aid kit, including the items listed below, and have one at home, one in your car, and take one on vacation. Just as important—make sure you know what all the parts are used for *before* an emergency occurs!

The following recommendations are not designed to replace veterinary care, and anything other than very minor problems should always be checked by your vet. Even some things that appear to be minor can actually be quite serious problems, so if your pet seems at all out of sorts, get it checked just to be on the safe side.

When do I call the vet?

Obvious things that need *immediate* veterinary care are (see also page 143):

- Any bleeding that is profuse or will not stop after a few minutes; also large or deep wounds.
- Any situation involving collapse.
- If the animal is unwell, lethargic or depressed.
- If the animal feels very hot, is restless or anxious.
- Difficulty in giving birth.
- Vomiting that continues for more than six hours, occurs more than two or three times, if the vomit looks similar to coffee grounds, or if the animal is very unwell.
- Diarrhea that contains blood or is very black and the animal is very unwell.

- Straining to urinate, vomit or defecate with nothing coming out.
- Respiratory distress (heavy breathing and gasping).
- The tongue going blue, extreme difficulty in breathing.
- Acute pain of any kind.
- Poisoning of any kind.
- Eye injuries, especially if the cornea is bulging.
- Whiteness and paleness of the gums and tongue, especially after an accident.
- Continuous fits (for more than a couple of minutes).
- If the animal has stopped eating for more than 36 hours.
- If the animal has a non-weight-bearing leg or severe limp.
- Basically, use your common sense and call the vet if you are at all worried.

It is impossible to list all the situations that require veterinary attention, but as a rule, if you are worried, have the animal checked. You may not always be able to get to a vet easily, and there are also things that can be done on the way to the vet clinic which can help save your pet's life. These are the things that are covered in this Chapter.

 Basic first aid kit

- Sharp scissors
- Cotton swabs, cotton balls
- Sterile gauze pads for cleaning wounds, as well as pads to act as wound dressings
- Bandage tape, about 2 and 3 inches wide
- Strapping tape, about $3/4$ inch wide, to finish off a bandage and hold dressings in place
- A "Vetrap" bandage or similar—this adheres to itself, and it can be reused
- Small tweezers for removing splinters, etc.
- A larger pair of forceps for removing bones or sticks from the mouth
- A couple of large blankets—one to keep the animal warm, one to use as a sling for carrying it
- A bottle of saline for flushing wounds

- Activated charcoal
- Baking soda

Essential remedies

- Homeopathic remedies:
    - ♣ *Aconitum (Aconite) 30c*
    - ♣ *Arnica 30c*
    - ♣ *Phosphorus 30c*
    - ♣ *Carbo veg 30c*
    - ♣ *Ledum 30c*
    - ♣ *Nux vomica 30c*
    - ♣ *Hypericum 30c*
    - ♣ *Ledum 30c*
    - ♣ *Urtica urens* tincture for burns
- Rescue Remedy (from the Bach flower range); have the mixture in a 30 ml dropper bottle ready to use—four drops of the mother tincture in 30 ml spring water, with 1 tsp good brandy to act as a preservative. Cats often hate the taste of the brandy, so I have suggested using slightly less brandy than is usually recommended. If you find the water is going murky sooner rather than later, you may need to add more brandy the next time.
- Manuka oil
- Wound-healing cream
- Aloe vera gel for burns

Emergency situations and what to do

Basic emergency care

- **Establish an airway**. Do this as soon as possible. Check the mouth to make sure there are no obstructions such as vomit or other foreign objects. Remove anything that shouldn't be there, using the large forceps. Pull the tongue forward to open the throat area. If the animal isn't breathing, try to perform mouth to mouth resuscitation by closing the animal's mouth and putting your mouth over its nostrils. Blow out to fill the animal's lungs (you should see the chest rise) and wait for the air to be released from the animal before the next breath. Do this every 10 seconds or so for dogs, and every five seconds for cats.

- **Make sure there is a heartbeat**—feel for a heartbeat in the area just behind the elbow, over the ribs, on the left-hand side (you can also feel it on the right-hand side but it is easier to feel on the left). You can also listen for a heartbeat by putting your ear to this area. If the heartbeat is not there, clear the airways first, then try external heart massage—lie the animal on its right side, place your hand over the heart area as described, and press firmly (but not so hard as to break a rib). Press and release in a rhythm every few seconds.
- **Apply pressure to any bleeding immediately**.
- **Check the color of the gums and tongue**. They should be a medium pinkish color, not pale, whitish or bluish. A healthy pink color denotes a healthy circulatory system.
- **Check the position and size of the eye pupils**. If they are fully open and there is no blink reflex when you lightly tap the inside corner of the eye, the animal may already be dead (especially if you cannot detect a heartbeat). Always check with your veterinarian to confirm this.
- **Stimulate the acupuncture points for resuscitation**. The main one, called GV 26, is in the middle of the nasal plate. Tapping on this point with the tip of a pen or your fingernail will stimulate blood pressure and heart rate. It can also be useful to squeeze the webs of skin between the toes, and to press the middle of the main pad on the hind feet (KI 1). Pressure at any of these points may help to revive the animal, and they are very accessible and easy to stimulate with pressure.

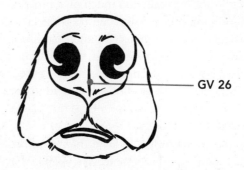

GV 26

KI 1
(hind paw)

- Once breathing begins and any bleeding has been attended to, give **Rescue Remedy** every five minutes until the animal is stabilized.
- **Homeopathic remedies**:
    - ❖ If the animal is unconscious, give *Aconitum 30c* every 15 minutes until it is conscious;
    - ❖ If the animal is not responding to resuscitation measures (going blue, looking like dying) try *Carbo veg 30c* (known as the "great reviver");
    - ❖ Use *Phosphorus 30c* (as well as direct pressure) if there is bleeding.
    - ❖ Use *Arnica 30c* for any accident involving bruising, shock or bleeding—use every 15 minutes until a response is seen, then every few hours until the animal is stable.

Emergency care for specific situations

Bee stings and insect bites

There is often considerable swelling following a bee sting or insect bite, which is not normally too much of a problem unless it occurs in the throat or mouth area and constricts the airways. Bee stings do tend to occur in the mouth, as cats and dogs like to chase and snap at bees, so always suspect a sting if there is any rapidly occurring swelling in this area. The tongue is a common site for stings, and can swell enormously, but the swelling does tend to go down quickly.

What to do

- Keep the animal quiet, to keep the respiration rate down.
- Use the homeopathic remedy *Apis mellifera 30c*. This remedy is

made from actual bees, and it is very useful for the treatment of stings, especially where there are puffy, itchy swellings. Other useful remedies are:

> ✤ *Ledum 30c* for most insect bites;
> ✤ *Urtica urens 30c* remedy; it is also good to bathe the area with the tincture.

- Remove the stinger by scraping it from the skin with a blunt knife (rather than tweezers, which may allow more venom to be discharged into the skin).
- If there is any difficulty with breathing, or swelling, get the animal checked by your veterinarian.

Burns

The main thing with burns is to cool the area as quickly as possible. Hot water, for example, is held on the skin for longer by the fur, so dousing the area with cold water immediately helps to slow the damage to the skin. Burns are very painful, so pain relief is essential. Always work under the guidance of a veterinarian. Some useful remedies are:

- **Rescue Remedy**—use this initially, until the shock of the event is over. Then use a dressing of *Urtica urens* tincture (diluted 1:10).
- **Lavender oil**—dilute 5 drops of lavender oil in 10 ml wheat germ oil (this is high in vitamin E, so it is very useful for reducing scarring); dab it onto the burn twice daily as it heals. Lavender is a good antiseptic and stimulates healing.
- **Aloe vera**—this can be squeezed onto the burn straight from the aloe leaf; it is very cooling and soothing. Apply twice to three times daily until the burn is healed.
- **Natural wound-healing cream (such as Nelsons Cuts & Scrapes Cream)**—useful for bathing the burn before applying the lavender or aloe.
- **Comfrey**—makes an excellent burn compress and helps with healing.

Car accidents

Being hit by a car can result in very minor damage if the animal is lucky, or at the other end of the spectrum, it can result in death. Prevention is the ideal; always make sure your dog is on a leash when it is out near traffic, and ensure your yard is fully fenced. If the unthinkable happens (and it does with alarming regularity) and your animal friend is hit by a car:

- **Try to pick the animal up carefully**, and move it to a safe area. If it is in severe pain it may try and bite (even very friendly animals will do this), so put a makeshift cloth muzzle around its nose and tie it behind its head (see diagram on page 249). If it is a cat, gently take it by the scruff and carefully place it in a cage with a firm bottom to transport it to the vet. With a dog you may need to make a temporary sling from a blanket, or even better, use a board, which will keep the body flat. Make sure *you* are not injured by other traffic or the injured animal while attending to your pet.
- **Check the heart and breathing** as outlined above, and give the remedies suggested, especially:
  - ♣ Rescue Remedy (this can be dropped in the mouth or, if the animal is very stressed, directly onto the fur, especially the point on the top of the head between the ears);
  - ♣ *Arnica 30c.*
- **Take the animal straight to a veterinarian** for a full checkup, as there could be internal injuries that may not be apparent in the very early stages after an accident.

Heatstroke

! *Never* leave your animal friend in the car if it is hot! Animals die very quickly when left in hot cars, but it is an easily averted tragedy—leave them at home on hot days.

Dogs and cats don't sweat all over as we do; they cool themselves by panting and some sweating around the pads of the feet and ears. A furry coat also insulates the body and slows cooling once the core temperature is up. If heatstroke occurs:

- **Get the animal out of the car** and into a cool place ASAP.
- **The main aim is to cool the body** as soon as possible; use a hose to run cold water over the animal or, if a hose is not available, use cold compresses on the ears, feet and the rest of the body.
- **Get to your vet quickly,** because treatment for shock will probably be necessary.

- Use **Rescue Remedy** on the way to the vet.
- **Homeopathic** *Belladonna* may be useful.

Poisonings

Each poison produces its own symptoms: there may be increased salivation, convulsions (as with slug bait), hemorrhaging (with rat bait), vomiting and diarrhea (with caustic or irritant poisons), or liver damage or failure (with antifreeze). The treatment depends on the symptoms shown.

Many poisons don't have antidotes, and if the levels in the body are too high or the subsequent damage is extensive enough, there is little chance of recovery. Supportive care is essential. *Always* contact your veterinarian for information on what to do. Time is of the essence here, and your vet can give instructions over the phone. Try and bring in some of the poison, for example the packet it may have been in, or the animal's vomit, which may still contain the poison.

- **Activated charcoal** can be very useful to mop up some poisons in the digestive system. Have some in your first aid kit, so if the vet recommends it on the phone you can give it immediately, rather than waiting until you get to the vet clinic. Use 5 tsp in 1 cup of water; spoon it into the mouth or syringe it into the pocket between the teeth and the cheek—see the diagram on medicating with liquids (page 243). Use approximately $1/4$ cup in small dogs and cats, up to 1 cup for larger dogs.
- **Washing soda or salt** (1–3 tsp in a cup of water) can be used to make the animal vomit if the vet recommends this (both taste terrible, so good luck!).
- **Homeopathic** *Nux vomica 3c* can be useful if there is vomiting, and stomach and liver pain. Use three doses 15 minutes apart, and stop if there is no improvement.

How to medicate cats and dogs

Restraining cats

Before you can administer pills or perform a procedure on your feline friend, you need to restrain the animal in a firm yet gentle way. First, settle the cat on a flat, non-slip surface such as a table top covered with a plastic or rubber mat. Ideally, have someone to help hold the cat, standing behind and holding each front leg with a hand.

The pin trick

Take three plastic clothes pins, the type with a metal spring and (ideally) smooth and flat ends. Take a good fold of skin (the scruff) on the neck and put the three pins in a row around this, side by side down the neck. Make sure you take a full thickness of skin right to the base of the pins. Don't just pinch the skin with the tips of the pins. This calms and sedates the cat for a few minutes, enabling you to administer pills or liquids, or trim claws. It works well on most cats, although some don't like it at all—it is best not to use the "pin trick" on these cats.

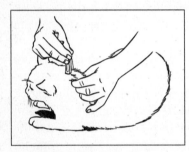 

Hand under the chin

You can cup the cat's head in your hand, holding it under the chin. You still need to hold the rest of the body, and to watch those teeth!

Wrap the cat in a towel

Firmly wrap a towel around the whole body, right up to the neck, enclosing the front legs and especially the claws.

Zip the cat into a small sports bag

Leave the cat's head out, but zip the rest of the body inside the bag. This restrains the legs and claws. Make sure it's not too tight around the neck though.

Restraining dogs

Ideally, you should have another person to help you. Make sure the dog has a strong neck collar on, with a leash attached. Hold the leash firmly, near where it attaches to the collar, and back the dog into a corner, right up against the wall.

Another method is to get the second person to put their right arm around the dog's neck and hold the muzzle and head with the right hand, while the left hand and arm steadies the dog.

How to give pills

The first thing to do is make sure the animal is restrained in some way.

- With **cats**, it is often necessary to have someone hold them from the back, hands on both front legs, tucking the cat's body into his or hers. A second person can apply the pins, as above, and then, with one hand over the top of the head, thumb on one corner of the mouth, forefinger in the other side, hold the head back so the nose is up in the air. The lower jaw automatically opens. Holding the pill between the thumb and forefinger of the other hand, open the lower jaw between the front lower canines and pop the pill right at the back of the mouth, in the middle over the top of the tongue with the forefinger. Give the pill a quick push back past the point of no return, remove your finger quickly, and release the head. When the animal swallows and licks its lips, the pill should be gone.

Restrain the cat's front legs to avoid being scratched.

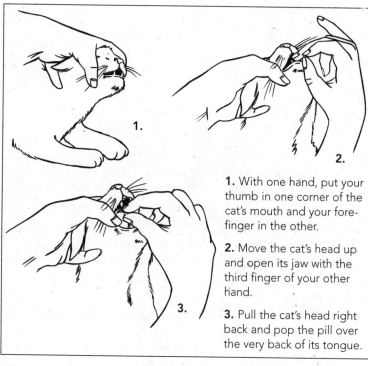

1. With one hand, put your thumb in one corner of the cat's mouth and your forefinger in the other.

2. Move the cat's head up and open its jaw with the third finger of your other hand.

3. Pull the cat's head right back and pop the pill over the very back of its tongue.

- **Dogs** may also need a second person to steady them, allowing the person giving the pill to use both hands. If this is not possible, back the dog into a corner and gently hold it there with your legs to stop it from backing away. The person giving the pill puts their hand down over the top of the nose and gently pushes the lips around the upper teeth, pressing gently into the mouth as they go. The mouth will open, since the dog will not want to bite its lips. Taking the pill between the thumb and the forefinger again, open the lower jaw with the third finger and place the pill as far back in the mouth (in the middle) as you can. Shut the mouth and rub the throat and the pill should be swallowed.

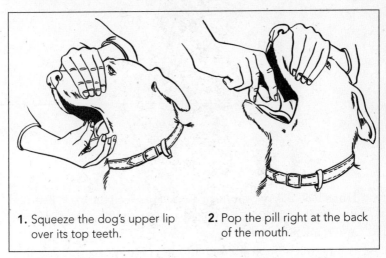

1. Squeeze the dog's upper lip over its top teeth.

2. Pop the pill right at the back of the mouth.

- **Pills can be secreted in food** at mealtimes, but only put a teaspoon or so of food in the plate, hide the pill, and give it to the animal at the very beginning of its meal when it is most hungry. The animal should eat the food quickly and not detect the pill.
- **You can wrap the pill in something yummy** like a piece of cheese or pâté. If you have a dog, and it wises up to the fact that there is something else in its cheese, try tossing a small piece of cheese or two for it to catch (with no pill in it) then quickly toss the piece of cheese with the pill in it. Usually the dog will be so excited at getting all the cheese that it won't notice the pill!

How to administer liquids

Restrain both cats and dogs in the same way as for giving pills.

- **With cats**, place your hand over the top of the head, with your thumb in one corner of the mouth, and gently open the lips and teeth, supporting the head and holding it to one side.

Gently insert the end of the syringe or spoon into the mouth and start dropping the liquid in slowly, so it can be swallowed easily. If it tastes bad, be prepared for the cat to jump a little!

- **Dogs** have a very convenient pocket between the back teeth and the cheek. This can be pulled out gently, a syringe inserted, and the liquid squeezed into the area. It should be allowed to run between the teeth and into the mouth cavity, rather than being squirted down the throat and possibly going down the wrong way and choking the dog. A reasonably large amount of liquid can be quickly administered in this way. Close the mouth around the syringe and hold the head up a little so the liquid runs back into the mouth.

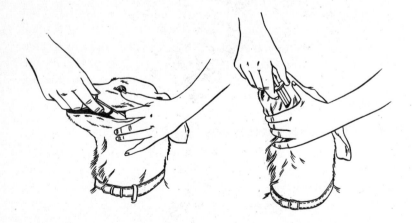

How to give homeopathic remedies

All homeopathic remedies work best if they are not given with food or water. Ideally, leave 15 to 30 minutes before and after giving a homeopathic remedy, since the energy of the food and even water interferes with the energy of the remedy. In some situations the only way to get the remedy into the animal is with food or water, and they still seem to work, but the optimal response is when they are given alone.

The liquid remedies are preserved with a small amount of alcohol, which can be unpalatable to some animals, especially cats, but they are definitely easier to administer than the pellets. I tend to suck some of the liquid out of the bottle with a sterile 1 ml syringe and squirt it onto the animal's gums or tongue. This is useful when you need to give repeat doses because you can draw up as much as you need for all the doses without having to reopen the bottle. Make very sure you don't touch the top of the bottle to the animal's mouth or lips, as once this happens the bottle is contaminated and can only be used for that particular animal.

For pelleted remedies, I suggest rinsing two teaspoons with boiling water, air drying them, then dropping two or three pellets onto one teaspoon and crushing them with the back of the other. You can then flick the powder onto the gums or tongue. An alternative is to make a small funnel out of clean paper by folding it in half, crush the pellets between the paper, then pour the remedy down the fold into the mouth. Again, make sure *you* don't touch the pellets when getting them out of the bottle as you will contaminate them, and they won't work for that animal. Simply flick them onto the spoon or the paper without touching them with your fingers.

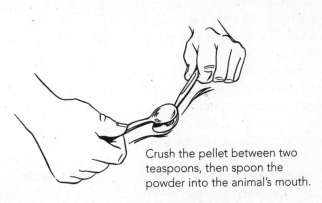

Crush the pellet between two teaspoons, then spoon the powder into the animal's mouth.

As a very general rule, for acute, emergency situations, give the remedy every 15 to 20 minutes for three or four doses, and as the condition stabilizes and improves continue once daily for four or five days. If there is no change or the condition worsens, revise the treatment (change remedies or treatments).

For not so acute situations try a dose every 12 hours for three days and again, if there is no change or the condition worsens, try a different remedy or treatment.

For very chronic (long-standing) problems, use once daily or every other day for three to four weeks. If there is an improvement continue the remedy as necessary.

Generally, use the remedy more when the symptoms are present, less as they improve. If they simply don't improve, you probably need to try another remedy. Again, always be guided by your veterinarian's advice.

How to apply acupressure

Applying pressure to an acupuncture point is known as acupressure. Often the most convenient things to use are your fingertips, as you can feel for the exact point and know how much pressure is being applied. Make sure your fingernails are not so long that they dig into the skin, and press firmly but not too hard on the skin with a straight (not bent) forefinger or thumb, whichever is most comfortable. Use an even pressure rather than an intense pressure, beginning slowly and lightly and gently deepening with a steady movement.

When the animal begins to resist or tense up a bit, relax the pressure and hold the point for five seconds. If the animal seems uncomfortable while you are doing this, tensing or moving away, you are probably pressing too hard and need to ease up a little. All this is a feedback experience, and with practice you will get good at noticing the signs that mean you can press harder or when you need to lighten up.

You can alter the technique for different individuals and conditions. For example, in frail, "deficient" individuals (prone to being cold, quiet, weak, thin and maybe nervous) use a light pressure for about one to two minutes at any one point. For "excess" individuals (robust, loud, hot) use a light to moderate touch. If the animal is very restless use a stronger pressure for a shorter time. Try and match the pressure with the animal and its condition, and use commonsense, for that is very much what traditional Chinese medicine is all about.

How to use the flower essences

As described in Chapter 4, the flower essence treatments are made up in 30 ml dropper bottles. Two drops of the mother tincture (four drops of Rescue Remedy) are added to the 30 ml bottle of spring water, with a teaspoon of good-quality brandy to preserve the water. Because these are energetic medicines working on the energy of the animal, they work just as well *on* the animal as *in* the animal. You can simply drop the remedy (approximately four drops per treatment) onto the fur, in the mouth, in the food or water, or even put it into a small glass vial and attach it to the animal's collar. A very useful (and accessible) place to drop them is the acupuncture point right on the top of the head, midway between the ears. If the animal is very nervous you can simply drop the remedy into the palm of your hand and stroke the drops over the top of the head or down its back.

> **The frequency of treatment is the important thing**, rather than the amount given—in other words, it is better to give just a few drops (about four) more often than half a bottle just once. The latter would equate to just one dose, and you would have simply wasted the remedy.

If the remedy is put into the animal's water and food, every time it eats or drinks it takes another dose. The flower essences are far more robust energetically than homeopathic remedies, which should not be given with food or water, and ideally need to be given orally.

Flower essences differ from homeopathic remedies in that the dilutions of the flower essences are much lower, and closer to the herbal end of the scale. Both are energetic medicines, but in other ways they are quite different. The flower essences tend to treat more of the emotional problems that may lead to physical symptoms, whereas the homeopathic remedies are more orientated toward physical symptoms (although they can be used for mental and emotional problems as well).

Use the flower essences more frequently when they are needed, reducing the frequency as the condition improves. For acute problems (such as shock or severe emotional distress) use them every 10 to 15 minutes until the animal has settled, then as necessary. For chronic problems, use four drops four times a day for four weeks.

The flower essences are completely safe and you cannot overdose or create any adverse effects with them. Overuse of a homeopathic remedy can lead to what is called an "aggravation" or worsening of the symptoms, which is why the dosing regime is more specific (and by stopping the use of that remedy, the aggravation will go). With the flower essences, you simply don't get this. The worst that can happen if you get the "wrong" remedy is that the condition doesn't improve, which means you need to reconsider the mix or try a different treatment.

How to apply a pressure bandage

A pressure bandage may be necessary when a wound will not stop bleeding, or to control swelling. The important thing is to make sure there is plenty of padding with something like cotton wool so that the strapping pressure is spread evenly over the area. The following directions are for a leg wound.

First, cover the raw area with a gauze pad; you may like to put some wound-healing cream on the pad to moisten it and act as a mild antiseptic. Then wrap a thick sheet of cotton wool (from a roll) over the entire area that needs bandaging, right down to the foot. Using a stretchy bandage such as Vetrap, and starting at the top, firmly wrap the leg right down to and over the foot. Put a couple of strips of bandage tape around the bandage at regular intervals to keep the Vetrap firm. If you leave the foot open and unbandaged, it will often swell and become very uncomfortable.

Leave the bandage on for 24 hours, then replace it. Remove it if the leg swells above the bandage, and leave a small window at the very bottom of the bandage so you can look at the quick of the claws. Check the color of the quick every few hours; if you squeeze the claw, pressing the blood from the quick, then release it, the blood should return immediately. The quick should be a nice pink color at all times. If the quick is blue or purply, remove and replace the bandage immediately because it is probably too tight!

Making a temporary muzzle for a dog

Take a strip of non-sticky bandage or cloth about 20 inches long. Tie a loop in the middle of the cloth, and drop it over the dog's nose, half to two-thirds of the way along the nose toward the eyes. Once it is in place tighten it quickly then tie again underneath the nose. Pull the remaining ends up behind the ears and tie them firmly in a quick-release knot or bow. Make sure you hold the dog's front paws and prevent it scratching the muzzle off, or keep your hand under the nose, holding it up.

This is useful as a temporary muzzle in an emergency, but don't leave it on for more than a few minutes at a time since it prevents the animal from panting and cooling itself. Use the muzzle when you need to move and lift the dog, from the road to the car, for

1. Tie a loop and drop it over the dog's nose.

2. Tighten the loop over the top of the nose.

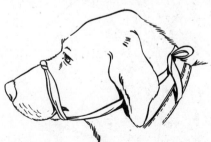

3. Tie again under the nose, then behind the ears.

example, or into the vet clinic. You need to be quick when putting it on since the dog usually only gives you one chance to do it—they soon wise up, then they won't let you near them!

Making an Elizabethan collar to prevent self-trauma

There are a couple of ways of making these collars, or you can buy one from your vet clinic, so you have it on hand when you need it.

One simple way to make a collar is to cut the bottom out of a plastic bucket, then punch holes around the bucket, about ³/₄ inch from the lower edge. Place it over the head of the dog and thread string through the holes, then through the dog's collar.

Alternatively, to make a custom-sized collar, take some firm plastic sheeting (an old x-ray plate makes a good Elizabethan collar) or firm cardboard. Cut out a largish circle of the sheeting, then cut into the center and cut out a smaller circle that will go round the animal's neck. Punch holes around the edge of the smaller circle, bend the sheeting into a cone shape around the animal's neck and staple or tape it together. It should reach to the end of the dog's nose. Thread string through the holes and the dog's collar, as before. The animal should be able to eat and drink, but not able to chew and lick at itself.

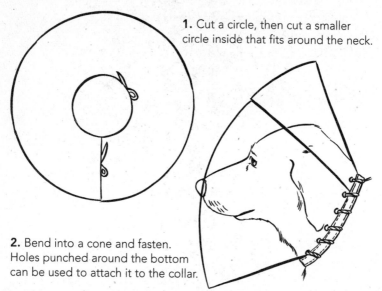

1. Cut a circle, then cut a smaller circle inside that fits around the neck.

2. Bend into a cone and fasten. Holes punched around the bottom can be used to attach it to the collar.

Chapter 7

Raising puppies and kittens holistically

With a holistic approach to pet care that focuses on prevention, regulating the cat and dog population by preventing random breeding is essential. I am a great advocate of spaying and neutering cats and dogs, since the number of animals needing good homes far outweighs the number of good homes available.

Although many attempts are made by animal shelters to rehome unwanted kittens and puppies, there is still a surplus that never get homes. It is a tragic thing that these unwanted animals are euthanized, all because of careless animal owners not being socially responsible and making sure their animals were spayed or neutered before they became sexually active.

However, if you do decide to breed your pets in a responsible way, ensuring the offspring have homes before they are even conceived, then the following information should be helpful.

Pre-conception care

One great secret of healthy puppies and kittens is making sure the health of the parents is as good as possible, before the offspring are even conceived. And this does not just mean physical health, but emotional and mental health, since these things are all passed on to the offspring. It is very important to try and select unrelated parents with as much genetic diversity as possible, to reduce the likelihood of gene-related problems.

While the health and vitality of both parents is important, the mother's vitality is paramount, because she has to contribute 50 percent of the genetic material at the same time as carrying the young to full term, and suckling them until they are able to eat on their own. In traditional Chinese medicine this genetic vitality is known as "Jing" essence, and each individual is born with a finite amount of this type of energy, which is stored in the kidneys. If an animal inherits a high level of Jing from its parents, it is more likely to live a longer, healthier life. Once the Jing has been used up then the animal dies, as it is vital for life.

Things that use up Jing quickly are having too many babies for your level of vitality; stress, poor diet and poor lifestyle habits. Therefore pre-conception care of both the mother and the father is important in making sure you have healthy offspring. Working at increasing the parents' health probably needs to begin at least a year before conception, as ovulation in the bitch only occurs approximately every six months.

Ensuring the parents' good health

To ensure the parents' good health examine the following areas:

Diet

Make sure your pet has a well-balanced diet with plenty of whole grains, vegetables and meat (raw, if possible), and the cat and dog powder and oil mixes where appropriate, or a high-quality commercial adult maintenance diet. Extra supplements for the homemade diet that are useful include zinc (from ground pumpkin seeds), which helps conception; calcium (from tahini, made from ground sesame seeds, or dried and ground egg shells; also in the powder mixes) and kelp (in the cat and dog powder mixes), which provides many of the minerals and vitamins essential for reproduction. If you are using a commercial diet ask your veterinarian to check that any extra supplements you are using are appropriate, as overuse can create serious health problems. The essential fatty acids in fish and plant oils (such as flaxseed oil), are also important in reproductive health.

Exercise

Getting plenty of exercise is important, so the mother is fit and more likely to have a natural birth.

Emotional health

Use the flower essences for emotional unrest and for helping to resolve emotional problems.

Constitutional homeopathic remedy

Go to a trained homeopath for a full consultation and to determine the constitutional remedy appropriate for your pet. This will increase overall health and help to reverse any negative influences in the animal's make-up.

Acupuncture

Acupuncture is very valuable as a way of increasing fertility and vitality as well as preserving and enhancing Jing essence. It is also very useful during pregnancy and at birth to help prevent problems.

Further points to consider

In addition to these basic care and management issues, consider the following:

- **Possible problems associated with a particular breed.**
- **Is this particular breed the best one for your lifestyle, home and family?** Get to know the breed characteristics and pros and cons of the breed with regard to health and wellness.
- **Get veterinary certification** for hip scores (which determine the degree of potential hip dysplasia problems), corneal health and any particular breed-related health problems.
- **Try to meet both the mother and the father** of your intended puppy or kitten if at all possible; note things like overall health, personality and emotional health, how often they are bred (stud animals may be worn out from too much breeding), and the state of their surroundings and lives.
- **Does your situation allow for a new puppy or kitten?** Do you have the financial means to feed and provide essential care for them, do you have a fully fenced area, and the time to walk, feed, groom, play and love a pet? Do you or any other members of the family have allergies to pets? Do you have young children? Some breeds of dog are very unsuited to children. Is your household relaxed and relatively stress-free? What about vacations? What will happen to the pet when you are at work all day (can you arrange company for your pet during the day?)

- **How toxic is your environment and home?** Using large amounts of household cleaners, soaps, laundry detergents, oven cleaners, insect sprays, herbicide sprays, deodorants, cosmetics and hairsprays, as well as fumes from new carpets and drywall, and a myriad of other environmental toxins leads to a daily assault on our own and our animal friends' bodies, sometimes resulting in immune dysfunction and congenital problems. Rectify this situation by using low-toxicity, eco-friendly cleaners, organic sprays and personal body preparations from eco-friendly companies such as Seventh Generation.

  Educate yourself about additives in foods and cosmetics, and learn to read the labels and small print. Recent research shows things like artificial sweeteners can damage health if they are used regularly, as can many other additives like MSG, colorings, preservatives and flavor enhancers. Even the air we breathe may be polluted with exhaust fumes and cigarette smoke, destroying our pets' health as much as our own. Applying chemicals to your skin and breathing them in can be as dangerous as eating or drinking them—the effects on the body are the same. In fact, transdermal uptake (skin absorption) is often faster than the absorption that occurs when a substance is eaten, something to remember when you are shampooing your hair (or using hair dyes) or applying face cream.

During pregnancy

- **Make sure the diet is excellent**. Talk to your veterinarian about how much and what type of food to feed your pregnant animal, as each animal has individual needs. Pregnancy requires approximately twice the amount of energy intake as the non-pregnant state, and lactation requires three times the amount. Either use a high-quality adult maintenance food for the first two-thirds of the pregnancy, then go to a growth formula for the final third (the last three to four weeks) as well as during lactation, or a growth formula can be fed throughout pregnancy, especially if the bitch is not holding her condition or is bred often.

  Don't allow the bitch to get too fat—this can mean big puppies, possibly resulting in a difficult birth. If the mother is being fed a highly nutritious diet, doubling the food may not be necessary. Each animal is an individual, and its needs are highly individual, so every case must be assessed according to its needs. If the mother is healthy, maintains an even weight, is active, and has a clean and shiny coat, then she is probably receiving all the necessary nutrients. However, do get regular veterinary checkups during pregnancy to monitor this.

- **Make sure you worm the mother** before conception, and at three weeks and 10 days before birth; this will ensure the puppies are not born with worms and you won't need to worm them until they are a month old.
- **Avoid insecticides, pesticides and heavy metals** (e.g., mercury, lead), and use eco-friendly or organic household cleaners.
- **Avoid unnecessary stress during pregnancy.**
- **Herbal remedies**:
    ✤ A strong dose of raspberry leaf tea with a spoonful of molasses stirred in is excellent in the last two-thirds of pregnancy, and especially the last week.[1] It helps tone the uterine muscles as well as prepare the body for birth.
    ✤ Nettles are also very useful as a tonic throughout pregnancy, and contain iron.
    ✤ Alfalfa is highly nutritive, and includes vitamin K, which is helpful in blood clotting and avoiding hemorrhage at birth.

At birth

If there is any problem, particularly a delay in the birthing, or retained placenta, contact your veterinarian ASAP. The following suggestions can be tried if the mother is well, and the babies are not distressed.

- **Herbal remedies**:
    ✤ Give shepherd's purse during labor and just after, to contract the uterus.
    ✤ If there is retained placenta or still some babies to be born and contractions have stopped, try a strong dose of raspberry leaf tea. If this fails, for a medium-sized dog give 2 tbsp of pennyroyal infusion with a tbsp of dissolved Epsom salts.

> **!**Pennyroyal is toxic to dogs at high doses, and *do not* use the essential oil. Pennyroyal can also be toxic in cats, so should not be used. Diane Stein's *Natural Remedy Book for Dogs and Cats*[1], from which this information is taken, is a useful source of advice.

- **Homeopathic remedies**:
  - ✤ Use *Caulophyllum 30c* in the last week of pregnancy and during the birth. It can also help with hemorrhage and retention of the placenta postpartum.
  - ✤ *Arnica 30c* will help with bruising, and help prevent infection.
  - ✤ *Sepia 30c*—a single dose can help the uterus return to normal after birth.
  - ✤ *Pulsitilla 30c*—use when labor contractions stop and there are still puppies or kittens to be born. Give a dose and stop when contractions resume.
  - ✤ *Carbo veg 30c* to revive collapsed and blue babies (*Arnica 30c* can also be used).
  - ✤ *Helleborus 30c* for weak babies that are having difficulty breathing.
- **Acupuncture** is very useful in the last week or so of pregnancy to help prepare the body for birth, loosening the ligaments and softening the cervix. There are also very useful acupuncture points for difficult births, and acupuncture can even be used to turn a breech birth (where the baby is coming backward).
- **Watch the mother closely for signs of infection** (fever, depression, very smelly dark vaginal discharges or sore, hard and inflamed mammary glands). Get to your vet ASAP if these are seen. If the babies are noisy and hungry it may mean there is a problem with the milk supply, so get this checked too. If there is simply no milk, you will have to feed the babies by bottle every three to four hours with special infant formula.
- **Do not stress the mother** by interfering and hovering around. Keep visitors to an absolute minimum and let her take care of it without too much interference. Personally, I think many birthing problems and mismothering result from too much owner interference.

Lactation

- **Diet**—Lactation requires a higher than normal energy intake, supplementation of important minerals and vitamins as well as extra protein. A growth diet is suitable to supply these needs. The better the nutrition, the better the milk and, more importantly, the better the mother's health. The mother will tend to "milk off her back" and will put the growth of the offspring and the milk to feed them before her own needs, so if a poor diet is fed, this will seriously undermine her health.
- **Herbal remedies**: A tea made with equal proportions of nettles, anise seed, fennel seed and caraway seed helps support healthy milk production and is beneficial for the digestion of both mother and babies.
- **Mastitis** is an infection of the mammary glands which must be checked by a vet, but you can also use:
  - ❖ *Phytolacca 30c*, a homeopathic remedy, for a hard, extremely painful mastitis.
  - ❖ *Belladonna 30c* where there is a fever, lots of heat and possibly excitement.
  - ❖ Make sure the mother has a stress-free environment, and don't fuss over and bother her too much. Make sure she has a quiet, safe bed or nest, away from the household noise and bustle.

Raising healthy puppies and kittens

Diet

Offer solid food to puppies and kittens from two to three weeks of age. Try a cereal-based product or oatmeal porridge to start with (commercial puppy and kitten "starter" foods are available) then offer more variety as they age. To begin with they may play with the food and walk through it, but persevere with smearing small amounts around their lips so they get used to the taste. As the mother's milk reduces in volume, they will want to eat more. Most puppies and kittens can be weaned from seven to eight weeks old. They should be freely eating various solid foods by this time.

Feeding

Recommended feeding frequency and techniques vary depending on who you ask, but the commonly accepted technique for puppies is to put down the food and take it up again after about 20 minutes if it hasn't been finished, allowing the puppy to eat all it wants in this time. Do this until they are nearly fully grown. Most breeds should be fed twice daily, except toy breeds which need three meals a day until they are about six months of age, then go to twice daily feeding.

Feed kittens little and often, because their stomachs are small and fill up and empty quickly. Up to five weeks of age feed every four hours; from six weeks to about six months feed three times a day, then move to twice-daily feeding. Alternatively, you can leave the food out so the kitten can "graze" when it feels like it. Use a growth diet.

Exercise

Remember not to overdo the exercise with the large, rapidly growing breeds of dog. Allow them to race around home in a well-fenced section, but restrict outside walks to no more than 20 minutes a day until they are a year old. Getting out and about is important for their social and emotional development, so make sure there are plenty of positive growth experiences, like fun car rides, meeting friendly dogs and people, getting used to traffic and crowds, as well as open spaces.

Allow kittens to explore inside the house, making sure there are plenty of toys and play things to chase and climb on. Take them on supervised outside tours, but don't let them outside on their own until they are about five months old or until they have been spayed or neutered at around this age. They are still very much babies and cannot be expected to know the dangers of roads and dogs, but let them have a scratch in the soil and get to know their backyard.

Behavioral considerations

Creating firmly defined boundaries that are consistently enforced by all members of the family results in a far more settled and relaxed dog, as they don't have any hierarchy disputes to worry about (see Chapter 5 for behavioral problems). If you don't have any idea about dog training it is highly advisable to go to dog obedience classes, puppy preschool (this is mostly for socialization) or employ a professional dog trainer to train you as well as your dog!

> For both puppies and kittens, make sure they have lots of toys that *don't* resemble your expensive running shoes, or anything you may not want them to scratch, chew or destroy. Have toys like Frisbees, rope chews and soft rubber pieces that are inviting to chew, and of course balls like tennis balls (or ping-pong balls in the case of kittens). You don't have to buy expensive toys; a kitten is just as happy playing with a ball of crunched up paper on a string as it is with a fancy store-bought toy.

It is important to have plenty of play time, with people and toys, because this is the way these youngsters learn about their environment and about pouncing and hunting. Chewing is vital for jaw and tooth growth as well as strength, and plenty of leaping and playing helps the bones develop and strengthen—the old saying "Use it or lose it" is true—the more you use your senses, the more they tend to develop. Make sure puppies learn basic skills like "Sit," "Come," "Stay" and how to walk on a leash. This comes from consistent commands by all family members, so make sure everyone uses the same words and command techniques.

Socialization

For many years, it was accepted that there was a crucial "socialization" period for puppies from eight to 12 weeks of age. This narrow time frame theory is now disputed, and it is accepted that this important socialization time lasts over a greater number of weeks and months, and begins earlier, perhaps from the age of three to four weeks. During this time it is considered vital for the puppy to have as many positive growth experiences as possible, such as meeting new people, going to different places, riding in the car, etc., which allow the puppy to get used to various noises, smells and sights in a positive way. It is believed that these positive experiences affect them for the rest of their lives, just as negative experiences affect them negatively for the rest of their lives.

Safe places

Make sure your puppy or kitten has a "safe" place to go to when everything gets to be too much for it. This is especially important in a very busy household, where they will need a quiet, out of the way place to go to get away from the hubbub of everyday life. A box in a back room, a quiet corner of the room to put their bed in, or even a sheltered, waterproof and warm kennel outside is sufficient—just somewhere they can go to rest and recuperate.

This also applies to feeding arrangements, since a stressful eating area can lead puppies and kittens to gulp down their food, with resulting stomach or intestinal upsets, or being too stressed to eat and developing an unhealthy attitude toward eating. I always suggest shutting the puppy or kitten in a separate room to eat, and leaving them well alone for at least 10 to 15 minutes, so they can have a peaceful eating experience and develop a healthy attitude toward food.

The importance of routine

Establish a regular routine for your new animal friend. It is comforting for them to eat, walk and play at similar times each day, and it also allows their body cycles to adjust to these routines. If you come home from work at a regular time each day this will train them to know that although you are away for that period of time, you are coming back. Some cats or dogs assume that when you leave the house you are not ever coming back, and this is where anxious behavior may possibly arise. Having another animal for company, or another human (for example, arranging for a neighbor or friend to have the puppy or kitten when you are out all day) may take away a lot of this anxiety.

I believe it is very unfair to expect any cat, and particularly any dog, to spend hours on end alone at home, waiting for you to return. If you are out all day, most days, I recommend you seriously reconsider whether you should be getting a cat or dog in the first place. It may be better to wait until your situation changes and you can take the animal to work or you have some company for it during work hours. So many anxiety problems, which can lead to potentially serious physical problems, arise from this very situation that it is not fair on either the animal or its owner. Cats are far more self-reliant and cope with separation much better than dogs, although some of the very gregarious breeds of cat such as Burmese and Abyssinians really need lots of human contact, so it is also unfair to expect them to spend a lot of time on their own.

Other health issues

- **Worming** is done:
    - ❖ Every two weeks until the animal is 12 weeks old;
    - ❖ Then every month until they are six months old;
    - ❖ Then every three months, as for adults, with a broad-spectrum wormer. Because roundworms are a problem mainly in young animals, treating adults for roundworms is not as critical.
- *Dr. Pitcairn's Complete Guide to Natural Health for Dogs and Cats*[2] suggests not treating young animals unless they have large numbers of worms (on stool examination by a vet) or are showing visible signs of the effects of worms (failure to thrive, pot belly, diarrhea). If you do need to treat for roundworms, Dr. Pitcairn suggests:
    - ❖ Using homeopathic *Cina 3x*, 1 tablet three times a day for at least three weeks.
    - ❖ Adding oat bran to the food daily ($1/_2$ to 2 tsp, depending on the size of the animal). Also feed the animal grated raw carrots, turnips or beets.
    - ❖ Adding $1/_2$ to 2 cloves of garlic (depending on the animal's size) daily in food.
    - ❖ Diatomaceous earth (see the section on treating fleas in Chapter 5, page 200); add $1/_4$ to 1 tsp of natural, unrefined diatomaceous earth to several meals in a row, then check again for worms. Make sure it is not inhaled, since it can irritate the airways.
- Tapeworms (or rather part of the tapeworm life-cycle) are ingested via fleas and prey such as rabbits, mice and rats, and it is necessary to treat these on a regular basis. You can use commercial tapeworm treatments or try Dr. Pitcairn's suggestions for treating tapeworms:
    - ❖ Pumpkin seeds—add $1/_4$ to 1 tsp freshly ground seeds to each meal, depending on the size of the animal.
    - ❖ Wheat germ oil—$1/_4$ to 1 tsp, depending on size.
    - ❖ Homeopathic *Filix mas 3x*, 1 tablet three times a day for three weeks, or you can also use the remedy *Cina 3x* as before.
- Fleas—see the section in Chapter 5 on treating fleas (page 200), especially the notes about using flea products in young animals and, most importantly, the toxicity issue in kittens.

Chapter 8
Saying goodbye and letting go—a holistic approach to euthanasia

Saying goodbye to an animal friend at the end of its life is something many of us will face at some stage. Our animal friends have a lifespan that is much shorter than ours, although some animals can live for up to 18 or 20 years (the oldest cat I ever met was 21 years old!).

It is never easy to face the reality that our faithful and loving friend is leaving its body and will not be there to meet us when we get home at night, to sleep on our bed, or accompany us on walks. The process can involve a quiet and very peaceful natural death, or we may need to make the often difficult decision to help our pet along the way with euthanasia. We are very lucky to be able to choose the euthanasia option for our animal friends, to end suffering or a poor quality of life, something that (for the most part) isn't available for us as humans—we have to wait until the (often) very bitter end.

Death and dying is something that tends to be swept under the mat in our society. The issue is often avoided, and is frequently given negative connotations. The reality is that death and dying are as much a part of the cycle of life as living—it is a natural progression of the course of things, for without death there can be no life, and without life there can be no death. When we look at life from a purely physical viewpoint, the loss of our body at death, the decomposition of the whole, it means the end of how we are. When we look at ourselves as having mental, emotional and spiritual bodies, we realize that we simply change forms at death. Our essence—our spiritual self—remains, albeit without a physical form, but still very much alive in a different form.

After years of observation and experience in helping animals move from their physical bodies to their spiritual bodies my impression is that our animal friends come into our lives to protect, help and, above all, teach us important lessons such as love, compassion and care for others. We are blessed and privileged if we have one truly special animal friend in our lifetime, and I believe these really special animals follow us from lifetime to lifetime, coming to us when we really need their friendship, help and guidance, and gracefully leaving us when we don't need their help anymore.

Time and time again I have seen the most incredible animals coming into people's lives when they really need help, providing companionship, protection and reassurance, and helping them through very sad times, only to die gracefully when the owner finds a new partner or gets through the hard times. These very special animals seem to know when their job is done and they can leave, but they remain connected to the person on a spiritual plane. People often hear and sense these special animals some time after they have left their physical bodies, and some are aware that they are still there, although not in a physical form.

Our animal friends, especially dogs, often provide completely unconditional love; they are there when life gets tough, and they never judge you or hold a grudge (for long!). This is why it is often a very traumatic event when your special animal friend dies, or starts the dying process. Not only do you have to decide on the ultimately unselfish act of allowing your friend to leave its body without undue pain and suffering, and while it still has some dignity, via euthanasia, but you may be losing an unconditionally loving friendship as well.

Spending time in meditative quietness with our animal friends when they are on their dying journey can be very enlightening. Our senses are often heightened by the imminence of their departure, and we can focus on every minute we spend with them. Wouldn't this be a great way to live each day, not with the grief, but with the appreciation of every minute, with a heightened awareness of the beauty and wonder of life? This special time can bring up other unresolved emotions around death and dying, including the loss of other loved ones. It provides us with an opportunity to grieve afresh for losses we have suffered in the past, and perhaps complete the grieving process this time around.

In her book *On Death and Dying*, Elizabeth Kubler-Ross identifies the five stages of grief that we may go through when confronted with death. The length and intensity of each stage depends on the individual situation, and the grieving process may even start before the death occurs, as is often the case when an animal has been diagnosed with an incurable condition. Although it can be difficult to accept that your animal friend is going to die, the positive side is that they are giving you the opportunity to get used to the fact, and even start your grieving at this time. When death is more sudden there is no opportunity to say goodbye and let go. In consequence, the grieving process can be very intense and it becomes more difficult to move through each level of grief in a healthy progression.

It is important to recognize each stage and allow yourself to go through them all. If any stage is suppressed the grieving process may possibly not be completed, and it may be revisited at a later date. It may also be internalized as a "stuck" emotion, which may lead to physical problems later on.

I have always been fascinated by the observation that our animal friends seem to know when and how to exit this world gracefully, and in a form their owner can tolerate. I have seen situations where some owners cannot bear the dying process, and the animal seemed to know this, and went away to die. Other owners needed to play an active role in the final run-down to the moment of death, and the animal held on until their owner was there. Alternatively, many animals give their owner plenty of warning that they are dying, allowing them to start grieving from that point.

When to euthanize

Every individual dies in its own way. The spectrum ranges from choosing to go on their own, by quietly slipping away in their sleep without any fuss, to being in a state of severe pain and distress, where it is very clear that euthanasia is necessary. Then there is a very large gray area in between, where the animal may not be in pain or distress, but their quality of life is poor and there is no hope of a recovery. The animal may look thin and unwell, or they may look normal but be depressed and lack the will to live. If your animal friend is in this gray area, you will need to ask your vet to help you decide on the best time for euthanasia. It is very important that pain and discomfort levels are assessed and appropriate medication is given to ease the process, so that it is as smooth and stress-free as possible. Constant pain undermines quality of life enormously, making the euthanasia decision even more important.

Quality of life

Everything boils down to quality of life, in the short and long term. When the end is near, my assessment criteria for quality of life are:

- Is the animal eating and drinking?
- Is the animal still moving about (i.e., not in pain, and still relatively active for its age and condition)? It must be able to get outside or to a litter box to urinate and defecate.
- Is there still a spark of life in its eyes? Is the animal reasonably alert and bright?

These things help us decide if quality of life is decreasing or non-existent. If you answer "No" to all these questions, it is pretty obvious that euthanasia is necessary. If the animal is still bright but not eating, then you may want to wait a while to see what unfolds, and tempt it with favorite foods such as tuna or chicken. When the animal cannot move, and is simply lying in its feces and urine, even if it is eating a little, but is depressed and the spark in its eyes has gone, then euthanasia is probably best done sooner rather than later. It is important to recognize an animal's right to die, searching your soul to make sure you are not keeping it alive for your own sake, when its quality of life is bad and there is little chance of improvement.

I often say to owners that their animal friend will "tell" them when they are ready for euthanasia. Although the owner may be a little confused by this at the time, when it happens, they often have no doubt that it is the right time to call the vet or bring their animal friend into the clinic to be euthanized. Many conditions have to be well advanced before the animal will die "naturally" (i.e., without intervention). Although many owners find euthanasia an extremely difficult decision to make, it can be made together with a sympathetic veterinarian.

I see no reason to keep animals with advanced and terminal organ failure on things like intravenous drips for days on end. Not only does it put them through the pain and discomfort of having a drip catheter in their leg, but it means separating them from their owners while they stay in a veterinary hospital that is foreign and often stressful for them. This is a special and important time in which your animal friend needs to be at home with familiar people and surroundings.

These advanced cases need constant monitoring by a veterinarian to ensure the animal is not suffering. The vet needs to be able to read each individual situation carefully, monitoring both the animal and the owner, to get the time just right—not too soon and not too late. Some owners rush into it, unable to cope with any part of the process, while others leave it too long and allow the animal to suffer. The aim is for a positive and peaceful event, leaving everyone feeling it was done well, with the timing just right. A negative experience of the death and dying process can haunt you for many years, while the death of an animal friend, handled in a gentle and positive way, can help you overcome negative emotions resulting from other deaths that have not been fully dealt with in the past.

How to make the process smoother

Once you have decided the time has come for euthanasia, the procedure needs to be carried out by a veterinarian. The drugs involved are restricted to veterinary use only, and the technique requires skill to be performed safely and correctly. Once euthanasia has been performed, a veterinarian needs to ensure the animal is clinically dead. Whether the animal will be cremated or buried at home is usually discussed before the procedure takes place, and if necessary the vet will arrange for cremation of the body.

This is a very important time in the animal's life (probably second only to being born), and I believe the euthanasia process needs to be carried out with extreme sensitivity to the needs of both the owner and the animal. Here are some suggestions to help make the process the best it can be.

• **Create peaceful, quiet and if possible familiar surroundings** for the animal. Often the veterinarian will come to your home, bringing a nurse to assist. This is probably the ideal situation, as the animal can be in its favorite bed, with familiar smells, thus reducing stress. If the vet cannot come to your home, another suggestion is to see if it can be done in the car at the vet clinic. If it has to be done inside the clinic, take in some familiar bedding or cushions for your animal friend to lie on. In my clinic there was a small garden at the back where euthanasia was occasionally performed, as some animals preferred to be outside. If the euthanasia was done in the consultation room, we always made sure there was lavender essential oil in the room (the oil was put in a ring that sat on the bulb of a table lamp, which heated the oil so that the vapor floated around the room). Lavender is very calming and soothing, and it helps animals and their humans relax in stressful situations. We also made sure there were no interruptions and that we had plenty of time for the procedure, and time for the owner to stay in the room with the animal afterward if they wanted to.

- **Have people there who are familiar to the animal**, who they know and trust. If the owner cannot be there, a gentle and sympathetic vet nurse can hold the animal securely during the procedure, since a few kind words and soothing pats go a long way to ease the transition.
- **If the animal is very distressed**, sedation can be used prior to euthanasia. The situation is much worse for everyone if the animal struggles or seems upset. A light sedative can prevent this and allow a quiet and smooth euthanasia.
- **The flower essences are very useful for calming the animal.** I routinely use Rescue Remedy before the procedure, usually on the top of the animal's head, which is as effective as in the mouth and less distressing for the animal. Other remedies that can help with the transition are aspen (for unknown fears), mimulus (for known fears such as going to the vet clinic) or walnut (for transition). The Australian Bush Flower Essences range has the remedies fringed violet, autumn leaves and lichen, which are really useful for integrating the death process, helping with letting go and moving on. For a week before euthanasia use these twice daily, then use one or two doses during euthanasia.
- **Homeopathic remedies**—these recommendations are for the last few hours before euthanasia or death, to help with a gentle transition. They will not cause death, but will ease an already occurring event.
    - ✤ *Arsenicum album 30c*—to ease suffering prior to euthanasia, especially where there is restlessness and frequent changing of position, and fearfulness that worsens closer to midnight.

❖ *Aconitum napellus 30c*—if the animal is very frightened and is reacting to everything that is different.

❖ *Pulsitilla 30c*—for the animal that is whimpering, cannot settle, and wants to be held. Also for the stage right before death, when breathing becomes loud and labored.

❖ *Tarantula cubensis 30c*—at the stage right before death, where the animal is tossing and turning and there is intense restlessness (much more so than where you would use Arsenicum, but without the fear).

The actual process of euthanasia

The drug used for euthanasia is a very concentrated form of anesthetic. It is drawn into a syringe by a needle. The animal's cephalic vein on the front leg has gentle pressure applied above the point of insertion so the blood pressure makes it stand up slightly (this is usually done by a trained vet nurse) and the needle is gently inserted into the vein by the veterinarian. The drug is injected directly into the bloodstream and goes to the heart and brain in the following few seconds. The drug acts very quickly, and almost immediately the animal will lose consciousness and relax, and heart and brain activity will stop a short time later.

Sometimes the animal will start to breathe a little more heavily and gasp a bit, but this is normal, and will only last 30 seconds or so. This is simply due to the muscles relaxing and the nerves firing in an uncoordinated way. Sometimes the bowels and bladder may relax and void their contents. Often the eyes remain open, and the mouth may sag open as well.

It is important that these things are explained before the procedure since they can be disconcerting to an already stressed owner if he or she is not prepared. Afterward the owner may want to stay with the animal for a while.

Time for reflection, and what to say

I generally recommend a funeral of some kind to say goodbye to your animal friend; it may be as simple or as elaborate as you want. These rituals have a real function in most cultures, providing formal recognition of the occasion and allowing the grieving process to be completed in a healthy way.

I believe it is really important to involve children in this process, as it is a valuable learning opportunity that can help them develop a healthy attitude toward death and dying. They can be encouraged to let out their feelings in a positive way, and perhaps to write a poem, draw a picture, say some words or lay some flowers. It is equally important not to rush out and get another pet right away, as this may send a message to the children that their animal friends are expendable and can simply be replaced when they die. I sometimes encourage parents to allow the children to be present during euthanasia, so it is a more real event for them, rather than the animal being taken to the vet and never coming back home.

I do not advise describing the procedure as "putting the animal to sleep," as children may associate the euthanasia death with going to sleep and not waking up, and be frightened about going to sleep themselves. It is better to refer to it as "euthanasia," a term that is not related to their commonly known activities. Usually the euthanasia procedure is a very peaceful and often positive event, and children are unlikely to find it scary. They can be encouraged to talk about the whole situation so you, or your veterinarian, can answer any questions they may have.

Talking about it all

There may also be a need for you to talk with someone who understands about the loss of a much-loved animal friend. This is not really a topic that is discussed much in our society, and people who have not been in this situation may not understand, brushing off the grief with a comment such as, "It was only an animal." A sympathetic ear from someone who does understand this acute grief can be really important. At my clinic a trained grief counselor was available for people who needed a little more help in dealing with the loss of their animal friend, and it was pretty common for people to go and see her. I believe the loss of a pet is not only about a devoted friend, and the physical and emotional company they gave, but also about the loss of the unconditional love these wonderful animals offer us. This love, freely given to us by our animal friends, is very special, and often not found with another human being. You will always remember these very special animals, as they are with you through all your life journeys, as true animal soulmates.

And finally . . .

Our animal friends are great teachers about life, love and companionship. They are there for us when we need them; they never judge us; they give of themselves freely; and they teach us important life lessons such as being in the present, playing, devotion, loyalty and, above all, unconditional love. They come to us when we need their company or the lessons they have to teach, and they gracefully leave us when their "work" is done. We are privileged to have known our truly special animal friends in this lifetime.

For those who have not yet met that special animal friend, you have a great and wondrous experience ahead. Watch out for these special friends, as they usually just come to you—it could be a wild stray that decides to live with you, the little puppy right at the back of the pen of 20 puppies at the animal shelter, or maybe the little old cat that no one wants. You know without a shred of a doubt when you see these animals—they seem to call out to you that they are the one.

Respect their right to be healthy, respect their ability to heal themselves given the right conditions, embrace all parts of their being—physical, emotional, mental and spiritual—and you can be part of the wonderful holistic experience that is life with our animal friends.

Suppliers

I have listed just some of the eco-friendly suppliers in the U.S. There are many more—look in your local directory or on the internet. Details were correct at the time of printing.

Eco-friendly suppliers

Botanical Dog, 843-864-9368; www.botanicaldog.com

Only Natural Pet Store, 888-937-6677; www.onlynaturalpet.com

PetAlive, 8773-289-1235; www.petalive.com

Seventh Generation, 800-456-1191; www.seventhgeneration.com

San Francisco Bay Area

Alpha Pet Supply, 960 San Pablo Avenue, Albany, CA; 510-525-7361

Happy Pet, 709 Taraval Street, San Francisco, CA; 415-566-2952

Holistic Hound, 1510 Walnut Street, Berkeley, CA; 510-843-2133; www.theholistichound.com

Noe Valley Pet Company, 1451 Church Street, San Francisco, CA; 415-282-7385; www.noevalleypet.com

Pawtrero Hill Bathhouse & Feed Co., 199 Mississippi Street, San Francisco, CA; 415-863-7297; www.pawtrero.com

Los Angeles area

My Pet...Naturally, 12001 West Pico Boulevard, Los Angeles, CA; 310-477-3030; www.mypetnaturally.com

Natural Touch 4 Paws, 21789 Ventura Boulevard, Woodland Hills, CA; 818-993-8910

Chicago area

Krisers, 2037 North Clyborn Avenue, Chicago, IL; 773-871-3663; www.kriserspetsupplies.com

Natural Pet Market, 263 Rice Lake Square, Wheaton, IL; 630-682-4522; www.naturalpetmarket.com

Boston area

Pawzitively Dogs, 3 Rockland Street, Canton, MA; 718-828-7299; www.pawzitivelydogs.com

The Pet Cabaret, 4404 Washington Street, Roslindale, MA; 617-323-7387; www.thepetcabaret.com

New York area

Whiskers Holistic Pet Products, 235 East Ninth Street, NY, NY; 212-979-2532; www.1800whiskers.com

A Natural Pet, 238 Third Avenue #1, NY, NY; 212-228-4848

Homeopathic pharmacists

Baileys, 175 Howard Avenue, Allston, MA; 617-782-7202

Boericke & Tafel, 2381 Circadian Way, Santa Rosa, CA; 707-571-8202

Hahnemann Labs, 1940 Fourth Street, San Rafael, CA; 888-427-6422

Santa Monica Homeopathic Pharmacy, 629 Broadway Avenue, Santa Monica, CA; 310-395-1131

Waleda Pharmacy, Inc., 841 South Main Street, Chestnut Ridge, NY; 914-352-6165

Flower essence suppliers

Pet Essences, 505-586-1607; www.petessences.com

Many health-food stores carry the full Bach Flower range and can make individual remedies for you. Look in your local directory or on the internet.

Herb suppliers

Herbal Remedies, 866-467-6444; www.herbalremedies.com

Chinese Herbs Direct, 800-608-9056; www.chineseherbsdirect.com

References and further reading

While every care has been taken to acknowledge reference sources in the body of the text, not every fact can be acknowledged directly. The references cited here have all been used in varying degrees as resource material. The author thanks all contributors, and has obtained permission for the use of large amounts of material cited. All material from A.M. Schoen and S.G. Wynn (Eds.), *Complementary and Alternative Veterinary Medicine, Principles and Practice* (Mosby, St. Louis, MO, 1998), is used with permission from Elsevier.

Chapter 1. What is holistic health?

Day, Christopher, *The Homeopathic Treatment of Small Animals.* C.W. Daniel, Saffron Walden, England, 1984.

McLeod, George, *Dogs: Homeopathic Remedies.* C.W. Daniel, Saffron Walden, England, 1989.

Wynn, Susan and Schoen, Allen M., "Fundamentals of Complementary and Alternative Veterinary Medicine" in Schoen, A.M. and Wynn, S. (Eds.), *Complementary and Alternative Veterinary Medicine, Principles and Practice.* Mosby, St. Louis, MO, 1998, Chapter 1, pages 3–13.

Chapter 2. The holistic approach

Thanks to Dr. Vicki Erceg, BVSc, at Massey University, Palmerston North, for checking the facts on behavioral issues.

Chapter 3. Nutrition and diet

1. Kronfield, D.S., *Nutrition: A Refresher Course for Veterinarians.* Proceedings No. 63, Post Graduate Committee in Veterinary Science, University of Sydney, 1983.

2. Piper, C., *Homemade Diets, Thought for Food, Feeding Your Pet.* Series of papers adapted by the author for use in this text.

3. With permission from Hand, M.S., Thatcher, C.D., Remillard, R.L., Roudebush, P., *Small Animal Clinical Nutrition.* 4th edition. Mark Morris Institute, Topeka, KS, 2000, Chapters 6, 9 and 11.

4. Pitcairn, R. and Hubble Pitcairn, S., *Dr. Pitcairn's Complete Guide to Natural Health for Dogs and Cats*. Rodale Press, Emmaus, PA, 2005.

5. Pitchford, Paul, *Healing with Whole Foods: Asian Traditions and Modern Medicine*. North Atlantic Books, Berkeley, CA, 2002. Reprinted by permission of the publisher.

Billinghurst, Dr. Ian, *Give Your Dog a Bone*. Ian Billinghurst, Bathurst, NSW, Australia, 1993.

——— "Creature Health Inescapably Reliant on Nutrition." *Chiron* (newsletter of the Australian Association of Holistic Veterinarians), Vol. 4 No. 1, February 1998.

Delaney, S.J., *Hey Doc, What Do You Think of My Home-prepared Diet?* Lecture notes from the North American Veterinary Conference, 2006.

Lewis, L.D., Morris, M.L. and Hand, M.S., S*mall Animal Clinical Nutrition*. 3rd edition. Mark Morris Associates, Topeka, KS, 1992.

www.petdiets.com

www.pettogethers.com

www.petsynergy.com

www.balanceIT.com (diet analysis software)

Special thanks to Dr. Sean Delaney, DVM, MS, Diplomate of the American College of Veterinary Nutrition, Davis, California, for diet analysis advice and use of his software; and Dr. Nick Cave, BVSc, MVSc, DipACVN, senior lecturer in small animal medicine and nutrition, Massey University, Palmerston North, for advice with diet analysis.

Chapter 4. Holistic therapies

Acupuncture

1. Schwartz, Cheryl, *Four Paws, Five Directions*. Celestial Arts Publishing, Berkeley, CA, 1996.

Kaptchuk, Ted J., *The Web that Has No Weaver: Understanding Chinese Medicine*. Contemporary Books, NY, NY, 2000.

Homeopathy

Day, Christopher, *The Homeopathic Treatment of Small Animals*. C.W. Daniel, Saffron Walden, England, 1984.

———— "Veterinary Homeopathy: Principles and Practice" in Schoen, A.M. and Wynn, S. (Eds.), *Complementary and Alternative Veterinary Medicine, Principles and Practice*. Mosby, St. Louis, MO, 1998, Chapter 26, page 485.

Macleod, George, *Dogs: Homeopathic Remedies*. C.W. Daniel, Saffron Walden, England, 1989.

Panos, M.B. and Heimlich, J., *Homeopathic Medicine at Home*. G.P. Putnam's Sons, NY, NY, 1980.

Pitcairn, R. and Hubble Pitcairn, S., *Dr. Pitcairn's Complete Guide to Natural Health for Dogs and Cats*. Rodale Press, Emmaus, PA, 2005.

Ulman, D., "Homeopathic Medicine: Principles and Research" in Schoen, A.M. and Wynn, S. (Eds.), *Complementary and Alternative Veterinary Medicine, Principles and Practice*. Mosby, St. Louis, MO, 1998, Chapter 25, page 469.

Flower essences

Blake, J.R. and Stephen, R., "Bach Flower Therapy: A Practitioner's Perspective" in Schoen, A.M. and Wynn, S.G. (Eds.), *Complementary and Alternative Veterinary Medicine, Principles and Practice*. Mosby, St. Louis, MO, 1998, Chapter 31, page 579.

Sheffer, M., *Bach Flower Therapy and Practice*. Thorsons Publishers, Rochester, VT, 1986.

Stein, Diane, *The Natural Remedy Book for Dogs and Cats*. Crossing Press, Freedom, CA, 1997.

Herbs

2. De Guzman, Enriqueta, "Western Herbal Medicine: Clinical Applications" in Schoen, A.M. and Wynn, S.G. (Eds.), *Complementary and Alternative Veterinary Medicine, Principles and Practice*. Mosby, St. Louis, MO, 1998, Chapter 20, page 337.

de Baïracli Levy, Juliette, *The Illustrated Herbal Handbook for Everyone*. Faber and Faber, London, England, 1974.

Duke, J.A., du Cellier, J., Beckstrom-Sternberg, S.M., "Western Herbal Medicine: Traditional Materia Medica" in Schoen, A.M. and Wynn, S.G. (Eds.), *Complementary and Alternative Veterinary Medicine, Principles and Practice*. Mosby, St. Louis, MO, 1998, Chapter 19, page 229.

Basko, Ihor J., "Over the counter herbal pet supplements: fact or fiction?" Proceedings of the 1995 American Holistic Veterinary Medical Association Annual Conference, page 139. www.drbasko.com

Chiropractic

3. Homewood, A.E., *The Neurodynamics of the Vertebral Subluxation*, Parker Research Foundation, 1962.

Willoughby, Sharon, "Chiropractic Care" in Schoen, A.M. and Wynn, S.G. (Eds.), *Complementary and Alternative Veterinary Medicine, Principles and Practice*. Mosby, St. Louis, MO, 1998, Chapter 12, page 185.

Aromatherapy

4. Werchon, Tonia, *Control of Fleas in Pets Using Essential Oils*. Annadale Publications, 1997.

Wynn, S.G. and Kirk-Smith, M.D., "Aromatherapy" in Schoen, A.M. and Wynn, S.G. (Eds.), *Complementary and Alternative Veterinary Medicine, Principles and Practice*. Mosby, St. Louis, MO, 1998, Chapter 30, page 561.

Chapter 5. Common problems

1. Pitchford, Paul, *Healing with Whole Foods: Asian Traditions and Modern Medicine*. North Atlantic Books, Berkeley, CA, 2002. Reprinted by permission of the publisher.

2. Pitcairn, R. and Hubble Pitcairn, S., *Dr. Pitcairn's Complete Guide to Natural Health for Dogs and Cats*. Rodale Press, Emmaus, PA, 2005.

3. Reprinted with permission from *The Natural Remedy Book for Dogs and Cats* by Diane Stein, © 1994 by Diane Stein. The Crossing Press, Freedom, CA, 1997. www.tenspeed.com

4. Casey, M., "Case Study: Neem Oil Treatment for *Demodex cati* in one cat." *Chiron* (newsletter of the Australian Association of Holistic Veterinarians), Vol. 4 No. 4, November 1998.

Schwartz, Cheryl, *Four Paws, Five Directions*. Celestial Arts Publishing, Berkeley, CA, 1996.

Chapter 6. Holistic first aid

Pitcairn, R. and Hubble Pitcairn, S., *Dr. Pitcairn's Complete Guide to Natural Health for Dogs and Cats*. Rodale Press, Emmaus, PA, 2005.

Schwartz, Cheryl, *Four Paws, Five Directions*. Celestial Arts Publishing, Berkeley, CA, 1996.

Chapter 7. Raising puppies and kittens holistically

1. Reprinted with permission from *The Natural Remedy Book for Dogs and Cats* by Diane Stein © 1994 by Diane Stein. The Crossing Press, Freedom, CA, 1997. www.tenspeed.com

2. Pitcairn, R. and Hubble Pitcairn, S., *Dr. Pitcairn's Complete Guide to Natural Health for Dogs and Cats*. Rodale Press, Emmaus, PA, 2005.

Special thanks to Dr. Vicki Erceg, BVSc, Massey University, Palmerston North.

Chapter 8. Saying goodbye and letting go

Pitcairn, R. and Hubble Pitcairn, S., *Dr. Pitcairn's Complete Guide to Natural Health for Dogs and Cats*. Rodale Press, Emmaus, PA, 2005.

Day, Christopher, *The Homeopathic Treatment of Small Animals*. C.W. Daniel, Saffron Walden, England, 1984.

Index